The Methuen Drama Book of Contemporary Uruguayan Plays

This work has been published within the framework of the IDA Translation Support Programme.

The Methuen Drama Book of Contemporary Uruguayan Plays

Ana Versus Death
They All Sleep at Siesta Time
Basic Principles for the Construction of Bridges
Prelude to Anne
I Will Give You Verses, Not Children
Emotional Terror

Gabriel Calderón, Leonor Courtoisie, Jimena Márquez,
Sandra Massera, Marianella Morena, Josefina Trías

Translated by
STEPHEN BROWN, WILLIAM GREGORY, CATHERINE BOYLE,
RACHEL TOOGOOD, KATE EATON, SOPHIE STEVENS

Edited by
SOPHIE STEVENS AND WILLIAM GREGORY

methuen | drama
LONDON · NEW YORK · OXFORD · NEW DELHI · SYDNEY

METHUEN DRAMA
Bloomsbury Publishing Plc
50 Bedford Square, London, WC1B 3DP, UK
1359 Broadway, New York, NY 10018, USA
29 Earlsfort Terrace, Dublin 2, Ireland

BLOOMSBURY, METHUEN DRAMA and the Methuen Drama logo are trademarks of
Bloomsbury Publishing Plc

First published in Great Britain 2025

Copyright © Sophie Stevens and William Gregory, 2025

Ana Versus Death © Gabriel Calderón, 2019; translation © Stephen Brown, 2025
They All Sleep at Siesta Time © Leonor Courtoisie, 2019; translation © William Gregory, 2025
Basic Principles for the Construction of Bridges © Jimena Márquez and Mario Benedetti, 2020; translation © Catherine Boyle, 2025
Prelude to Anne © Sandra Massera, 2017; translation © Rachel Toogood, 2025
I Will Give You Verses, Not Children © Marianella Morena, 2014; translation © Kate Eaton, 2025
Emotional Terror © Josefina Trías, 2018; translation © Sophie Stevens, 2025

The Authors have asserted their right under the Copyright, Designs and Patents Act, 1988, to be identified as authors of this work.

Cover design and illustration by Megan Wilson

The translation of these works has been supported by the Baroness von Schlippenbach Endowment and by IDA, the Translation Support Programme of the Ministry of Education and Culture of Uruguay.

All rights reserved. No part of this publication may be: i) reproduced or transmitted in any form, electronic or mechanical, including photocopying, recording or by means of any information storage or retrieval system without prior permission in writing from the publishers; or ii) used or reproduced in any way for the training, development or operation of artificial intelligence (AI) technologies, including generative AI technologies. The rights holders expressly reserve this publication from the text and data mining exception as per Article 4(3) of the Digital Single Market Directive (EU) 2019/790.

Bloomsbury Publishing Plc does not have any control over, or responsibility for, any third-party websites referred to or in this book. All internet addresses given in this book were correct at the time of going to press. The authors, translators, editors and publisher regret any inconvenience caused if addresses have changed or sites have ceased to exist, but can accept no responsibility for any such changes.

No rights in incidental music or songs contained in the work are hereby granted and performance rights for any performance/presentation whatsoever must be obtained from the respective copyright owners.

All rights whatsoever in these plays are strictly reserved and application for performance etc. should be made before rehearsals to Permissions Department, Bloomsbury Publishing Plc, 50 Bedford Square, London, WC1B 3DP, UK. No performance may be given unless a licence has been obtained.

A catalogue record for this book is available from the British Library.

A catalog record for this book is available from the Library of Congress.

ISBN: HB: 978-1-3505-2531-3
PB: 978-1-3505-2530-6
ePDF: 978-1-3505-2533-7
eBook: 978-1-3505-2532-0

Series: Methuen Drama Play Collections

Typeset by RefineCatch Limited, Bungay, Suffolk
Printed and bound in Great Britain

For product safety related questions contact productsafety@bloomsbury.com.

To find out more about our authors and books visit www.bloomsbury.com
and sign up for our newsletters.

Contents

Foreword by Adam Versényi vi

Introduction by Sophie Stevens 1

Ana Versus Death by Gabriel Calderón, translated by Stephen Brown 11

They All Sleep at Siesta Time by Leonor Courtoisie, translated by William Gregory 49

Basic Principles for the Construction of Bridges by Jimena Márquez, translated by Catherine Boyle 83

Prelude to Anne by Sandra Massera, translated by Rachel Toogood 119

I Will Give You Verses, Not Children by Marianella Morena, translated by Kate Eaton 149

Emotional Terror by Josefina Trías, translated by Sophie Stevens 183

Foreword

Adam Versényi

Sandwiched between Argentina and Brazil, Uruguay, South America's second-smallest country, is often overshadowed by its larger neighbours. As this collection of contemporary Uruguayan plays in translation ably curated by William Gregory and Sophie Stevens amply demonstrates, however, Uruguayan culture is as rich as that of its larger neighbours. With a performance culture reaching back to pre-colonial days and encompassing music, dance, theatre, *murga*, carnival, and the literary arts, Uruguayan artists have distinguished themselves on both national and international stages. This anthology of twenty-first-century Uruguayan plays in translation brings its contemporary vibrancy into English for the first time, showcasing the eclectic and diverse nature of Uruguayan theatre today.

The plays presented here deal both with universal themes—the nature of death (*Ana Versus Death*), how cultural memory operates (*Basic Principles for the Construction of Bridges*; *I Will Give You Verses, Not Children* and *Prelude to Anne*), and particular intimate stories that open out into communal shared experience (*Emotional Terror* and *They All Sleep at Siesta Time*). Whether dealing with titans of Uruguayan letters such as Mario Benedetti or Delmira Agustini, historical figures of worldwide renown such as Anne Frank, or ordinary people coping with the loss of a loved one, the break-up of a relationship, or the search for safety and comfort, each of these plays is theatrically compelling, employing various techniques in innovative ways.

Gabriel Calderón's *Ana Versus Death* employs a mixture of monologue, dialogue, and direct audience address as Ana's attempts to protect her son from death due to cancer become increasingly desperate. In Leonor Courtoisie's *They All Sleep at Siesta Time*, a great deal of the play is actually narrated in the poetic stage directions as The Girl, The Younger Girl, and A Little Girl take their picaresque journey to save an armadillo, a dog, and themselves as they lumber towards the sea and their celebratory demise aboard a tractor,

> *Suddenly the monstrous sea and silence. [. . .] Naked they reach the sea and wade in as if they were dressed and with stones in their pockets. They sink, hug, and kiss each other on the mouth. In the distance, sirens.*

In Jimena Márquez's *Basic Principles for the Construction of Bridges*, a company of actors tasked with creating a piece celebrating Mario Benedetti's centenary instead explore their inability to bridge the gap between themselves and Benedetti by presenting their non-completed commission as they un-act it for us. Through quoting from the work of both Benedetti and Idea Vilariño, poems composed by the actors themselves, and their own reactions to these interventions, the play delves into the legacy of the Uruguayan dictatorship and the memories it both forged and erased,

> **Flor** Then we had a story. The story of the bridges, because we're bridges there and back, bridges of memory and forgetting. And acting is militancy and to fight is to commit completely. Bridge.

Sandra Massera's *Prelude to Anne* depicts a playwright attempting to write a new play about Anne Frank aided by Frank's ghost and, in the course of the play, becoming a ghost herself as her final spurt of creativity results in a fatal heart attack. Anne and the playwright look on as the theatre company produces the new play to honour both of their legacies. Marianella Morena's *I Will Give You Verses, Not Children* is an investigation of the life and death of Uruguayan poet Delmira Agustini, and like Márquez's *Basic Principles for the Construction of Bridges*, interrogates the nature of the theatre-making process itself, although in Morena's play the playwright rather than the actors asks the questions as each of the three acts is given a subtitle: "Towards Life", "Towards Realism", "Hyperrealism", and extensive stage directions that establish the performance style for that act, while the characters themselves question the nature of what they are engaged in doing:

> **Father** [...] How does one do a reconstruction? Does it go slowly, quickly, does one speak or is it done in silence? Is there an archaeology of memory, a museum of poetry, a theatre of the lost?

All of this strives to illuminate Agustini's life and death, while also shining light on our own participation in the process as audience members and readers. Finally, Josefina Trias' *Emotional Terror* employs the cycle of the seasons from summer to spring to chronicle a young woman's loves, heartbreaks, and ability to heal through a series of monologues. Each of these plays is theatrically alive and provides multiple opportunities for creative approaches to performance.

Theatrical translation's primary importance is to enrich our own theatrical cultures by exposing theatre professionals and audiences to a kind of theatricality lacking in our own environment. Through a discerning selection of plays, and commissioning of both well-known and lesser-known theatrical translators to bring those plays to life in English, Gregory and Stevens bring us a cornucopia of twenty-first-century Uruguayan playwrighting. Unpack it. Sate yourself. Let it bloom.

Adam Versényi, Professor of Dramaturgy in the Department of Dramatic Art, Senior Dramaturg for PlayMakers Repertory Company
The University of North Carolina, Chapel Hill

Introduction
Sophie Stevens

Why this Anthology?

Uruguayan theatre is dynamic, inquisitive, reflective, and formally innovative. However, to date, an anthology of plays from Uruguay translated into English has not been published as a collection which is available to researchers, theatre-makers and students. This book seeks to fill that gap. It features the writing of six contemporary playwrights, all published in English for the first time; they range from emerging to established authors and all continue to produce new work.

The anthology aims to introduce a diverse range of Uruguayan plays to English-speaking audiences. The fact that an anthology of this kind did not exist before is not reflective of a diminished or recently established theatre scene in Uruguay. Theatre in Uruguay is rich, varied and an important part of the country's cultural and artistic production. There are venues which receive state subsidies such as Uruguay's oldest theatre, the Teatro Solís, as well as independent venues such as the Teatro Circular. There are training opportunities through theatre schools, the most famous being the Escuela Multidisciplinaria de Arte Dramático Margarita Xirgu (EMAD) in Montevideo, and a range of theatre festivals which take place in Montevideo and across the country, including the Bienal de Teatros del Interior which specifically celebrates, stages and promotes the work of the theatres based outside of the capital city. This means that it has been both a joy and a challenge to curate and edit this volume with my co-editor William Gregory; we had such a diverse range of material to choose from precisely because new work for the stage is constantly emerging and being produced. In order to select the plays, we undertook an extensive reading project, connected to and informed by my ongoing research into Uruguayan theatre, and William's continued work with international and UK-based theatres and arts institutions. We both have experience of translating theatre from Latin America into English and are active in our translation communities, especially theatre translation networks, and we have consulted and discussed the development of this project with colleagues to whom we are very grateful. Further details of the criteria that we applied will be given below but for now, I want to emphasise that, above all, we decided to prioritise the quality of the plays. This anthology of six exciting, intriguing, well-written plays by six contemporary Uruguayan playwrights provides a snapshot of a playwriting culture that is relevant to our twenty-first century world and enticing for English-speaking audiences.

What is Uruguayan Theatre?

Contemporary Uruguayan theatre frequently engages with issues facing society within the current political context and theatre plays a crucial role in examining these issues through a critical lens. The plays in this anthology engage with topics such as misogyny, public health, and the role of the creative arts; they also interrogate the legacies of individuals and of political movements and periods of change. This type of critique is deeply embedded in Uruguay's theatre traditions: one of the most celebrated playwrights in the history of the River Plate region is Florencio Sánchez (1875–1910) and the Premios Florencio (Florencio Awards), a prestigious set of awards from the Asociación de Críticos Teatrales del Uruguay (ACTU, the Uruguayan theatre critics association) now bear his name. He worked in both Argentina and Uruguay and his writing brought to life the cruelty, conflict, challenges, and rural-urban divide faced by Uruguayan society at the start of the twentieth century. This was a time during which leaders sought to establish Montevideo as a modern intellectual and cultural hub, offering opportunities for training in new professions, whilst still depending on the rural export economy from Uruguay's vast, rich land. Whilst these questions and critiques are rooted in experiences in Uruguay, they resonate beyond this immediate context. Theatre in Uruguay raises challenging questions about our place in the world, our duty of care towards others and the environment, and our responsibility to think across generations to understand our present reality and what we can change in the future. The works included in this volume will broaden audiences' perspectives on our responsibility to tell the stories of others (or not), to reappraise and rewrite historical moments, and to address structural inequalities. Whilst these are serious issues, this anthology demonstrates how Uruguayan authors approach and explore them in creative ways by using humour, self-critique and scrutiny of the theatre-making process itself to invite audience members to reflect on and engage with these topics.

Theatre from Uruguay shares some of the stylistic features of other theatre traditions in Latin America; this is particularly true of the River Plate region and specifically Buenos Aires because many writers, performers and artists move across the region to share and develop their work. Uruguay has a long carnival tradition linked to the African diaspora, and the carnival itself is often considered to be the longest in the world. It includes processions, competitions between dance groups and satirical shows called *murgas*. For a study of carnival theatre, including translations of *murga* songs, see Gustavo Remedi's (2004) book in the Further Reading section.

The origins of modern-day theatre in the region are frequently traced back to the Podestá family of circus performers who worked across Uruguay and Argentina and whose circus shows were renowned and attracted large audiences. In 1884 José Podestá was cast by the theatre company of the Carlo brothers as the lead in *Juan Moreira*, about the heroic humble *gaucho* (nomadic herdsman), at the Teatro Politeama Argentino, Buenos Aires. It was an adaptation of the story by Argentine author Eduardo Gutiérrez which had been published as a weekly serial in the Argentine newspaper *La Patria Argentina* in 1879. When in 1886, Jose Podestá decided to re-stage the play and add dialogue to the performance, based on the text by Gutiérrez, the performance was transformed and gradually his company started performing in theatre spaces within cities and attracting new audiences (Versényi 1993: 73–7). The opportunities offered by the city and its spaces were transformative for the development of theatre in both Uruguay and Argentina. The experiences of *gauchos* and the tension between the new opportunities in the city and the rural ways of living and working would continue to exist and to be prominent themes of theatre and literature, including in the works of Florencio Sánchez. He also adapted Spanish and Italian forms of theatre, which were a cultural and literary inheritance from the waves of immigration to the River Plate region in the nineteenth century. Whilst Sánchez was inspired by these inherited forms of theatre, such as the *sainete* (short one-act plays, often using satire and humour), he adapted them and wrote for Uruguayan audiences with a focus on local concerns.

The period of the 1930s and 1940s was a prosperous time for Uruguay during which the export economy was successful and the country's cultural, artistic and academic offerings were expanded. The country received immigrants from Spain who were fleeing the unrest of the Spanish Civil War and the onset of Franco's dictatorship. These connections to Europe through different waves of exile and migration have had an important impact on Uruguay's theatre traditions, but artists have constantly modified and reshaped theatre styles to make them their own. Actress Margarita Xirgu was one of those who left Spain and settled in Montevideo where she established her career and contacts in the artistic and political spheres; this enabled her to establish Montevideo's drama school in 1949, now the aforementioned EMAD, which bears her name. In 2016 a Tecnicatura Universitaria en Dramaturgia—a degree-level award in playwriting—was created through an agreement between the EMAD and the Facultad de Humanidades, the humanities faculty established in 1945 at the Universidad de la República, the state university. Many academic and arts institutions were founded during this period including theatre companies such as the Comedia Nacional (the national theatre company of Uruguay, funded by the city of Montevideo) in 1947 and theatre spaces such as the independent theatre El Galpón (1949) which also had a theatre school. However, from the mid-1950s, Uruguay experienced civil and political unrest and clashes, leading to increased trade union activity and strikes, political repression and economic instability.

Between 1973 and 1985 Uruguay experienced a repressive civic-military dictatorship. Many artists went into exile and many theatre spaces were closed as large public meetings were banned. Repression also took the form of abduction and long-term imprisonment, and prisoners were often subjected to torture. This was at a time when there were repressive regimes in other parts of Latin America, and Operación Cóndor (Operation Condor) allowed for concerted action across countries and sharing of intelligence to find, imprison, and in many cases murder, those who were seen as subversive. There are many unresolved cases and ongoing searches for those people who were forcibly disappeared during this period and whose whereabouts remain unknown. For a clear and illuminating account of the factors influencing the lead-up to and onset and experience of the civic-military dictatorship in Uruguay, see Francesca Lessa's book in the Further Reading section; the chapter on "The Downward Spiral toward Dictatorship" (pp. 31–47) provides a very clear and succinct account of this difficult period.

The return to democracy in 1985 enabled theatre artists to begin staging work again, and some returned from exile. However, it is important to recognise that theatre did not cease to exist during the period of the civic-military dictatorship and artists who stayed found innovative ways through parody and folklore to perform stories, some of which critiqued the oppression and violence, whilst others called for resistance. In the 1990s and 2000s writers such as Carlos Liscano, Raquel Diana, Mariana Percovich, Carlos Manuel Varela, as well as Sandra Massera and Marianella Morena who are both included in this anthology, created work which reflected on the injustice, impunity and ongoing impact of the dictatorship period by exploring questions of memory, legacy and identity. In his study of theatre and dictatorship, Roger Mirza

(2009: 42–3) points out that the number of plays which sought to explore the experience and repercussions of the civic-military dictatorship increased as time passed, creating a certain distance from the events themselves. This distance allowed for critical reflection and multiple types of representation. The artistic concern with the civic-military dictatorship was compounded by the many unanswered questions and the lack of formal processes for justice, commemoration and memorialisation in Uruguay, something which has started to change more recently. See Stevens (2023) in the Further Reading for a study of Estela Golovchenko's work in the context of theatre and commemoration in Uruguay. Uruguay experienced an economic crisis in 2002 which led to increased levels of poverty and an increase in emigration, particularly amongst young people. Writers and theatre-makers continued to adapt and invent, and to be resilient in order to find ways to make new work.

As I am writing this introduction in November 2024, Uruguay has just elected a new president, Yamandú Orsi of the Frente Amplio (Broad Front), the centre-left coalition party who were previously in power with presidents Tabaré Vázquez (2005–2010 and 2015–2020) and José Mujica (2010–2015). Whilst it is not possible to say what will change or remain under this leadership, it is important to note that previous Frente Amplio governments paved the way for the creation of a series of competitive grants for artists and theatre-makers and helped establish the Instituto Nacional de Artes Escénicas (INAE), the national institute for the performing arts which coordinates the Festival International de Artes Escéncias (FIDAE), an annual international performing arts festival. The INAE has also played an important role in raising the profile of Uruguayan visual art, theatre and performance within and beyond Uruguay. Therefore, there are reasons to remain optimistic that the arts will continue to flourish in Uruguay and that there will be opportunities for playwrights to work and have their work produced through international collaborations. I hope that this anthology can be a starting point for generating interest and curiosity about Uruguay's cultural production and that it paves the way for new theatre practices, new productions, new research, and new translations.

What were the Criteria for Selecting these Plays?

The primary motivation behind this anthology project was to share exciting, innovative and stimulating work by contemporary playwrights from Uruguay who had not previously been translated into English and to place it in dialogue with contemporary playwriting from the English-speaking world. This anthology will expand the range of plays available in English and so be a valuable resource for students, practitioners, researchers, teachers and theatre-makers. Following an extensive period of research and reading of plays in Spanish, as co-editors, William and I quickly took the decision to prioritise the quality of the plays, as well as to include a variety of topics and styles, rather than to create a particular thematic or stylistic link. The selection of six playwrights in this anthology, Gabriel Calderón, Leonor Courtoisie, Jimena Márquez, Sandra Massera, Marianella Morena and Josefina Trías, encompasses writers with more established careers and those whose plays published here are their first. They come from different generations in terms of their ages and how long they have been creating work for the theatre. A unifying factor is that they are all still creating, and so there is a possibility to access more of their work, in Spanish in the first instance.

There is a growing interest among theatre-makers and theatre audiences in plays from Uruguay in translation. This is evidenced by the staging of the works of Sergio Blanco in London at the Arcola Theatre (2016, 2017, 2024) and the Pleasance Theatre (2020) all translated, adapted and directed by Daniel Goldman. Goldman has also showcased and developed Blanco's works at the Edinburgh Festival. The event "Celebrating Uruguayan Theatre" held at Barons Court Theatre in 2023 included a rehearsed reading of Raquel Diana's *Dancing Alone Every Night* (translated by Sophie Stevens and directed by Leo Bacica) which had been developed through a series of previous readings, including with Out of the Wings, a UK-based, interdisciplinary collective focused on researching, translating and platforming the theatre of Ibero-America for Anglophone readers and audiences. Out of the Wings has showcased work by Raquel Diana and Estela Golovchenko at its monthly table reads and at the annual Out of the Wings festival (see the festival webpages for more details), and a full staging of *Her Open Eyes* by Raquel Diana (translated by Sophie Stevens and directed by Giovanna Koyama) took place at Omnibus Theatre in 2022. The London Spanish Theatre Company produced *The Reality* by Denise Despeyroux (translated by Sarah Maitland and directed by Raymi Ortuse Quiroga) in 2019. This is a brief summary of some recent readings and productions which have provided an important insight into Uruguayan theatre and generated curiosity amongst audiences. Many of them have been the fruit of ongoing collaborations and relationships established between playwrights and translators and their joint efforts to find spaces to share their work (such as Goldman and Blanco, and my own work with Raquel Diana). Some of them have resulted in the publication of individual play texts (see Further Reading at the end of this chapter) and in my own book, I included three new translations as part of a larger study of Uruguayan theatre (Stevens 2022). Through this new anthology, we have created a resource which will increase and diversify the range of work from Uruguay available to English-speaking audiences. We believe this anthology demonstrates the richness of theatre from Uruguay and hope that these new translations will form the basis of future stagings and projects.

All of the playwrights included in the anthology have actively contributed to developing and promoting Uruguayan theatre in recent years through their participation in national and international theatre festivals, their roles in contributing to actor and director training, and through leading theatre companies and arts institutions. Most of the writers included here occupy or have previously occupied multiple roles across creative practice and theatre-making including teaching, acting, directing, arts management and publishing (see the biographies of each of the playwrights included before each of the plays for specific details). In addition to their national profile, many of them have established a reputation for creating work internationally, having participated in festivals and writing residencies in Latin America and Europe. This, in turn, has added to the richness of their work: it has afforded them the opportunity to see both Uruguay and the issues that they take on in their work from new perspectives as they have developed their work in dialogue with theatre practices, artists and audiences around the world.

It is noteworthy that some of the playwrights choose to explore creative and artistic processes within the plays themselves and this is perhaps inspired and informed by the range of creative roles that they themselves have carried out. For example, Massera's and Márquez's plays both explore the complex process of staging a play and the negotiations and tensions that can arise in the casting and rehearsal processes as creative decisions are made. These works, as well as Morena's, which features a character who is a "Maid-Stage Manager", include meta-theatrical elements which invite the audience to reflect on these choices and constructions, rather than to see this as realism. The protagonist in Trías' play explores how to nurture a process of creative writing in order to help her to make sense of her recent break-up and her identity as writer and woman. Both Morena and Trías focus on the role of women as creative writers, meaning that the plays are also self-reflexive in asking what the costs are of developing a writing career. Trías' play is a monologue; the anthology also includes plays with larger cast sizes, such as those by Morena and Calderón, with possibilities for doubling-up of actors.

The book is comprised of work by majority women playwrights, and many of the plays deal with the experience of women in the present day and in the past. Both Massera and Morena choose female historical figures as their subjects, Anne Frank in Massera's play and Delmira Agustini in Morena's. The connection to Agustini is significant as her legacy lives on in multiple ways. Delmira Agustini (1886–1914) was a Uruguayan poet who wrote erotic poetry exploring female sexuality, which has become increasingly recognised and studied since her death at the hands of her ex-husband Enrique Job Reyes who murdered her and then took his own life. Uruguay became the first country in Latin America to allow divorce initiated by either party in 1913 and Agustini divorced Reyes soon after, although they maintained a relationship until their deaths in 1914. See Further Reading for the article analysing Morena's play by Sarah Misemer (2020) which also contains details of the murder and the context in Uruguay. The significance of Agustini's violent death has been emphasised by feminist movements and those protesting against the prevalence of feminicide and structural inequalities; a plaque in Montevideo which commemorates Agustini's life is also dedicated to victims of gender-based violence. A performance space at the Teatro Solís is named after her and is where the *Nosotras en la Delmira* Festival (*We Women in the Delmira*; formerly called *Ellas en la Delmira* [*Women in the Delmira*] between 2017 and 2022) takes place annually during the month of March to mark International Women's Day. Trías and Massera have both had plays programmed in this festival.

In addition to Anne Frank and Delmira Agustini, this anthology also introduces audiences to novelist, poet and playwright Mario Benedetti (1920–2009) through Jimena Márquez's play about a company of actors from the Comedia Nacional seeking to create a new piece to commemorate the writer. Benedetti was part of the literary "Generation of 1945"—a year when many writers began to publish and to be in dialogue with each other and the public, thanks to the importance of literary magazines such as *Marcha*. This generation is also sometimes referred to as the "Generación Crítica" because of their critiques of society (Ángel Rama used this term in the title of his 1972 book about writers of this generation, including Benedetti). William and I saw this anthology as an opportunity to introduce readers and theatre-makers to other aspects of Uruguayan literary and cultural history and so we were particularly intrigued by and keen to include these plays which took as a starting point the work or lives of other authors and reimagined them in new ways for the stage. Therefore, the plays selected demonstrate the richness of contemporary Uruguayan writing whilst also providing an insight into the work of other creative artists and Uruguayan authors, as well as connections to Europe, making the plays intriguing and captivating.

Another thread running through this anthology, connecting many of the plays and playwrights, is the Comedia Nacional, Uruguay's highly prestigious national theatre company. As well as being the named company in Márquez's play, the real Comedia Nacional produced and staged the play in 2020. All of the writers included in this book have had works staged by the Comedia Nacional and some have also directed productions for the company. Gabriel Calderón was Artistic and Managing Director of the Comedia Nacional from 2022 to 2025 during which time the company staged a range of work, included international theatre, and ran a series of premieres outside of the capital city, Montevideo.

Some of these connecting threads were not at the forefront of the criteria but came up as William and I sought to make our choices. We believe that they create links between these works and serve to paint a picture of a dynamic network of authors whose contributions shape contemporary theatre in Uruguay. This means that the richness of the literary and cultural production of this country can be understood in greater detail by reading this collection as a whole.

The process of translation is a demanding one and it is also one which can sometimes highlight inconsistencies and weakness within plays. Based on our previous experience of translating theatre, William and I selected plays which were dramaturgically robust and which could undergo this process of intense reading and scrutiny, development and testing in another language, and the transformation into new plays in English. At the time of writing, these plays have not had full stagings in English. As part of the process of producing this anthology, William and I facilitated opportunities for the six translators involved to meet together to share extracts and read from their translations as a way to test them. We were also invited to do this at an Out of the Wings monthly table read which enabled us to receive further feedback from translators, directors, actors, and researchers. Therefore, sharing has been part of the process of developing this work to create stage-ready translations and we are delighted to share them with you now in the hope that they will inspire future work and productions.

The Plays

In this section, I will give a short overview of each of the plays and their key themes in the order that they appear in the book.

Ana Versus Death (*Ana contra la muerte*) by Gabriel Calderón, translated by Stephen Brown: Ana's son is diagnosed with cancer for a second time, but she remains determined to keep him alive. This play, like many of Calderón's previous works, explores the themes of violence, mortality and family. It depicts the pain of living with a child who is ill with cancer and the extreme risks a mother will take to save her child. But when protecting one person means endangering others, how far does a parent's love for their child justify their actions? *Ana Versus Death* explores the impact of poverty and desperation, and the meaning of sacrifice.

They All Sleep at Siesta Time (*Duermen a la hora de la siesta*) by Leonor Courtoisie, translated by William Gregory: in this tale of adventure, determination and independence, three friends embark upon a road-trip to save the life of a dying armadillo by stealing a tractor from the local brothel. Soon they become embroiled in a spree of misadventure, with an increasing body count and fresh injuries. A sense of power and possibility fills the play, as does the responsibility and ingenuity of the three friends; at the same time, does anyone even notice if all this happens whilst everyone else is enjoying a siesta?

Basic Principles for the Construction of Bridges (*Nociones básicas para la construcción de puentes*) by Jimena Márquez, translated by Catherine Boyle: this play depicts a company of actors working to devise a play about Mario Benedetti, who published prolifically in poetry and prose and is one of Uruguay's most respected and well-read authors. However, the process is a challenging one because they struggle to reconcile the image of this literary great with his relationship to the darker side of Uruguay's history. As artists born during the dictatorship period, they question how their own personal narratives fit into the dramatic narrative. The play creatively raises questions about the limits between fact and fiction in theatre-making, and what we prioritise when staging a play. *Basic Principles for the Construction of Bridges* draws on the experiences of the play's original cast to expose the complexity, creativity and care involved in remembering great literary figures and dealing with the aftermath of dictatorship.

Prelude to Anne (*Preludio de Ana*) by Sandra Massera, translated by Rachel Toogood: in this play, the theatre-making process is also explored; this time the protagonist seeks to create a work about Anne Frank. How can a Uruguayan writer in the twenty-first century do justice to the life of one of the previous century's most enduring historical figures, whose story carries a symbolism of almost unimaginable weight? As Elena struggles to finish the play and opening night approaches, it is through an encounter in the theatre with Anne Frank herself that the protagonist gains a renewed sense of clarity, creativity and connectedness to her subject matter, and understands the role that her work can play in Anne's legacy. *Prelude to Anne* is the first of three plays about Anne Frank written by Massera; it is followed by *Ana después* (*Anne Afterwards*) and *Tulipanes para Hermine* (*Tulips for Hermine*).

I Will Give You Verses, Not Children (*No daré hijos, daré versos*) by Marianella Morena, translated by Kate Eaton: the play takes as a starting point the life and death of Uruguayan modernist poet Delmira Agustini who was killed by her ex-husband in 1914. Agustini's erotic poetry and desire for independence posed a challenge to norms at the time. Morena's play shows how Agustini's experience can shed light on patriarchal structures which continue to exist today in Uruguay and beyond. The play draws on songs, poetry, and documentary material to depict Agustini's defiance, resilience and creativity and raises the question: what is the price we pay for artistic freedom?

Emotional Terror (*Terrorismo emocional*) by Josefina Trías, translated by Sophie Stevens: the protagonist Clara finds herself back at her parents' house after a traumatic break-up. She is filled with sadness, frustration and many questions about why her relationship ended, what it means to be a single woman in society today and how to transform mourning into creativity. Set across four seasons, the play is a funny, frank and moving insight into the intertwined processes of writing and defining one's identity in a world of body-shaming, activism or slacktivism and social media. Clara asks: what happens if we manipulate language so that our identity is imagined and formed through our art?

We hope that there is something in here for everyone and that if not, you will be inspired to search for what interests you amongst the wealth of playwriting from

Uruguay that we were unable to showcase here for lack of space. Do consult the Further Reading list where you will find other Uruguayan plays published in English. This anthology shows that Uruguayan theatre deserves more critical and creative attention. As well as more stagings of plays from Uruguay, William and I hope that this anthology may inspire new lines of investigation and critical inquiry to generate analyses to accompany these theatre texts. Above all, we hope that this anthology can pave the way for the richness of Uruguayan theatre to occupy a greater space in theatres, universities and drama schools.

Works Referenced

Mirza, R. (2009), "Escenificaciones de la memoria en el teatro de la postdictadura: *Pedro y el Capitán, Elena Quinteros. Presente* y *Las cartas que no llegaron*", in R. Mirza and G. Remedi (eds), *La dictadura contra las tablas: Teatro uruguayo e historia reciente*, 37–81, Montevideo: Biblioteca Nacional.

Rama, Á. (1972), *La generación crítica 1939–1969: 1. Panoramas*, Montevideo: Arca.

Versényi, A. (1993), *Theatre in Latin America: Religion, Politics and Culture from Cortés to the 1980s*, Cambridge: Cambridge University Press.

Further Reading

Articles, Books and Book Chapters about Uruguayan Theatre

Buffery, H. and C. Levey (2023), "Transnational Embodiments: Staging the Trope of Transgenerational Transmission in the Theatre of Victoria Szpunberg and Sergio Blanco", *Bulletin of Spanish Studies*, 100: 1–28.

Bulman, G. A. (2022), *Feeling the Gaze: Image and Affect in Contemporary Argentine and Chilean Performance*, Chapel Hill, North Carolina: University of North Carolina Press. (This book contains a study of Sergio Blanco's *Tebas Land* [*Thebes Land*] staged in Buenos Aires, directed by Corina Fiorillo [2016–2019]).

Lessa, F. (2013), *Memory and Transitional Justice in Uruguay: Against Impunity*, New York: Palgrave Macmillan.

Mirza, R. (1991–1992), "El sistema teatral uruguayo de la última década ¿Un cambio de paradigma?", *Latin American Theatre Review*, 25.2: 181–190.

Mirza, R. ed (1992), *Teatro uruguayo contemporáneo: antología*, Madrid: Centro de Documentación Teatral: Sociedad Estatal Quinto Centenario: Fondo de Cultura Económica.

Misemer, S. (2013), "Tragedy and Trauma: *Antígona oriental* de Marianella Morena", *South Central Review*, 30 (3): 125–42.

Misemer, S. (2017), *Theatrical Topographies: Spatial Crises in Uruguayan Theater post-2001*, Lewisburg, Pennsylvania: Bucknell U.P.

Misemer, S. (2020), "Over Her Dead Body: Marianella Morena's Delmira Agustini in *No daré hijos, daré versos*", *Revista Canadiense de Estudios Hispánicos*, 43 (2): 403–23.

Out of the Wings Festival website: https://www.ootwfestival.com/

Remedi, G. (2004), *Carnival Theater: Uruguay's Popular Performers and National Culture*, trans. A. Ferlazzo, Minneapolis: University of Minnesota Press.

Stevens, S. (2016), "Distance and Proximity in Analysing and Translating *Bailando sola cada noche* (*Dancing Alone Every Night*) into English", *The Mercurian: A Theatrical Translation

Review, 6 (2): 81–99. Available at: https://the-mercurian.com/2016/11/16/distance-and-proximity-in-analysing-and-translating-bailando-sola-cada-noche-dancing-alone-every-night/

Stevens, S. (2022), *Uruguayan Theatre in Translation: Theory and Practice*, Cambridge: Legenda.

Stevens, S. (2023), "Representations of Transition, Memory and Crisis on Stage in *Punto y coma (Ready or Not)* by Uruguayan Dramatist Estela Golovchenko", in A. Balduino P. Fernandes, M. Haughton and P. Verstraete (eds), *Theatre, Performance and Commemoration: Staging Crisis, Memory and Nationhood*, 65–78, London: Methuen Drama.

Versényi, A. (1993), *Theatre in Latin American: Religion, Politics and Culture from Cortés to the 1980s*, Cambridge: Cambridge University Press.

Plays

Benedetti, M. (2009), *Pedro and the Captain*, trans. A. Aron, Tiburon Belvedere, California: Cadmus.

Benedetti, M. (1985–87), "Pedro and the Captain (translation from Spanish)", trans. F. Beberfall, *Modern International*, 19 (1): 33–52.

Blanco, S. (2016), *Thebes Land*, translated and adapted by D. Goldman, London: Oberon.

Blanco, S. (2020), *The Rage of Narcissus* translated and adapted by D. Goldman, London: Oberon.

Blanco, S. (2024), *Divine Intervention or The Celebration of Love*, translated and adapted by D. Goldman, London: Bloomsbury Methuen.

Blanco, S. (2024), *When You Pass Over My Tomb* translated and adapted by D. Goldman, London: Bloomsbury Methuen.

Despeyroux, D. (2019), *La Realidad, Reality*, trans. S. Maitland, Madrid: Antígona.

Despeyroux, D. (2017). *Black Tenderness: The Passion of Mary Stuart*, trans. S. Breden, ed. and intro. M. Laera, Imola: Cue Press.

Diana, R. (2020), "Her Open Eyes", trans. and intro. by S. Stevens, *The Mercurian: A Theatrical Translation Review*, 8 (2): 183–206. Available online at: https://the-mercurian.com/2020/11/24/her-open-eyes/

Ana Versus Death

Gabriel Calderón

Translated by Stephen Brown

Ana contra la muerte (*Ana Versus Death*) premiered on 23 July 2019 in the Espacio Palermo at the at the Instituto de Actuación de Montevideo (Montevideo Institute of Acting). It was directed by Gabriel Calderón and performed by Marisa Bentancur, Gabriela Iribarren and María Mendive. The play was published by Criatura Editora in 2020.

About the author and translator

Gabriel Calderón is a playwright, director and actor. He has written over 30 plays and has twice received the Uruguayan Ministry of Education and Culture National Literature Award. His plays have been translated into French, German, English, Italian, Catalan, Greek and Portuguese. In 2022, *Ana contra la muerte* won the Florencio Awards for Best Production, Best Direction, Best Leading Actress and Best Supporting Actress. In recent years he has worked increasingly in Europe, with productions at the Théâtre des Quartiers d'Ivry (Paris), and becoming the first Uruguayan playwright to have productions at the Teatre Nacional de Catalunya (Barcelona) and the Teatro Nazionale di Modena (Modena, Italy). He has been the Director of the Instituto Nacional de Artes Escénicas (National Performing Arts Institute), Director of the Executive Office for the Uruguay Bicentenary, and Coordinator of University Programmes in Playwriting at the Universidad de la República, the state university of Uruguay. Between 2022 and 2025 he held the role of Artistic and Managing Director of the Comedia Nacional, the national theatre company of Uruguay.

Stephen Brown translates from German, French and Spanish into English and completed the MA in Literary Translation from the University of East Anglia with Distinction. He is interested in translating contemporary fiction, including theatre plays, as well as non-fiction. His translation of Luis Edoardo Torres's play *On the Edge* (*En la margen del río*) was performed at the 2022 Out of the Wings festival (Omnibus Theatre, London) and published in 2023 by Inti Press. He currently translates alongside his full-time job as a technology manager for a London-based charity.

For my parents, who with love, pain and dignity, survive my sister.

Characters

Ana, *f*
Doctor, *f*
Best Friend, *f*
Dealer, *m*
Police Officer, *m*
Lawyer, *f*
Assassin, *f*
Other Friend, *f*
Judge, *f*
Nurse, *f*
Doctor Two, *f*
Cellmate One, *f*
Cellmate Two, *f*

There are thirteen characters but all of these can be played by three actresses or, as ever, not.

Scene I

Ana *and the* **Doctor** *are in the consulting room at the hospital.*

Ana Well I just don't know where he got that passion for horses.
He used to like watching them run.
Because he liked running.
And that broke my heart.
When you told me you were going to have to remove his leg, that broke me in two.
No, I thought, not his leg.
What with him liking running so much.
He used to come into the house running,
he would leave the house running,
he would dash about inside and out at the speed of light.
"One day you're going to fall and you're going to break every bone in your body,
one day you're going to clatter into something",
I would tell him, but he just kept on running.
It was as if life was getting away from him, you know, so he had to live it all in a hurry.
. . .
OK right . . .
So when he woke up from the operation he said:
Did I tell you what he said to me?
He said: "Mamá, when a horse loses a leg, they put it to sleep."
"You're mad", I told him.
"You're not a horse.
You're a man", I said.
"You're much more than a leg.
Don't say that.
Don't think about it anymore."
And so he didn't mention it again,
never said a word to me again.
I don't know if he kept on thinking about it.
But he never mentioned it to me again.

Doctor (*to the audience*) And despite all this, he didn't say a word to his mother, even though the boy was a boy and was sad and disappointed, just like any boy would be, on being told they were going to remove one of his legs, even though he was as sad as any soul that innocently cries when hope is ripped from its grasp. Despite all that world of pain, that boy, in front of his mother, doesn't cry. He is left looking at his mother, a suspicious expression on his face, his brow furrowed, listening to the arguments given by those who are going to amputate his leg. And it's moving, you know, seeing that boy, who still isn't ready for this world, how he sadly, yet courageously, accepts the idea of the amputation. How he nervously bites the inside of his lip, trying to figure out the options they have, despite not really understanding everything he and his mother are up against. Because when they told him he was going to end up bald like a little old man, well that he could understand, because he knew his hair would grow back and the boy would come back to eclipse the old man, when they told him he would vomit a lot, that he would lose weight and not want to eat, he understood and accepted all that, in the hope that one day he might again be able to stuff his mouth with sweet things, and put behind him this illness which can only be felt and not seen. But, for now, it was all about where they were going to take his leg, and more importantly, why they weren't going to return it. Because something that final, something that permanent, is beyond a boy's tiny, miniscule capacity for understanding. He still doesn't understand what "forever" means, rather he does know it will be for a long time, and that to run like he liked to run he would need both his legs, and for the girl he liked to tell him he was really fast he needed both his legs, and to win the football back off his best friend he needed both his legs, to steal sweets and not get caught, to wear fashionable shoes, to climb the stairs, get out of the house, get out of school, get out of his chores, for all that you needed two legs. And it's right at that moment he sheds a warm tear out of the corner of his eye, he who had tried to live up to the name "little man" his mother had given him. And it's then his mamá, who up until that point had been thinking her son was maturely accepting everything life was putting in his way, she sees that tear, and knows that that's only to be expected, that he's a boy and amputating his leg is like tearing out his soul. So the mother intercepts the path of the tear with her work-worn fingers, lifts up the boy's chin and tells him: "Don't cry about this, leave crying for important things."

Ana So I can still remember the day our luck changed.
It was you, Doctor, who changed our luck.
The day you first told us there were these things called prosthetics.
I thought they were something for your teeth.
But you made us see there was hope, Doctor.
And that it wasn't easy, it wasn't cheap, it wasn't straightforward.
It was like a miracle though.
Friends, relatives, neighbours, all of them collecting every little peso they had.
And I was afraid, yeah.
That after all that effort.
I had so many doubts.
What if they don't work?
What if he can't use them, what if he doesn't like them, what if he falls and breaks the only leg he's got left?
But yesterday when I opened the door and saw him there, standing all upright.
Proud, imposing.
Like he was a horse, Doctor.
And I started crying, you know.
On the inside, not on the outside.
But I was crying.
At seeing my little foal there, so noble.
So proud.
Standing so tall.

The **Doctor** *makes as if to speak, but* **Ana** *continues.*

Ana OK, so I know you want to tell me something,
but today I want to tell you something first,
because I know I never said much.
But today I told myself
I've got to tell you a few things.
Do you know what he said to me today?
He said:
"Mamá I'm going to a dance,
I'm going to a dance to break in my leg."
As if he were breaking in new shoes;
you just miss the silliest things.
And I swear I got all emotional.
My son dancing again.
He's going to a concert tomorrow.
Next week he wants to start doing sport.
I told him: "Be careful, take your time."
Honestly though it makes me feel so good seeing him dashing about everywhere.
And that's when I remembered I was seeing you today.
So I told myself: "Ana, you need to give the doctor a present."
I didn't have any money,
but I never do have any money
well, you already know that.
What am I going to say to you?
What with everything you did to help me
so I told myself: "What does it matter?
One day of life is still life."
Because you helped us
you always gave me hope.
So yesterday I told myself:
"Do something for the doctor, knit her something, cook something for her."
So I made you a little something.
I don't know how to cook but I made you a few biscuits.
They won't taste nice, but they're a present.
If they're horrible, just think of them as a gesture.
Because it's about time we starting feeling good again,
that we start cooking again,
thinking about what we will eat for dinner,
for breakfast,
making plans,
going out again,
going to dances and concerts,
getting worried when I don't know what time he's going to get home,
feeling afraid, afraid in a different way though, afraid of silly things, of everyday
things, feeling afraid for no reason.
I missed not feeling afraid like that.
I was tired of feeling that other fear,

that deadly fear.
You know . . .
That . . . fear . . . That overwhelming fear.

Doctor Ana.

Ana Oh, I'm talking too much.
Doctor, you know what you mean to me, to us, to everyone.
You mean life, Doctor.
People don't want to see doctors.
My mother used to say you killed the healthy.
But you lot kill the dead, don't you . . .
You kill death.
You kill sorrow.

Doctor Ana.

Ana Let me speak, I'm all worked up, but what I'm saying is important stuff.
Stuff I need to say
about this whole story, of pain
of sadness
and most of all of injustice.
Because this story was unjust, it made us do and live through things that no-one should be made to live through, and I won't forget that. I won't forget the role you played in this story. And now that this story is ending . . .

Doctor Ana, let me speak.

Ana No, let me speak, please, it will only be for a second and then you can speak. Just like when you speak to me and I always listen. You always used to ask me what I was thinking, and I wasn't thinking at all, I was just inundated with information, overwhelmed with information. That's right. Drowning in it. I couldn't say a word. But now it's finally all over, it feels right, before everyone forgets and goes their separate ways, and perhaps, who knows, we never see each other again. It's right I say thank you to you, Doctor, for everything. Thank you.

Doctor Ana, I need you to listen to me and calm down.

Ana Yes, Doctor, thank you Doctor. You're great, Doctor. I'll be quiet.

Doctor Ana . . . It came back . . .

Ana What came back?

Pause.

Doctor . . . It came back . . .
. . .

Ana . . . Came back where?
. . .

Doctor Into your son's body.

...

Ana But . . . How? Didn't they get it out?

Doctor Yes, but it's reappeared.

...

Ana What do you mean, "it's reappeared"?

Doctor Well, sometimes that can happen . . .

Ana But how could it have reappeared? Where did it reappear? How did it get back in?

Doctor Sometimes it can happen.

Ana No, but this can't happen now. There must be something wrong with the tests. The last time, when something really happened, when all this started, he had a lump on his leg, and he was in pain and . . . No, no, he doesn't feel any pain now. There's something not right.

Doctor The routine checks we did last time showed it had reappeared, there is metastasis in various places, it's rare in a cancer of this type, but it does happen.

Ana In what sort of places? There's nothing wrong with him though, he's not in any pain. Yesterday he went out, yesterday . . . he went out dancing, with his prosthetic leg, with friends and he was happy and breathing fine. No, no, there's something not right, you must be reading someone else's report, you're mistaken. It hasn't come back. He's already better, he went out yesterday and he's just got back in, he's at home and today he's going out again to see a concert of a group he likes, he doesn't look ill at all. There's nothing come back, nothing's ever going to come back.

Doctor He's going to have to come in to the hospital so we can carry out more tests.

Ana No. (*Becoming very agitated.*) No. No, not more tests. He, I, his body won't cope, none of us will be able to cope with that. He's happy because this was all over, don't ruin that for him. None of this is right, Doctor. What you are trying to say? What are you telling me? Why are you doing this to me? Why are you doing this to us? What's wrong with all of you? What have you got against us? My son is at home, with both his legs, don't confine him to a bed again, don't admit him to hospital again, he doesn't want to vomit again, we can't, we can't go through all this again. (*She is struggling to breathe.*)

Doctor Calm down, Ana.

Ana Calm down? How I am supposed to calm down? Calming down is absolutely the last thing you can ask of me, I feel totally desperate.

Doctor Right now though the most important thing is for you to calm down and remain strong.

Ana I'm not calm, I'm not strong, I haven't got any strength left because we barely survived what happened the last time. If I had, ever did have any strength, that's all gone and all I feel now is afraid, afraid.

Doctor Do you want us to call someone?

Ana What am I going to do? I just don't know what I'm going to do. I don't think we can do all this again.

Doctor The new treatment might be more expensive, but there are sources of funding.

Ana Sources I've already called on, sources I've already used, there isn't any money, there isn't a door I haven't banged on. This isn't fair!

Doctor We're going to help you, we're going to support you through this.

Ana What good is your help going to do me? Ever since you all started helping me, all I've done is fall downhill, faster and faster, and I don't know now if I'll be able to crawl back up, I haven't even got the strength to look my son in the eye and tell him . . .

Doctor You've got to be strong.

Ana No, you all have to be stronger, you all have to improve, be better. What are you all doing? What's wrong with you all? You removed my son's leg, you removed his hair, you pumped him full of chemicals, inserted cables into him and everything, all to get rid of something we couldn't even see. And now you tell me it's come back? What kind of doctors are you anyway? What did you study? What good did all your studies do if you can't even prevent a boy suffering like this?

Doctor We can't do everything, Ana.

Ana You should be able to, you're all liars. You all go on about medical advances yet you can't even save a boy's leg. All your studies go to help rich people, you spend hours inventing creams for wrinkles, so their hair doesn't fall out, so they can just sit there and get slimmer, but when you need to invent something to save a poor boy's leg, that's when all the constraints start appearing, that's when you start saying we did everything we could, we don't know everything. Perhaps rich people are satisfied with you getting rid of their dandruff or stretching their skin, but I want more from you, I expect more, I want you to conquer this, don't ask me to be strong, ask it of yourself, call your friends, get a group of you together, because you swore you would protect my son so now it's up to you to make him conquer death. Not just lose a leg, lose his hair, or stop vomiting. I want you to make him conquer death, if you can't, then you're not doctors, you're . . . you're . . .

Scene II

Ana *and* **Best Friend** *at her friend's house.*

Best Friend What bastards!

Ana They're not bastards, they're doing what they can.

Best Friend Not again?

Ana Yes, again.

Best Friend I haven't got any more money, I . . .

Ana I didn't come here to ask you for money.

Best Friend No, I know, it's just if I did . . .

Ana Yes, I know.

. . .

Best Friend We'll help you.

Ana Yes, that's why I came, because I knew you would help me.

Best Friend We'll all help you, here in the neighbourhood we're poor, but we're good people. Not everyone though, some people aren't good, some are messed up, others are lost. But those who aren't either messed up or lost, those who know very well where they're at, who they are and most of all who you are, those people, the good ones, they'll help you. We'll help you. What's more, your family always helped you . . .

Ana My family can't help me this time around.

Best Friend What do you mean, "they can't help you"?

Ana When you say family, that sounds like something enormous, but we're only talking about two or three people. Some of them have already helped me a lot, others only a little, but as for money, which is what I need, they don't have any. I really can't ask them to pull out all the stops for me again.

Best Friend So how much money do you need?

Ana A lot.

. . .

Best Friend And the hospital won't cover it?

Ana They covered the first treatment in its entirety, the second one as well, then after that they covered the medication. But now they're already saying this is incurable, that this is a different field altogether, that this is an experimental treatment which is expensive and which they don't cover.

Best Friend But can that save him?

Ana For now it's the only option I can see, however expensive it might be, however experimental it might be, it's the only way out I've got.

. . .

Best Friend So, how can I help you?

Ana I know you've already helped me a lot. Like many people have. You've already lent me money and I know you haven't got any more and that if you did have, you'd give it to me without a second thought, I know that. That's why I've not come to ask you for money or anything else that awkward. I just need one simple thing and I know you'll be able to help me.

Best Friend Of course, what is it?

Ana I just need the number.

Best Friend What number?

Ana I mean just his number.

Best Friend Whose?

Ana You know very well whose.

Best Friend No, no, I don't.

Ana The only number I don't have that you might have.

Best Friend The only number I might have, that I do have but you don't have, OK, well it's a good thing I do have it and you don't.

Ana I need it.

Best Friend No, it's your son who needs you, he needs you to be clear, alert, strong and that number isn't going to help you with any of that.

Ana That number is going to help him.

Best Friend What's wrong with you? Have you gone mad? I'm missing something here, is there something I don't know?

Ana All you need to know is that I've thought this through, I'm convinced, I'm certain, I know that number is the only chance I've got.

Best Friend It feels like you don't know a thing.

Ana I know how I can help my son.

Best Friend Not like that.

Ana Come on, please, make it easy for me, I need help and you yourself can't help me.

Best Friend I'm helping you by not giving you the number.

Ana Give it me.

Best Friend Why are you going back to all that shit? Sorry, but I'm your friend and I'm looking out for you.

Ana I'm looking out for my son, I've been up to my neck in shit for a long time now, not to mention my son.

Best Friend I need you to think clearly, ask me for anything apart from that number.

Ana You know I can get that number another way, don't you? You know I can get hold of that number, or any other number, elsewhere, that the shit you're trying to keep from me I can get hold of on any street corner.

Best Friend Yes, but for some reason you came here to ask me for it, because in some way you understand this is bad news and you know it, and perhaps you need me to remind you of that. That I make you think a bit about the state you were in, about what a wreck you and everyone else was who loved you, about how much your son needed you and cried when you were far away. Have you forgotten about that already? And how during all that time when you were far away, when you were a wreck, nearly dead, not knowing whether you would ever come back one day, throughout all that time I waited for you with your son, I looked after him so you could be with him today. So here's why you're going to hear me out. That mess already led you astray once and I'm not going to let that shit do it to you again.

Ana That mess, as you call it, has a debt with me and it's going to pay me back.

Best Friend That shit doesn't pay, it only takes from you.

Ana Will you cut the lectures and all the comebacks, just give me the number!

Best Friend I won't give it you.

Ana I'll get it another way.

Best Friend So why did you come here and ask me for it?

Ana Because I wanted to do this the right way, I wanted it to be discreet, I wanted your son to help me.

Best Friend My son can't help anyone.

Ana He can help me, and my son.

Best Friend You're not thinking clearly.

Ana That might be true, but I still want the number because I've long got used to thinking unclearly. I don't think I've ever thought clearly, my mind isn't clear, my mind's all mixed up, fogged up, it's always fogged up and I have to think my way through it. I've long got used to looking only a few metres ahead of me, and since my mind only thinks a few metres ahead of me, that's how I've become, fogged up. And the only thing I can see through all that thick air is the face of your son, who, whatever you might think, is the only one who can help my son.

Pause.

Best Friend (*to the audience*) We skirt round and round the subject, as if in fear, avoiding it, we don't even want to say its name, because to name it would be to bring it out into the open, to give it a presence, and both of us, even though she wouldn't accept it, even though she wanted to go back to that place, the pair of us want to keep it, the unnameable, at a distance. And for that reason, we don't name it, not to make poets out of ourselves or because we didn't know the words, rather we avoid it, because to say it out loud hurts, it awakes in us a really tangled, complex labyrinth of memories. Dangerous memories, because there are such things as dangerous memories. Just like there are beautiful memories, ones that when a word brings them to mind, they make you smile, your soul feels joyous and you breathe more easily. And so there are dangerous memories, which a word can spark into life, like something that is set on fire inside you and can't be extinguished, as if the curse word lets go a millilitre of poison into your bloodstream and spreads throughout your whole body. Dangerous memories are those you struggle to live with, which you try and keep in a little room in your head that's difficult to access, behind a door you keep closed, a door which can still be opened, for by simply mentioning the word, remembering the word, the door would open, and the word would then contaminate your blood, rip your muscles to shreds, break your bones and tear apart everything inside you, and that complex machinery of tendons and guts will then be liquified along with your teeth and skull, and all that will be left of you is a bag of skin filled with your own liquid. And there is nothing worse than seeing a friend liquified, confused, not knowing which part of them was soul and which sternum. That's why we don't mention that evil word, so we avoid pressing the button on the liquidiser, so the ghost remains within its sphere of non-existence and we are, at least for today, safe.

Ana The liquidiser was already switched on and it's now all spurting out all over the place. There's going to be one big mess. Of that I am sure.

Scene III

Ana *and the* **Dealer** *are in a squatters' apartment.*

Dealer You're the last person I would have expected a call from . . .

Ana Right, of course, I thought the same, I mean . . . You're the last person I would have wanted to call.

Dealer Still . . .

Ana Still.

Dealer To what do I owe this honour?

Ana I need money, lots of it.

Dealer Welcome to the twenty-first century, nowadays everyone needs lots of money.

Ana My son is dying.

. . .

Dealer Welcome to the twenty-first century. Nowadays children always die before their parents.

Ana You're still alive.

Dealer I'm neither dead or alive. I'm a ghost, you might say. I'm in a domestic and material limbo. I'm like the reflection of everything I used to be, but only a reflection at that, when people go to hug me, they're left hugging nothing.

Ana You seem really alive to me.

Dealer That's just lies. I'm lying to you and you're lying to yourself, that's what drugs do to you, don't you remember?

Ana Are you using now? I thought you didn't use, at least when you were selling to me you weren't using.

Dealer I'm not a user, this might sound strange though, but it feels like all these years I've been used.

Ana That doesn't sound strange to me, it sounds a shame.

Dealer It's not a shame, it is what it is. When you look hell in the eye, you don't realise it but hell is looking back at you too. And hell doesn't forget, it remembers you, it seeks you out and invites you back in again (*he takes out a small bag containing drugs*), you can't avoid it, I understand you better than anyone, there's no way out.

Ana I did get out.

Dealer Yet here you are again.

Ana If your mother were to find out, she'd kill you.

Dealer You can't kill a ghost, you can only exorcise it and my mother doesn't want to exorcise me, or rather she doesn't want to exorcise herself of me.

Ana No mother wants to exorcise herself of her children.

Dealer That's true, it's the children who want to get our mothers off our backs, but they're really clingy.

Ana Don't be stupid, put that stuff away.

Dealer I'm not as stupid as I look, so said Plato to his disciples . . . (*He puts the small bag away.*) So if you didn't come for that, why have you come?

Ana I need money.

Dealer And what's that got to do with me?

Ana You can give me money.

Dealer I haven't got any money, what I have isn't mine, it's other people's, and even if I did have some, why should I give it to you?

Ana You've got money, you owe me money, and you're going to give it me back.

Dealer Give it back? If I weren't the one selling the drugs, I'd think you were high right now.

Ana Five years.

Dealer Ah, well.

Ana Five years in prison, can you imagine what that was like?

Dealer I know what it's like to be in for one, multiply by five and yes, I can imagine, more or less.

Ana And I never said anything, not a word. And let's be clear, they did ask.

Dealer If you'd talked, you wouldn't be here.

Ana And then I got out and I didn't come back looking for a single thing.

Dealer Because you were always intelligent.

Ana Not a single peso, or help, nothing.

Dealer Better that way, I say.

Ana But now I do need help, and you all owe me, and if you haven't got the means to pay me, you'll have to find a way, because I missed five years of my son's life and I'm not going to miss a single one again. And if I missed those years and didn't get out any earlier, it was because I helped you, by not exposing you, by not naming names, by not opening my mouth, by being fair and you all need to acknowledge that now. I was fair, I lived by the codes, I behaved well. But now I feel like behaving badly, because the codes are being broken, and injustice is about to take my son away from me for not having enough money to pay for his treatment. He deserves to get that treatment and I'm going to get that money, whatever it takes, whatever I have to say, whoever I have to name. If injustice wants to take him away from me, I'm going act justly for him.

Dealer Justly? Justly? What's this justice you're talking about, you fucking mule? You were a fucking mule, a run-of-the-mill one at that, another bloody carrier, a disposable meat wrapper, you stupid, screwed-up woman. What's this justice you're talking about, you junkie? You served up your arse for a hit and now you come here talking to me about justice. What do you think this is? A trial? That there are codes here? There's nothing here, only drugs, if you want them, you pay for them, if you don't have anything to pay for them, serve up your arse, and if your arse has exploded from all the drugs, just like your face and your life, then stuff all the drugs you can in that exploded arse and get it over to the other side, putting on your nicest face, and if they catch you, close your arse and your mouth, because if you don't, we'll explode it for you. That's what you did, that's what you're doing right now and that right there is justice, you got that, you fucking leech?

Ana I need the money.

Dealer And I need you to get lost. I promised my mother I wouldn't help you. Promises are made to be kept.

Ana I promised my son he wasn't going to die.

Dealer Some promises are made to be broken.

Ana Well, still.

Dealer Still.

Scene IV

Ana *and the* **Police Officer** *at the border.*

Police Officer Reason for the journey?

Ana Sightseeing.

Police Officer For how many days?

Ana Two.

Police Officer Sightseeing for two days?

Ana . . .Yes.

Police Officer Where are you going to stay?

Ana In a hotel . . .

Police Officer The name of the hotel?

Ana No, at a friend's house.

Police Officer What's your friend's address?

Ana Ah, well, wait a moment, I don't know it.

Police Officer Your friend's name?

Ana I'll tell you right away.

Police Officer You don't know the name?

Ana I've got it written down here.

Police Officer You're going to stay at a friend's place but you don't know her name.

Ana Yes, I do know it, Juana, it's written down here.

. . .

Police Officer What are you carrying in the suitcase?

Ana Clothes.

Police Officer For two days?

Ana Yes.

Police Officer For sightseeing?

Ana Yes.

. . .

Police Officer Wait here a moment.

. . .

Come this way.

Ana What's wrong?

Police Officer Nothing, come this way please.

Ana But I haven't done anything.

Police Officer No-one said you've done anything.

Ana You can check my case, I'm only coming for two days.

Police Officer Can you come this way?

. . .

We're going to talk for a bit.

. . .

Tell me again your reason for coming here.

Ana To stay at a friend's house.

Police Officer Didn't you say you were coming to go sightseeing?

Ana Yes sightseeing, but I'm staying at a friend's place.

Police Officer Whose name you don't know.

Ana I do know it . . . It's Juana . . . It's on the card I gave you.

Police Officer Yes, the card . . . So where did you meet this friend?

Ana She's a friend from school.

Police Officer And your friend's surname?

. . .

A friend from school whose surname you can't remember.

. . .

Ana It's just . . .

Police Officer No, no, don't go on, we're going to spare ourselves all this, most of all since I've been a border police officer for years and I've long got bored at playing at cross-examinations and . . .

Ana The thing is . . .

Police Officer No, look here, I'm going to tell you what the thing is. Better still, I'm going to tell you what's going to happen and why what's going to happen is going to happen. First, we're going to open the travel case you packed for your two-day sightseeing trip and we're going to tear it apart, turn it over looking for any suspicious signs, as if we hadn't got enough of them already. Then, I'm going to ask you to strip off and we're going to search, feel, poke around in every little piece of your clothing, then we're going to ask you to get on all fours, I'm going to professionally place one or two fingers inside you and I'm going to search, feel, poke around and that's when your real friends will start to come out, those whose address or name you don't know either, but there's bound to be various little pellets, little white ones, like ants' eggs. And do you know how I know that's going to happen? Not because you've got a suspicious look on your face, not because you're a woman who's going sightseeing on her own, not because you know neither your friend's name nor her address, not because you're carrying a suitcase for a two-day trip or because you're going for two days' sightseeing. I know because you gave me that little card. And that little card means that someone gave it to you so you would give it to me. No doubt whoever it was who put the little ants' eggs inside you told you: "When they question you at the border, you show them this little card." And do you know why they told you that? Because they've got an agreement with us, because they prefer us to catch a skinny little mule like you, with a few capsules inside you, because that's the real issue, knowing whether you've got lots or only a few of those little pellets inside you, because they never deliver me anyone with much inside, but sometimes they know they need to give us more than just two or three little pellets, and then we wait for you like someone waiting for an Easter egg, for the shell to break and see what present we're going to get, we're hopeful, we've got high expectations of you, even if it's only a little or a lot for the photo, it'll be enough, then we bust you because we're really smart, and that way no-one dies, everyone can get on with their lives and, at least for today, justice has been served. Doesn't it make you happy seeing how well this all works?

Scene V

Ana *and the* **Lawyer** *are in the prison visiting room.*

Lawyer I've heard you were inside before and as a result, to repeat, you're going to get more years inside. It's true what they pulled out from inside you wasn't much, but it was enough. For that reason they can only help you if you help them, if you give them a name, an address.

Ana *goes to say something.*

Lawyer I've already told them what you told me, I gave them those names, it sounds like they went there yesterday and they didn't find anything or anyone. You're in a tricky spot, a really tricky spot. I know you want to protect your loved ones, but the people who did this to you conned you and now you're all alone, do you understand? I don't want to give you any false hope, I'm going to defend you, but if you don't help me a little by demonstrating you want to cooperate, it's very likely you'll be locked up for quite a few years, and well, look, the prisons here are tough, they're not like the ones back over there, over here it feels like it would be in your best interest to talk, you know what I mean? I can try and get them to send you back to your country, there's the whole thing with your son's treatment, that might make them sit up and take notice a little, but the drugs seizure was carried out by the border police, and they're harder here on foreigners, you know how it is. You do realise, don't you, what a real mess you're in?

Ana *nods.*

Lawyer I'm not sure you realise just how big a mess you're in. Look, this is how I like to think of it: if the ocean was poisoned, let's just imagine that, imagine today that the ocean was poisoned and that as a result, all the seas, the rivers, the streams, the lakes were also poisoned, and that the rain and the plants and the food were also now poisoned, and that you were thirsty and hungry, that everything was poisoned and people were dying of thirst, but you had to avoid all contact with water because that would be fatal, can you imagine that? Well, that's the situation you're in, that's how precarious your situation is. I'm offering you a glass of water and you're telling me you're not thirsty, because you think you can get hold of water someplace else, but the oceans are all poisoned and cleaning all this up is going to get you years in prison along with loads of other things I wouldn't wish on anyone. It would be better to die poisoned.

Ana What a great piece of advice.

Lawyer What I'm trying to tell you is that you've got one shot. A small one, but it's a real one. We're all equal in the eyes of the law and that always gives us a chance.

Ana Really?

Lawyer The law is blind, but it does listen.

Ana OK, well in that case I do have something to tell you, to tell you and the law.

Lawyer Don't worry, this will stay between the two of us, the relationship between a client and their lawyer is a privileged one.

Ana Exactly, this is about privileges.

Lawyer What do you mean?

Ana Have you always been pretty?

Lawyer Sorry?

Ana Yes, sorry, the question should be: were you ever ugly? Really ugly? When you look yourself in the mirror and you know you're ugly, do you know what that feels like? Do you know what I'm talking about? When you put your make-up on and you realise that it makes your face look worse, you buy clothes and you realise they don't fit, that a poor person's face, and I believe I was born with one, always remains. I'm poor and I'm ugly, they might even be the very same thing, I struggle to tell them apart. You, on the other hand, are pretty, what with your watch, your mobile phone, your clothes, your profession, everything tells me you've got more money than I have. But try being poor and ugly. Try sitting in a chair like this one, being ugly and poor, on the point of going to prison, and a pretty woman with money tells you that everything is going to be alright, that we're are all equal in the eyes of the law.

Lawyer No, no, no! You're wrong! I might look pretty to you, but I don't look like that to me, or to many other people, for instance my second husband from whom I've just got divorced. Ask him if I look as pretty as that bitch he's going out with now. Do you think that's what beauty is about? What I'm like now is nothing by comparison, not even a distant echo of how I once was. I was much prettier, I used to be really pretty. People would turn their heads to look at me and once they'd looked at me, they wouldn't be able to take their eyes off me. My beauty was contagious, people would look far prettier in my company than when they weren't. You're looking at me and thinking how pretty I am, I'm thinking how pretty I used to be. Beauty isn't something we have, rather it's something we had, it's something that slips from our grasp, it's a promise or a memory. It's never something current. You think it's unfortunate not having a virtue like beauty, but I'm sure you have other virtues which aren't as susceptible to time. Beauty, youth, are virtues we all had, believe me, you've just got to find one that will last the course of time.

Ana Nothing lasts the course of time. Of the few virtues I've had in my life, the majority, if not all of them, have disappeared with time. And all that remains are flaws. And what's more, flaws feed on time. Every flaw that used to be small is made bigger by time. And all the while your virtues fade, they rot, collapse, become forgotten. Before we die, before it kills us, time takes hold of our virtues, and it's for that reason, and no other, that time is taking my son away. My son doesn't have any time left, and he's being taken away from me very quickly as if he was the last of my virtues, and what will be left, I warn you, let this serve as a warning to you, what will be left of me will be of no good, of no virtue whatsoever. That's why we have to remember the virtues we had, because as long as we can remember them, then in some way we won't lose them. And we mustn't forget we were all beautiful once, for a moment, at some moment in time. But when we forget, as I am now forgetting, then that's when we are dangerous, really dangerous.

Scene VI

Ana *and an* **Assassin** *in the cell.*

Assassin So what's your story?

Ana It's a sad story.

Assassin Do you want to tell me it?

Ana No.

Assassin So what are you in here for?

Ana To try and change my story, not tell it.

Assassin Sometimes it's better not to resist.

Ana Resisting is the only thing I'm good at.

Assassin So are you gonna resist me?

Ana Resisting is the only thing I'm good at.

Assassin Woah, you're a really tough cookie.

Ana That's what they've turned me into, it's not what I'm really like.

Assassin Have you got an answer for everything?

Ana No.

Assassin Don't you like me?

Ana You're OK.

Assassin You'd do well to have friends in here.

Ana I'd do well to get out of here.

Assassin That's not gonna happen, they've given you a long stretch from what I heard.

Ana Oh, really? What else have you heard?

Assassin I've heard you're a good girl, so for that I'm not gonna make your life impossible.

Ana Oh, really?

Assassin No, you're a young mother looking out for her son, we understand things like that in here. It's those on the outside that don't understand, but me, along with many of the other women here, we do understand. You've got a son on the verge of death, so what are you gonna do for him?

Ana My son isn't going to die.

Assassin You're resisting, that's what you're good at.

Ana My son isn't going to die.

Assassin Alright, look, that's what any mother would do, any mother who wasn't mad. We've had a few mad women in here, those that kill their children because they're mad, those that hit their children and break their bones. Awful people. Well, we didn't treat those women very well, we treated them like crazy women, but apart from that you can make friends in here, OK?

Ana I've heard things as well.

Assassin Oh really? So what have you heard?

Ana That you're no angel.

Assassin No, girl, there are no angels in here. Don't be confused. The angels are the ones in the convents and in the cemeteries, we're all alive in here . . . Survivors, if you like.

Ana Assassins.

Assassin There are some, yes, others are thieves, drug mules, nutcases, some are innocent and just unlucky, there are others who are traffickers, addicts, what do I know, we've got all sorts.

Ana I'm nothing like that.

Assassin If you ask around in here, no-one is anything like that, but everyone is, including you. You're a bit of everything, you're a poor little drug-trafficking mule who's on the verge of going mad.

Ana But I'm not an assassin.

Assassin No, I'm the assassin and a really good one at that.

. . .

Ana Are you going to kill me?

Assassin If someone pays me . . .

Ana Do you only do it for money?

Assassin Yes, and because I do a good job, no-one pays you to do a bad job.

Ana How many people have you killed?

Assassin Uh, I don't know. You lose count, that's a cliché but it's true. Especially when you've always had as much work as me. At the beginning you do keep count, OK, don't think that anyone can be insensitive to that. The first ten I'd say you count, you keep an exact count, up until about twenty I could remember clearly. Then, one day, you forget if you were at twenty-six or twenty-seven, and since it already feels like that's not the exact number, there's no point keeping count any more. And one day you realise that if you were keeping count, you would know if you had already passed two hundred or not, I mean, you would know if this had got out of hand.

Ana Interesting.

Assassin If you think about it, the same must happen to God.

Ana Do you believe in God?

Assassin Very much so. Don't you?

Ana I have my doubts.

Assassin OK, well, He loves you no matter what.

Ana So you're saying God loves an assassin?

Assassin You're quite the aggressive one, aren't you? . . . Of course He loves us, very much. He likes us best, I think we're His favourite assassins, mark my words.

Ana Why's that?

Assassin Because we put a price on death for Him. Which means that dying isn't for free, at least not with us. The world is full of crazy people who hand out deaths like they were sweets, they rob you and blow your brains out, you cross the street and they run you over, you eat genetically modified food and they kill you, you fall in love and they kick the shit out of you, you go to school and they machine-gun you to death, and all for the same amount of money: zero. Living is difficult and dying is so easy. It should be the other way round. But that's just how it is, dying is easy and it's free. That's why God likes us best, because we even things out a bit, girl. Nothing is easy with us, nothing is for free, if you don't come up with the right money, I won't even load the bullets. God likes us best because we make dying a little more difficult than living. I don't mean we're solving anything. But, look, we're also resisting, in our own way.

Ana Sometimes it's better not to resist.

Assassin Really? OK, suit yourself . . .

Scene VII

Ana *and* **Another Friend** *are in the prison hospital.*

Another Friend Oh my God, what did they do to you?

Ana Funny you say that, I think God is involved in all this.

Another Friend Are you alright?

Ana I'm coping.

Another Friend What happened?

Ana Stuff that happens in here.

Another Friend But, why though?

Ana It's nothing, the people who gave me the drugs on the outside must have been worried and thought I'd be better off dead than unreliable. So that's why they paid for three bullets.

Another Friend They shot you with three bullets?

Ana Luckily. It seems like they pay per bullet. They fire one at you if they want to scare you, two if they want to scare you a lot, three if they want to kill you, but they won't go crazy if you survive. This means they paid the minimum needed to kill me, luckily. If they had paid for one more bullet, I don't know if I'd still be here. When it's between four and six bullets, that's when they really hate you, I'm lucky they don't hate me.

Another Friend Are you going to be alright?

Ana That depends on how much they pay the next time.

Another Friend Please take care, we need you, we all need you, we love you, your son needs you.

Ana I know, that's why I didn't die. Only because other people need me. It would be easier dying if there was really nothing left of you, wouldn't it? Not even a body, or a memory for someone else, or a will. If you just disappeared, for good. Dying would be like never having existed and that's when it would become something powerful. But this death is almost . . . incomplete. Half-done. It leaves a really painful, unjust trace for those left behind. Recently I've come to see death not only as unjust, but defective, almost clumsy, lazy I would say. Perhaps it's the medication they've been giving me here that's making me think such thoughts.

Another Friend How much longer are you going to be here?

Ana Hopefully for some time yet, I don't know what might happen to me when I go back to my cell.

Another Friend Are you afraid?

Ana Not for myself, no.

Another Friend What are you afraid about then?

Ana What do you mean, "what about"? About my son, if I don't get out of here, who's going to prevent him dying?

Another Friend We're all helping.

Ana Don't get angry, but the last friend who helped me couldn't prevent her son sending someone to fire three bullets at me.

Another Friend You're being unfair, she told you not to approach him.

Ana It was the only way of getting the money for my son.

Another Friend Well now your son has neither the money nor you.
. . .

Ana How is he?
. . .

What's up?
. . .

Tell me, how is he?

Another Friend He's not doing well.

Ana I know that already, he's got cancer, but what about the treatment?

Another Friend What the hospital is able to provide isn't very effective and as for the other stuff . . .

Ana It's expensive, I know that, but I don't even have the means to pay for it, not least whilst I'm in here.

Another Friend To be honest with you, the treatment they're giving him slows down the cancer, but it doesn't stop it let alone cure it.
. . .

Ana Is he in pain?

Another Friend A little.

Ana If you're telling me a little, that means he's in a lot of pain.

Another Friend It won't do you any good thinking about it.

Ana So what do you want me to think about?

Another Friend About getting out of here.

Ana I think about that all the time. I'm asking them to send me back over there, to a prison back over there, I think over there I'd have more chance of working, studying, and I could exchange that for reducing my sentence.

Another Friend And when might that happen?

Ana I don't know, I'll have to work for at least a couple of years to demonstrate good behaviour.

Another Friend We haven't got all that time though.

Ana I know.

Another Friend How about you send them a letter and ask for permission to go and see him?

Ana They're not going to let me, everyone in here has some sick relative.

Another Friend But your son is dying.

Ana Yes, but he's not going to die imminently.

. . .

Another Friend Well . . . I think it will be imminent.

Scene VIII

Ana *and the* **Judge** *in a courtroom.*

Judge You stand before this hearing today so that we can consider your case and give you an immediate reply. Do you understand this?

Ana Yes, Your Honour.

Judge And from what I understand, your son has a terminal cancer in its final stages and you are requesting special permission to go and see him. Is that correct?

Ana Yes, Your Honour.

Judge The applicant has been in prison for approximately six months, during which time her son's health has significantly deteriorated. Accompanying the request, we have the corresponding medical reports which attest to his current condition. Regardless of what happens here today, let me say, Madam, that I'm very sorry to hear this.

Ana Yes, Your Honour.

Judge The applicant is requesting a temporary exit permit for thirty days, which is the maximum life expectancy of the boy. After completion of this period of time, or if the boy dies before, the applicant will return immediately to the penitentiary centre and serve the totality of the rest of the sentence. Is that correct?

Ana Yes, Your Honour.

Judge Nonetheless, cognisant of the tragedy which is set to befall you, I must clarify several points which are important under law and which, I believe, are relevant to consider today to justify my decision, regardless of whether the response to the request is positive or negative.

Ana   Yes, Your Honour.

Judge   You understand that you committed a crime in trying to bring in drugs to this country in an illegal manner and that your action, perhaps inconsequential for you, though no less serious, causes great harm to this society. I understand, believe me when I say I understand, that your behaviour was a desperate act, but it is exactly in moments of desperation when we have to remain focused and aware of our actions. I would like to know, and I would like you to reply honestly, were you aware of the harm you were causing other people by your actions?

Ana   Yes, Your Honour.

Judge   Are you aware that actions like yours, whether justified or not, be they understandable or not, cause harm to thousands of people? Because drugs enslave workers in the fields of our country, murder people in our neighbourhoods and lay waste forever to our young people on the streets. You understand that in the act of saving your son, you were putting in danger many other sons of other mothers who likewise grieve for them, care for them, yet who do not commit crimes to save them.

Ana   Yes, Your Honour.

Judge   So, then . . . are you sorry?

. . .

Ana   No, Your Honour.

Judge   Pardon?

Ana   Why should I be sorry for my actions?

Judge   For having brought in drugs, I've just explained this to you. Does it seem fair to you that in order to save your son, you brought in drugs which, year on year, damage, lay waste to and kill thousands of young people in this country?

Ana   Fair? No, it doesn't seem fair to me, but neither is it fair that my son is dying from cancer which in eighty per cent of cases with good treatment, that is to say with money, is curable. It doesn't seem fair he has to spend the last years of his life without his leg, in and out of hospitals, with chemicals attacking his mood, and without his mother. It doesn't seem fair I have to be here when you all know that I'm not the real problem. None of this seems fair to me.

Judge   You are justifying yourself, yet I asked you a different question.

Ana   What did you ask me, Your Honour?

Judge   I want to know whether you are aware of the dangers your actions represented for other people and whether you would do this again.

Ana   I don't understand your technical language, ask me concrete questions.

Judge What would you be prepared to do for your son, if this situation presented itself again?

Ana With all due respect, Your Honour. You ask me that question but you don't want to know the answer. You don't want to help me, you want to justify your rejection of my application and force me to say this on your behalf. You've already made your decision, but so that you can have an easy conscience, you want me to give you a motive, a reason. You're in luck, because I've got plenty of motives. Because if the question is about what I would be prepared to do for my son, write this down very clearly. The applicant replied: "Anything." I would be prepared to do anything so that my son doesn't die. If they came tomorrow and told me that if I robbed a shop, a bank, a school or a poor pensioner, my son wouldn't die, then I would start planning the theft. What do you want me to tell you? Do you believe there are things that can't be done? Do you believe the law prevents me from doing something for my son? Do you seriously believe the law is something I consider when I think about my son? I would do anything for my son, I would cross any line. Like a stubborn mule carrying my life's possessions, I would cross any boundary carrying bombs and explode them without a care for who or what this impacts. I'm a mule, I just carry stuff and move on, that's what I do. And anything I have to do, anything I have to carry out in order to save him, seems trivial by contrast. I would cut off one of his arms, or both of them, or both his legs if you told me that was going to save him. I would eat his shit and make him eat mine and collect everyone's shit and give it to him every day, even though he would hate me for it, because if he hates me that means he's alive and that's the only thing I care about. Listen, write this down, I would abuse him, rape his friends, rape my friends' sons, I would commit evil, I would pay for this evil, I would harm my son, let others do him harm, let him have a miserable life, if someone assured me he had a chance of living. Does it sound like I'm going too far, that I'm exaggerating? Do you think the world isn't like this? Perhaps you think, from your perspective, that the whole world is a courtroom where everything is weighed on the scales of justice? No, Your Honour, the world is a broken scale. It's a jungle where everyone is trying to survive and no-one considers the law. And my words are my preparation, when I say something, I think about it, prepare my argument, I say it and that's how I prepare. That's how I prepare myself. Because the day the disgust comes for everyone and everything, because one day the disgust will come, that day, whilst all of you will stand there, in a daze, vomiting at all the horror and pestilence, dumbfounded at the arrival of this disgust, I am going to be ready, the disgust will find me standing bolt upright, ready to fight, for my son. You ask me what I am prepared to do for my son, I am prepared to put all of my disgust into battle, not just half of it, not a little of it, not just what I might be able to muster up. All of my disgust. Have you, Your Honour, ever thought how you would react in your disgust? Be prepared, because if you don't consider this, someone will consider it for you. And then tomorrow the nausea will come and overwhelm you.

Judge Overwhelm me? Do you think I am so off-guard that wind, rain, storms, a tsunami of disgust as you describe it, will overwhelm me? Look, let me say one thing to you before I pass my verdict. And believe me that I'm not doing this as a judge to a prisoner, or as one woman to another or one human being to another. I'm doing this as one mother to another. Because we are both mothers and we are a race apart from the rest of humanity. The disgust isn't going to come, the disgust is already here and if you can't see it, it's because it hasn't yet sufficiently overwhelmed you. Disgust at watching this comedy play out every day in these courtrooms, I see people telling themselves things, like you just did, justifying their crimes, their betrayals, their friendships, their loves, their hatred, and all this generates is disgust. People don't want to save their sons any more, neither do they want to save themselves, they don't want to speak, listen to anyone else or even think. They just want to wallow in their disgust and listen to themselves, they want to make everyone else applaud their disgusting thoughts, and if this doesn't happen, they become angry and puke all over them. If I let you out, let one thing be clear, mother, I'm not letting you out into the world, I'm throwing you out in amongst all the mess, for that filth dirties everything and once you've touched it, you'll no longer know who's who and from what you have to protect yourself. You think that people are running away and preparing for the storm, well it's we who are the storm.

Scene IX

Ana *and the* **Nurse** *face the son who is asleep.*

Nurse He spends the day asleep now, he's very tired.

Ana Before he used the spend the day doing stuff and when he was little, it was a battle to get him to sleep.

Nurse I thought you weren't around when he was little.

Ana I was at the beginning, Who told you that?

Nurse He did.

Ana Ah, what did he tell you?

Nurse He said that when he was little he missed you a lot, but now he misses you even more. He said something really lovely, he said that beforehand he missed you because of your absence, that he needed his mother. But now he needs your presence. He needs you.

Ana I'm here now.

Nurse It's going to do him good.

Ana Not enough though.

. . .

Nurse He's handsome.

Ana Yes, he is.

Nurse But even in his condition, he doesn't look sick.

Ana He was much more handsome before.

Nurse Well, now, let me tell you something, and don't take this the wrong way, I know this might seem trivial but it isn't. I've seen many people in this situation, in their last moments like this, who are on the way out, they go on being mistreated, weakened, the treatment destroys them and then death is proclaimed. I've seen it an infinite number of times, they are unrecognisable in their last seconds. Your son seems unchanged however, he's strong, handsome, he looks full of life.

Ana He is full of life, he didn't waste his life, life didn't give him time.

Nurse I've seen children very quickly transformed into old people . . .

Ana But he's going to die all the same, before me, that feels really quick to me.

Nurse It is quick, yes.

. . .

(*To the audience.*) If you want to know though what makes me most anxious, it's not that we're going to die, rather it's that as a result of that death we're going to rot. I can't stop thinking about it. Where are we going to rot? Because the question isn't about who, we're all going to rot. The question isn't how, because whether the process is quicker or slower, we're all going to rot. When? Sooner or later, we're all going to rot. Rather, it's where? I'm obsessed by this. Who is going to watch us as we rot? Who is going to clean up our mess when our stomach dissolves in its acid, when our skin withers and everything inside spews out. When the insects channel their way in and we become a feast of worms and a nest of flies. When our bones start protruding and all that's left is hair and nails. That's when you understand why we are buried or burned, it's not a spectacle worthy of applause. But look at your son, he still belongs to his world, this lad looks ready to get up and get on with his life. I know everyone is saying there's little time left, and that's why they let you come here, but I've already seen too many things I don't understand, and this boy here is still with us. A mother can sense these things. Neither you nor he are ready to start rotting. It's a cliché, but don't lose hope.

Ana Death is a cliché, in every sense, you're right about that.

Nurse You've got to keep it together, stay in one piece. Don't destroy yourself.

Ana Death has always destroyed me, I've never understood why. And that's why, to some degree, I've always admired people like you. Especially people like you. Nurses, not doctors, or surgeons or therapists. A nurse doesn't cure anyone, but they are always there to support you. I don't know how anyone can work this close to death. After all this time I guess you become friends with death, you learn to accept it. Become resigned to it.

Nurse There might be something in that, yes.

Ana Nevertheless, I think we have to prevent people dying, at all costs, no matter what. I feel sure, it's not an impression rather a certainty, that with every death we become worse; because we carry the burden of our dead from the past. Every breath has been preceded by so many dead children, such that breathing out is almost an injustice, just like not atoning for this injustice with pain and evil. And so we resist death, here we are on the edge of tragedy, at a sort of wake, and we're laughing, we're making a little joke out of this and looking at one another to instil courage. I want to resist it all though, and for that I need courage. Because when my son wakes up, I'm going to grab his hand and I'm going to hold it for that long, and that firmly, no-one, not even death, will be able to rip it away from me. If you don't believe me, just stay here and watch.

Scene X

Ana, **Doctor Two** *and the* **Nurse** *along with, to a certain extent, her son.*

Doctor Two (*to the audience*)   So then a doctor arrives who the mother doesn't know but is seemingly someone who has recently cared for her son and knows a lot about the situation.

Nurse (*to the audience*)   The nurse is just about to leave to allow the mother and doctor to speak, when her son wakes up and says . . . "Mamá."

Doctor Two (*to the audience*)   He said "Mamá" and that "Mamá" lit up the whole room, the night.

Ana (*to the audience*)   He's saying "Mamá" to me, just like that first time when he wasn't even a year old and I welled up on hearing that fragile little word, that babble I would recognise in amongst any wall of noise.

Doctor Two (*to the audience*)   That universal "Mamá" is enough to bring a dead person back to life.

Nurse (*to the audience*)   So the mother throws herself on her son, then kisses and hugs him.

Ana (*to the audience*)   Then my son kisses and hugs me, weakly but firmly.

Doctor Two (*to the audience*)   And it feels like justice has been done, that at least in this little corner of the world, in this little moment in time, a mother and her child are as they should be: together.

Nurse (*to the audience*)   Because children are born to be with their mothers and mothers to be with their children and what is happening now, finally, is a good thing.

Nurse (*to the audience*)   And the doctor, to crown the moment, wants to take the opportunity to tell them about the tests they did recently, which, without being totally encouraging, give good reason for hope, she encourages both of them to remain strong, "because you mustn't give in, these things do happen and you can overcome them, you never know we might all soon be laughing about this."

Nurse (*to the audience*)   The son's eyes are fixed on those of his mother, as if he had come home.

Ana (*to the audience*)   And the mother's eyes relax in those of her son, as if her son had come home.

Nurse (*to the audience*)   As if the doctor has just given them an injection, of what I don't really know, but anything is better than nothing, anything . . . An injection of hope!

Ana (*to the audience*)   Of more than just hope! A chance. What the mother has been asking for since the first day, a real chance, however small, however slender or unlikely, a chance in a thousand or one in a million, because if it was one in a million, that means there is a chance, that that chance exists, and if it exists then it might happen.

Doctor Two (*to the audience*)   And then the son, as if wanting to protect his mother, starts cracking jokes.

Nurse (*to the audience*)   And they aren't very funny, but the three of them laugh, because seeing him cracking jokes in that situation is really moving, you know.

Ana (*to the audience*)   And then my son looks at me, just as a child looks at you when they're going to ask you one of those complicated questions you doubtless won't know how to answer, and out of nothing he asks me: "Mamá, do superheroes die?"

Doctor Two (*to the audience*)   And the mother laughs, giving off a mix of surprise and worry, she laughs. She tells him she doesn't know for sure, but she thinks so.

Nurse (*to the audience*)   And the son says yes, that he once read a comic strip where Superman was dying and if Superman died then it made sense that we too would all die.

Ana (*to the audience*)   "Of course, my love", I told him, not understanding a word of what he was saying.

Doctor Two (*to the audience*)   And as if the three of us had fallen into the trap, the child then presents the second part of his theory.

Nurse (*to the audience*)   "But then he comes back from the dead, Mamá", he says, seeking his mother's approval. "I have a magazine", says the son, "where Superman comes back from the dead."

Doctor Two (*to the audience*)   And the three of them just stood there dumbstruck, until the mother says what is needed to be said.

Ana   You're not going to die, my love.

. . .

Nurse (*to the audience*)   So then I say I have to leave, that they should excuse me, it feels like I should leave you to talk alone, that you should have this time to yourselves.

Doctor Two (*to the audience*)   And I do the same, there will be time enough to talk about options, hopes and the next steps.

Nurse (*to the audience*)   But even though this is bad, we stay on the other side of the door.

Doctor Two (*to the audience*)   Because at times we are lucky enough to experience these rare moments when everything makes sense, death, life, and we all understand everything more clearly.

Ana (*to the audience*)   So I hug my son and hold him against me just like I used to hold him when he was really little, as near as possible to my heart, and I rock him so he knows we are still together and that I'm still his mother.

Nurse (*to the audience*)   And from the other side of the door we don't know if the silence is because they are talking in a low voice or because they had fallen asleep or because they were just enjoying being with one another without speaking.

Doctor Two (*to the audience*)   There are silences that are screams of joy and pain, as if all the throats of the world were united in a choked silence.

Nurse (*to the audience*)   As if the population of the world had moved to another planet. As if they were the last inhabitants of Earth and didn't need to say another word to each other. Only feel the emotion . . .

Ana (*to the audience*)   And I feel like I've come home, that even though I'm in a hospital, in a damp room at a state hospital, in a break between prison and death, far from returning home, with my son in my arms, I do feel like I've come home. That now I can relax, now that, at least for today, I've prevented my son from dying, I did my job today and that great big body which came out of me, which I helped assemble from minute one, cell by cell, is whole, is strong, is alive. And having him here in my arms, wriggling all over the place, it feels like being pregnant again, like giving birth to him again, like I'm still giving him all the life I can.

Nurse (*to the audience*)   At this point she considers whether years of life could be given to each other as gifts, that if we can't stop death, then at least we should be able to choose whether to extend or shorten life. And that were she able, right then and there, she would use every last drop of her remaining life to ensure her son could live out his years, that if it was down to her, she would cut off her own leg and give it to him, she would snatch her son's illness away from him and suffer it herself with love and satisfaction, that if she could, if there was a chance, that if the mind was powerful and love was strong, she, by doing this right now, with every fibre in her being, would be saving him forever.

Doctor Two   And right then, the son, in an almost calm, inaudible whisper, such that even his mother has to calm her breathing to hear, says: "Mamá, I had a dream. In the dream I was dying and suddenly I was in a house a bit like Grandma's, not like the one she has now, but like the one she had when I was little where we all used to get together to eat, you know? It was full of people. In my dream it was a sunny day and my grandparents were introducing me to people there, Mamá, and all those people were happy to come and greet me, they were all happy to see me: some of them were little old people, some younger, because all of them had died at different times, and that's when I realised we all die at different ages so that death is really fun, so the other side doesn't just get filled up with little old people. The table was big, Mamá, it was full of people from our family I had never known but who were now happy to see me, our grandparents' parents, your parents, a never-ending procession of relatives, some of them looked like me, Mamá, some looked like you, Grandpa was drinking whisky and telling jokes and Grandma was saying the food was nearly ready and everyone was gazing at me, they loved me and were all so keen to wait for me that I felt good and it made me feel like leaving. Death is going back to Grandma's house, Mamá. We'll be waiting for you there, Mamá, the food will be nice and hot, don't cry Mamá."

Ana (*to the audience*)   That's when his heart stopped beating.
The doctors came in.
People came in.
They wired him up.
They tried to resuscitate him.
But he was no longer in the building.
When your son dies,
it's like a building collapsing.
You are on the ground floor and your son is on the top floor.
And you tell him to come down quickly.
Meanwhile planes crash between you and him.
Meanwhile the stairs go up in flames and the lifts grind to a halt.
Your son's death is like the towers falling.
And you're left in shock, searching among the ruins of masonry, iron and dust.
The death of a son is a terrorist attack that God carries out against you.
To fill you with terror, so you remain afraid for all eternity.

Epilogue

Ana *and her new* **Cellmates**.

Cellmate Two   What I heard is that the nun was telling her about a saint, and the nun is really going on about this saint, and well, you know how it is with saints, she had performed a miracle, or had suffered a lot or I don't know what . . . What was the saint called again? Teresa?

Cellmate One   Teresa is the name of a saint, but you're not going find any Teresa here.

Cellmate Two   OK, doesn't matter what she was called, the important thing is that the little nun is coming over all heavy, giving her a speech about the king of the heavens and the little angels and who knows what nonsense.

Cellmate One   That's not nonsense.

Cellmate Two   OK, the thing is when the nun started coming out with all that nonsense, that's when Ana started talking about ants.

Cellmate One   Oh, yeah, they did tell me about the ants. She's crazy, that one.

Cellmate Two   Mate, tell us about the ants, that's a good one, I can't remember.

Ana   I'd like to be reincarnated as an ant.

Cellmate Two   That's it, that's what she said.

Cellmate One   So why do you want to . . .

Ana Does an ant get cancer? I've never heard it does. I don't believe ants get cancer. I don't think ants even get what illnesses are, they never catch a cold or anything like that. Rip one of their legs off and they keep walking, you kill the next one in line, they all surround him and carry on, you destroy their house and they keep on walking, your steal their little eggs and they keep on walking, you step on them, you crush them and they look dead, then a few seconds later they come back to life and just keep on walking. They're strong, they keep on forging ahead and will keep on going just like that, almost immortal, they'll keep on going like that forever, devouring the flowers in our garden.

Cellmate Two Well, OK, it went something a bit like that, it sounded nicer now though although I was told it a bit differently. They told me she asked to be buried in an ants' nest. She wants to be devoured by ants, not worms. That's what she told the nun. Devoured by ants, that ants are sort of immortal, you know?

Cellmate One Ants die too.

Cellmate Two The thing was, they were arguing about all that, and it was getting quite heated and it sounds like at one stage she told the nun she felt like God was biting her, that God had grabbed hold of her, had her between His teeth and like a rabid dog wouldn't let go of her. Amazing yeah? The bite of God. And for sure the nun didn't quite know what to say to her, so goes and says: "God moves in mysterious ways."

Cellmate One What a bitch.

Cellmate Two No, they're not bitches, they just clueless. That's all.

Cellmate One Now I understand why she hit her, I thought it was because she was mad, but now I see the nun too was . . .

Cellmate Two No, she didn't hit her. It's better than that. It sounds as though she asked the nun to pray for God to let go of her, but the nun told her God didn't bite. And that's when, I don't know if it was out of madness, fatigue or pent-up rage, well, the thing is that tipped her over the edge and she pounces on her and bites her face. The nun screams and there she was like a red ant, like a rabid dog, like the wrath of God, snagged, clamped on the nun's face and the nun was screaming in desperation.

Cellmate One She bit her face?

Cellmate Two That's what they say.

Cellmate One Is that really true?

Cellmate Two I don't know, let her tell you.

Cellmate One Why did you bite her face?

Ana God moves in mysterious ways.

Cellmate One I see.

Cellmate Two They had to give the nun seven stitches.

Cellmate One If you bite me, I'll kill you.

Cellmate Two Anyway, she looks a bit calmer now.

Ana I'm never calm.

. . .

Cellmate Two That was last year, on this very date. That's why we have to be careful, it's a nonsense, but on the anniversary of his death we have to be careful. It's that date today, isn't it?

Cellmate One She's not going to agree with you, but she looks calmer.

Cellmate Two We can see you look better, that it would be OK to talk with you now.

Cellmate One You're brave, aren't you, and I've seen some brave ones here, but you really are brave.

Cellmate Two You seem better, yeah?

Ana I am better, yes. Much better. (*To the audience.*) It's five years today since my son died, it feels to me like it could have been yesterday, could have been five days ago, five centuries ago. But it is five years ago and what I think is how can it be possible that I've already lived another five years and he didn't even live another day. I'd like to go to his grave and dig him up with my own hands, with my nails and my teeth, open the coffin and sit there and reassemble every little part of his body. I want to pull his muscles over his bones and then connect up his nerves, I want to put him back together bit by bit, no matter how complicated a task that might be. He deserves for me to take the time to reassemble him. And I want to go and find all the people who knew him, who spent time with him, so they'll tell me every single word that ever came out of his mouth. I want to put his voice back together, starting with his crying when he was born right up until the silence of this day. I want to go to all the places he visited, sit down where he sat and look in all the mirrors where he was once reflected. I want to feel all his emotions. I want all the happiness, the anger, all the sadness he once felt. I want to hold in my chest all the feelings my son had, swallow with my breath all the air that once passed through his lungs and with my eyes look at all the people and places he once looked at. I want to lend him my body, so that he can walk with my legs, live for a while, here. I know he's dead, but I'm never going to accept it.

Cellmate Two Are you alright?

Ana (*replying to some extent to her cellmates but still talking to the audience*) I'm tired, for one day I'd like not to think about death. I'd like to hear the word as if I didn't understand it, as if I was being told about it for the first time and I didn't remember its name, I'd like to forget it and in that way be a little dead, only more alive than now.

Cellmate One Seriously, are you alright?

. . .

Ana I'm alright today, yes, I'm happy.

Cellmate Two Well, finally, there's a smile on your face.

Ana Well yes. Seeing as my sorrow couldn't stop death, let's see what happens with my laughter. I'm going to try and prevent it, I'm going to try and stop it, I'm going now to seek it out, to hunt it down, we're going to play for a while and have some fun.

Cellmate Two You're frightening me.

Ana It's OK to be afraid, because this world is spinning round and now I'm spinning round.

Cellmate One She's gone mad, it was bound to happen one day.

Cellmate Two Things like this happen.

Cellmate One Yes, but you can't do this to people.

Cellmate Two Well, how else do you want it then, people have to die. Flies die, as do ants and dinosaurs. We too have to die.

Cellmate One Yes but there are ways and there are ways, she's right about that, in any case, in the end it's this that turns you bad. Bad or crazy, there is no other way. We're bad because we're going to die, but we're worse because those we love are going to die as well.

Cellmate Two There are things we just don't understand.

Cellmate One There might be loads of things, but for a child to die doesn't feel right. Let old people die, or let people like us die, we're already past fifty, at least we've had some kind of life. What I've lived was already enough for me.

Cellmate Two For me too.

Ana Not for me, though, that's not enough for me. We should live for longer. I'm not asking for immortality, I don't need that much, but it doesn't feel like there's much between having to choose between being immortal and these miserable years we've been given. I don't want eternity but I expect more from life, I want another go on the merry-go-round. I still don't understand what this is all about. I understand that everyone makes do, that they'll say that's just how it is, that it is what it is, but I feel rotten it's like that. I'm not going to surrender to that. I'm not going to make do. I get it that mosquitos, fleas and elephants die, but it doesn't help me understand death any better. I don't understand why this happens to us, why we die like this, why people die like this, I think that's why we're killed off, so we don't understand it all. We die to confuse everyone else. Someone wants to confuse us. But I've got this straight now, I know now what I've got to do . . . They're not going to confuse me . . . Hey, Death, I've already worked out your plans and I'm coming to disrupt them, I'm aiming right between your eyes and the hunt is about to begin.

Cellmate One She's mad.

Cellmate Two To be expected, what with all . . .

We start to hear music in the distance which is upbeat, well-known. As the scene progresses, the music increases in volume until the end.

Ana Today's the day death stops happening, from the ant to the mule, from dogs to women, from this day forward the hunt begins, the rewards are plentiful and we're all hungry.

Cellmate Two Look, let's turn the radio on, a little music will do us good, calm us down . . .

Cellmate One Do you want to dance?

Ana Can't you feel it? I think God is getting ready to serve us up the final blow, look out, look out, He wants to bite again.

Cellmate One I love this song.

Cellmate Two Listen, isn't this the song your son liked?

Cellmate One Don't talk to her about her son, can't you see that's making her feel worse?

Ana Here I am, standing firm, waiting.

Cellmate Two Come on, dance, don't be bitter.

Cellmate One Dance with me, leave her.

Ana Yes, I've already got a dance partner, I've got two dance partners, but neither of them feels like dancing. They've got a guilty conscience. God and death versus Ana. Come on, Papá, come on, Mamá, here's your daughter ready to dance to this song.

They dance.

None of those tears, none of that pain, just death and happiness. Come on then! What's wrong? Are you afraid of me?

They dance.

One day they're bound to come and that's when we'll dance. One day I'm going to pounce on their faces and devour them. I'm going to rip those divine hands off them and make a necklace out of their milk teeth. I'm going to spit in their ear and gouge their eyes out. One day death is going to die and I'll be here to dance on its grave. I'm rehearsing for that moment and I'm going to find the right words so God will feel ashamed of me and death will cover its ears in fear, God will have to ask for forgiveness in my name and death will give up its work of making us suffer so much. And from that day on, no-one will ever die again. For now though, I'm going to eat them up, with this cannibalistic smile, with this eternal hunger, with this craving to swallow on the tip of my tongue. That's why I'm dancing, that's why we're dancing, that's why we're laughing: because we're determined, because we're going for broke, and because I'm immortal.

They dance.

Ready.
Steady.
Go!

END

They All Sleep at Siesta Time

Leonor Courtoisie

Translated by William Gregory

Duermen a la hora de la siesta (*They All Sleep at Siesta Time*) won the 2019 Uruguayan Ministry of Education and Culture National Literature Award.

About the playwright and translator

Leonor Courtoisie is a theatre artist and writer. She is a graduate of the Escuela Multidisciplinaria de Arte Dramático Margarita Xirgu and the Universidad de la República, Montevideo, where she completed a BA in Playwriting, and of the Diploma in Creative Writing at the National Autonomous University of Mexico. In 2019 she received the Premio Molière, awarded by the French Embassy in Uruguay. She was resident at the Cité International des Arts, Paris, in 2022, and has been a member since 2019 of the Directors Lab at the Lincoln Center, New York. Her credits as a playwright and director include *Estudio para La mujer desnuda* (*Study for The Naked Woman*, Comedia Nacional, Montevideo, 2022) and *Casi sin pedir permiso* (*Almost without Asking Permission*, Montevideo, 2019), among others. Her published works include the play *Corte de obsidiana* (*Obsidian Cut*, 2017), the poetry collection *Todas esas cosas siguen vivas* (*All Those Things are Still Alive*, 2020), and the novel *Irse yendo* (*Leave, Going*, 2021).

Productions of **William Gregory**'s translations include *A Fight Against . . .* by Pablo Manzi (Royal Court, London), *B* by Guillermo Calderón (Royal Court), *The Bit-Players* by José Sanchis Sinisterra (Southwark Playhouse, London), *Cuzco* by Víctor Sánchez Rodríguez (Theatre503, London), and *Chamaco* by Abel González Melo (HOME, Manchester). A Visiting Research Associate at King's College London, he was Translator in Residence at the British Centre for Literary Translation and a finalist in the Valle-Inclán Award for *The Oberon Anthology of Contemporary Spanish Plays*. Other publications of his translations include *Selected Plays by Cuban Playwright Abel González Melo* (Methuen), *The Children of Taltal* by Bosco Israel Cayo Álvarez (Laertes), *The Uncapturable* by Rubén Szuchmacher (Methuen), *The Widow of Apablaza* by Germán Luco Cruchaga (Inti), *An American Life* by Lucía Carballal (Antígona), and contributions to *Mexican Plays* (Nick Hern) and *The Oberon Anthology of Contemporary Argentinian Plays*. He is a member of the Ibero-American theatre and translation collective, Out of the Wings, and in July 2024 joined the artistic team of the Orange Tree Theatre, London, as Literary Associate.

Characters

Three Girls
An Armadillo
A Village
The Road Out
And The Story

The Three

The asphalt burns. **The Girl** *crosses the highway, runs across it, knows in the distance something. There's soy and sorghum. And just as it all is almost all too much, that. Silence. Season where the wind does not exist. Village like a heart sunk deep into the grass.*

Opposite **The Younger Girl** *static. Her city-hubbub nerves keep her from crossing, copying the country custom of going here and there, unbothered by it all, lest something knock her down dead.*

The Girl *has all that. No older than fifteen. No younger. Tight trousers, short. Flimsy tee-shirt, nothing underneath. Padded bra, waist-length hair. Large, dark eyes. Moody. Endearing. And menstruating. It doesn't show, there's no way to tell, but she's menstruating.*

The Younger Girl *is fat and wears a long-sleeved tee-shirt over a dress. Frizzy hair fringe cut by herself. At twelve years old she holds, barely, a weakly-tied rope an Armadillo's shell.*

"Not by the neck, she'll get away."

The Girl *laughs and chides from the other side of the highway. Makes faces* **The Younger Girl** *does not understand. Confused* **The Younger Girl** *squeezes her hands in fear and suddenly dreadful the thing approaches.*

Bored **The Girl** *flickers early-teen ennui then snaps back to being* **The Girl**.

A white gust springs up lightly, **The Younger Girl** *watches, turns her head stunned glued to the spot, forgets for a moment to hold on. Tries to tighten her grip but it slips cuts her burns slightly. The friction immediate blister and a loud bang second.*

Armadillo breaks forcefully away a Trinidad-registered four-by-four strikes its body at top speed leaving it barely alive.

Nothing happens.

The engine at full speed.

The girls' vision flooded with a cloud of dust.

Three

The Younger Girl   She's dead.

The Girl   Things don't die just like that.

The Younger Girl   It really hurts.

The Girl   It's bleeding.

The Younger Girl   It's a cut.

The Girl   It's swelling up.

The Younger Girl She was scared to death.

The Girl You have to keep her tied up properly.

The Younger Girl She went off on her own.

The Girl She threw herself under the truck.

The Younger Girl She didn't throw herself, it came really fast.

The Girl No she threw herself, it was suicide.

The Younger Girl There was a white thing moving.

The Girl It was a hare.

The Younger Girl I didn't know there were hares in the countryside.

The Girl They taste really good.

The Younger Girl It's so hot.

The Girl Have you never eaten hare?

The Younger Girl It stings.

The Girl The meat's soft.

The Younger Girl I need to get it wet.

The Girl You'll like it.

The Younger Girl I'm thirsty.

The Girl I'll give you some.

The Younger Girl Let's go to the hospital.

The Girl It's really far.

The Younger Girl If we go you can find someone to treat it.

The Girl It's not that simple, if they find out—

The Younger Girl You said we'd go as far as the water tanks and come back—

The Girl And you were meant to hold onto her.

Ther Younger Girl It really hurts.

The Girl I'll be scolded.

The Younger Girl I'll say it was my fault.

The Girl She was the last one.

The Younger Girl We'll get another one.

The Girl Oh, will we? How?

The Younger Girl We'll buy one.

The Girl You can't buy them.

The Younger Girl Someone must sell them.

The Girl You can't buy an armadillo.

The Younger Girl We'll hunt one.

The Girl It's not that simple.

The Younger Girl We'll go to the village and ask for help.

The Girl No. They might find out we hurt her.

The Younger Girl We'll hide her under my dress.

The Girl She won't fit.

The Younger Girl We have to get away from here.

The Girl I'm not gonna do what you say.

The Younger Girl Listen to me.

The Girl And you'll do what?

The Younger Girl Whatever you want.

The Girl Look she's trying to lick herself.

The Younger Girl It's boiling, let's go.

The Girl I bet you daren't lick the blood off her shell?

The Younger Girl I feel really dizzy.

The Girl Suck on the wound, it'll feel better.

The Younger Girl Give me your bra.

The Girl What are you doing?

The Younger Girl I'm making myself a bandage.

The Girl Give it to me.

The Younger Girl What are you doing?

The Girl I'm making a bandage for her.

The Younger Girl I'll get infected.

The Girl She's the one who'll get infected, poor thing.

The Younger Girl Let's go to the doctor.

The Girl She hasn't got much time left.

The Younger Girl You said things didn't die just like that.

The Girl Well she's dying now.

The Burrow

Closed space asphyxia. A building left to ruin. Alcohol and dregs from endless nights before. A faint light barely. Sol negro plays quietly Sonido Caracol ambience climate-change accordion. Damp catacomb contrast to the face-chapping, back-peeling midday heat. **The Younger Girl** *claps her hands, there is no reply.* **The Girl** *sneezes allergy.*

The Girl So anyway she left a mosquito coil switched on. A blanket fell on it, she woke up in the middle of the night with everything on fire.

The Younger Girl Are there prostitutes?

The Girl She started screaming but no-one woke up 'cause they didn't believe her.

The Younger Girl I've never seen one.

The Girl She sleepwalks, she talks in her sleep.

The Younger Girl She's moving a lot.

The Girl There's like five of these.

The Younger Girl Do they have little girls?

The Girl Some do.

The Younger Girl Are you sure there's no-one here?

The Girl She's asleep.

The Younger Girl She needs water.

The Girl She might wake up.

The Younger Girl It's not siesta time yet.

The Girl I can't find any.

The Younger Girl Where do they get them from?

The Girl You have to find the source.

The Younger Girl It's really hot.

The Girl Made of iron.

The Younger Girl There's a puddle there, look.

The Girl That's not water, it's whisky, do you want some?

The Younger Girl Alcohol?

The Girl I bet you daren't.

The Younger Girl She's dead.

The Girl She's not dead, she's asleep.

The Younger Girl Lying on the floor?

The Girl It's a mattress, put some on your cut.

The Younger Girl Don't talk so loud, there might be more.

The Girl She's only a prostitute.

The Younger Girl It really stings.

The Girl Trinidad isn't a woman.

The Younger Girl Trinidad?

The Girl She was a man and now she's a woman.

The Younger Girl She made up her own name?

The Girl Yeah, like the town . . . If I keep following this this way I'll find the tap.

The Younger Girl I want to make up my own name.

The Girl You can't, you've been baptised with yours.

The Younger Girl I'm not baptised.

The Girl I'm gonna take communion and then I'm gonna be confirmed.

The Younger Girl I've got a godmother.

The Girl But you're not baptised.

The Younger Girl She's pretend.

The Girl You can't do that.

The Younger Girl I can, my mum said I can choose when I'm older.

The Girl Water. It's high up.

The Younger Girl There's no glasses.

The Girl Did you never go to catechism?

The Younger Girl Once, but I didn't understand anything.

The Girl You don't have to understand, you have to believe.

The Younger Girl I can't believe a load of stories that don't exist.

The Girl There, in the rubbish.

The Younger Girl No, not dirty ones.

The Girl You're scared of the dark.

The Younger Girl What's that got to do with it?

The Girl You're scared of ghosts.

The Younger Girl Ghosts are dead people that aren't here any more.

The Girl She's opened her eyes.

The Younger Girl Let's go.

The Girl She's asleep, she's sleeping with her eyes open.

The Younger Girl You're right, sleepwalker.

The Girl That's what catechism is, dead people that aren't here any more.

The Younger Girl So why's my grandma not in the Bible?

The Girl *climbs onto a stool and places her mouth against a tap.* **The Younger Girl** *opens her mouth.* **The Girl** *spits water.* **The Younger Girl** *swallows.* **The Girl** *does it again, drinks some and shares the rest.* **The Younger Girl** *takes out the Armadillo, her clothes are stained with blood, she takes off her dress, takes off her long-sleeved tee-shirt, puts on her dress, fills her mouth and shares it among the shell, the red stains and her cut. She unties the bra, washes the bandage, washes the tee-shirt, wrings out the water. The Armadillo convalesces.*

The Girl The retreats are good, we all go to the park and have picnics.

The Younger Girl Do the nuns go?

The Girl No, the catechists.

The Younger Girl And what are they like?

The Girl The nuns?

The Younger Girl No, the catechists.

The Girl Normal.

The Younger Girl Normal how?

The Girl Like her, when she's asleep.

The Younger Girl Like how?

The Girl Normal, like you and like me.

The Younger Girl Oh, normal.

The Fat Man bursts in. Throws open the door. He is seen only in silhouette. He barks instead of shouting. Trinidad stands, approaches him, kisses him. They climb onto a motorbike and speed off. **The Girl** *and* **The Younger Girl** *hide. The Armadillo slowly creeps away.*

The Younger Girl Did you hear what he said?

The Girl She's escaped.

The Younger Girl They're looking for us.

The Girl The door's stuck.

The Younger Girl They're trying to keep us here.

The Girl She's going to die, help me.

The Younger Girl I don't want to be a prostitute.

The Girl The window.

The Younger Girl No, we can't get out.

The Girl We have to rescue her, if they see her, they'll take her.

The Younger Girl They don't want her, they want us.

The Girl Didn't you want to change your name?

The Younger Girl Yes, but I don't like this place.

The Girl Then help me get out.

The Younger Girl I don't like alcohol, or damp.

The Girl The bench.

The Younger Girl I can't reach.

The Girl *jumps through a high-up hole.*

The Younger Girl Don't leave me.

The Girl Don't shout, you're putting me off.

The Younger Girl The bra.

The Younger Girl *throws the bra through the hole.* **The Girl**'s *clothes slide down the wall, all tied together.* **The Younger Girl** *holds on tight as* **The Girl** *strains from the other side.*

The Girl I can't you're too fat.

The Younger Girl The tractor.

The Girl Where?

The Younger Girl At the entrance.

The Girl I don't know how.

The Younger Girl You live in the countryside, you must know how to use a tractor.

The Girl I'm frightened.

The Younger Girl She's dying.

The Girl *climbs into the tractor, naked, ties the rope of clothes to it and starts it up.* **The Younger Girl** *gets stuck in the hole, wriggles free.* **The Girl** *loses control of the vehicle,* **The Younger Girl** *is dragged along for half a block. The Armadillo runs behind them.* **The Girl** *catches her with a finger and ties her up with the ragged remains of the bra.* **The Younger Girl** *cries and laughs.* **The Girl** *unties the rescue device and begins to get dressed.*

The Girl That was the only bra I had.

The Younger Girl They're looking for us.

The Girl She doesn't have much time.

The Younger Girl We have to get out of here.

The Girl We stole a tractor.

The Younger Girl Let's go to the town.

The Girl She's dying, look at her.

The Younger Girl Let's go in the tractor.

The Girl I don't know how to drive.

The Younger Girl I'm getting infected and she's dying.

The Girl They mustn't see us.

The Younger Girl We'll ask for help.

The Girl If we get caught—

The Younger Girl We'll tell them they were trying to kidnap us and turn us into prostitutes.

On the Three

The vehicle pings along the highway that starts to connect the drawn-out comments the anxiety barricades all life. Heavens ahead and hell above. Stitched-up clothes aged yellow with ground-in dirt aplenty. A second taking-off putting-on taking-off putting-on. All dressed up now, heat in their throats and desire unconsumed. Sunstruck two in the afternoon. **The Girl** *at the wheel.* **The Younger Girl** *holds back* **The Girl***'s hair so nothing in her eyes. Tractor. Highway. Earth. Wheel.*

The Girl When they brought the first ambulance the doctors started the siren, turned on the lights and went out to drive around the village. The people who were in the square and at the doors of their houses heard the siren and started following it. The ambulance went ahead, and behind it, motorbikes, cars and bicycles. A whole convoy built up to see who the person was who was having an emergency, but they weren't going to help anyone, they were just showing off.

The Younger Girl What's your point?

The Girl Things attract too much attention here.

The Younger Girl Did you ever put a plastic bag over your head?

The Girl Do you think that's strange?

The Younger Girl If she dies we'll have to put her in a bag.

The Girl If she hasn't died by now she's not going to.

The Younger Girl But what if they're waiting for us?

The Girl We can't drive up in a tractor at three in the afternoon.

The Younger Girl The fat man and Trinidad, and there must be more of them, I'm sure there's more of them.

The Girl The fat man works this time of day.

The Younger Girl No-one works this time of day.

The Girl How do you know?

The Younger Girl They all sleep at siesta time.

The Girl We're not asleep.

The Younger Girl Don't you realise there's nobody here?

Agrarian businessman's truck two grandsons and farmhand passengers. Sun in their eyes. They see nothing.

The Girl We might get sent to jail.

The Younger Girl We can't get sent to jail, we're still little girls.

The Girl What's that got to do with anything?

The Younger Girl Little girls don't get put in jail.

The Girl They let a dog out last week. They'd kept it prisoner for like two months. Its owner had chained herself to the door of the police station. They hadn't fed it, and they wouldn't let her see it. It was tied to a tree for two weeks and finally they let it go. When it came out it was so skinny the woman didn't recognise it, they say she said it wasn't her dog and left, she walked all the way home and left her dog abandoned, thinking it wasn't hers.

The Younger Girl What if they put us in jail and don't feed us and then no-one recognises us and we get left on the street?

The Girl Like the chicken girl. When she was born she got left in the henhouse, she grew up in the pen. By the time they found her she was big, twelve or fifteen years old. She couldn't talk or walk, she had really long nails and she moved around and pecked like a chicken.

The Younger Girl What's that got to do with anything?

The Girl Because she'd been locked up, no-one recognised her as human. They had to take her to the zoo. They say she ate insects and one day a viper bit her and she was never heard of again.

The Younger Girl But was she a girl or a chicken?

The Girl Both.

The Younger Girl You can't be both.

The Girl Yes, you can. Like Trinidad.

The Younger Girl No, you're either a girl, or you're a chicken.

The Girl You're so symmetrical.

The Younger Girl What?

The Girl I'm a bird girl and you're a dog girl. Understand?

The Younger Girl I'm not—

The Girl You have to be careful, they might put you in jail.

The Younger Girl For what, I haven't done anything.

The Girl For committing offences, like the dog they put in jail, who wasn't recognised and got left alone.

The Younger Girl What offences did the dog commit?

The Girl Livestock theft. They say it killed some sheep.

The Younger Girl Killing and stealing aren't the same.

The Girl No, they're not the same, but they're similar. If they can put a dog in jail, they can put a girl in jail.

The Armadillo an unbearable smell invades. **The Girl** *speeds up. Abduction velocity the voices shout through the stinking sound of the wheel scratching the centre of the gravel ground.*

The Younger Girl We'll get to the village and they'll put us in jail or they'll kidnap us and she'll bleed to death because we'll never be able to get to the hospital in time because we'll be prisoners. And they'll put us in a plastic bag. And I won't be able to breathe and I'll want to scream. Like when you dream you want to scream but you can't. And they'll look for us all over the country and they won't find us. And then they'll feed us through a hole in a locked door and we'll hear the police coming and we won't be able to communicate. And they'll make us drink alcohol straight from the bottle there.

Sudden brake. **The Girl** *wets her index and middle fingers on* **The Younger Girl**'s *blood-soaked, heat-stiffened belly and like a little Indian girl finger-painting makes up her cheeks with the flesh of the Armadillo.*

The Girl Alcohol straight from the bottle?

The Younger Girl I saw it in a film, the prostitutes drank alcohol straight from the bottle, it's normal.

The Girl I'm thirsty.

The Younger Girl I need to get my hand treated first.

The Girl Stop telling me what to do.

The Girl *wets her fingers in the blood again and makes up* **The Younger Girl***'s chubby face. Motionless* **The Younger Girl** *lets her, trying to understand what's happening already immersed in what has never mattered to her and never will.*

In the distance **A Little Girl** *hitchhikes brandishing an open umbrella. She's seven years old, no older, no younger. Shoulder-length hair, blonde. Tee-shirt and short trousers. Worn espadrilles. Dirty hands, mouth, face. Teeth with cavities. Insistent and calm. She frowns. Breathes. Imagines a song she made up herself. Gust of wind.*

The Younger Girl It might be dangerous.

The Girl She's just a little girl.

The Younger Girl A little stranger.

The Girl The most dangerous thing would be if they find out you stole a tractor.

The Younger Girl I didn't steal anything, we stole it together.

The Girl I didn't do anything, I don't even know how to drive it.

The brakes skid the engine stops. **A Little Girl** *looks in.*

The Girl Where are you going?

A Little Girl I'm going to the village.

A bus speeds past. The driver and conductor wave. The girls wave back.

A Little Girl To buy spares.

The Three of Them

In the distance some houses a nearby shanty-town a roadside neighbourhood. The three of them on route three. **The Younger Girl** *observes* **A Little Girl** *with suspicion. At the wheel* **The Girl** *seems like a lady of twenty-five.* **The Younger Girl** *barely smiles.* **A Little Girl** *runs her tongue across the edge of her lips, takes a piece of bread from her pocket and puts it in her mouth.* **The Younger Girl** *digs her hand into* **A Little Girl***'s mouth and finds nothing there.*

The Younger Girl I thought . . .

A Little Girl You thought . . .

The Girl What are you talking about?

The Younger Girl How old are you?

A Little Girl What have you got under your dress?

The Younger Girl Nothing.

A Little Girl Is your tummy like that?

The Girl Yes, she's fat and she doesn't like people telling her.

A Little Girl   Can I touch it?

The Younger Girl   No, I don't like being touched.

A Little Girl   Can I plait your hair?

The Younger Girl   I don't like being touched.

The Girl   Yes.

A Little Girl   It's moving.

The Younger Girl   I'm hungry.

A Little Girl   It moves like that when you're hungry?

The Girl   Yes, she's got a disease.

A Little Girl   Is she going to die?

The Girl   Yes, she's going to die.

A Little Girl   I'm sorry.

The Younger Girl   Christians says sorry.

A Little Girl   What?

Tractor breakdown. **A Little Girl***'s head against* **The Younger Girl***'s belly.*

A Little Girl   It's hard.

The Younger Girl   Get off.

The Girl *jumps out of the tractor, ducks a wire fence, eucalyptus plantation, crawls across, hangs from a branch, tears it off, comes back calm, slow, quiet, in some kind of mood.*

A Little Girl   What have you got there?

The Younger Girl   Nothing, get off me.

A Little Girl   I haven't seen one for ages.

The Younger Girl   She's covered in blood.

A Little Girl   She's dead.

The Younger Girl   What do you mean dead?

A Little Girl   You've got it here on your face too.

The Younger Girl   She's gonna kill me.

A Little Girl   Did you two kill her?

The Younger Girl   Don't shout.

A Little Girl It's against the law to hunt them.

The Younger Girl She's not dead.

A Little Girl She is, you suffocated her.

The Younger Girl Shut up, we can't tell her.

A Little Girl You're murderers.

The branch, **The Girl** *beats the wheels.* **The Younger Girl** *slips the Armadillo back beside her belly, an invisible wake, holds the mammal with her left hand, with her right covers the mouth of* **A Little Girl** *who still has her umbrella open. Open-grave silence.* **The Girl** *climbs on. The tractor doesn't work it doesn't start up it doesn't work.*

It seizes up, a sound like machine gun going off.

A Little Girl It's catching fire.

The Girl It's normal, it's just a bit of smoke.

The Younger Girl We have to get out right now, she'll suffocate.

The Girl It's breaking down.

A Little Girl We'll all be choked to death.

The Girl What?

The Younger Girl The sun, the sun can make the accident worse and the fire can spread more quickly.

A Little Girl The trees will catch fire.

The Younger Girl And they'll cut the road off.

A Little Girl And we'll have to go via my shortcut.

The Younger Girl And the firemen won't be able to come because there are no firemen in the village.

The Girl What shortcut?

The Younger Girl Let's walk, we can't waste any more time.

A Little Girl There's shade that way.

The Younger Girl She's all infected.

The Girl This isn't going to work.

The Younger Girl She's moving, she can sense the smoke.

The Girl Is it shorter?

A Little Girl Yes, before you reach the village, past the Tomasito Molina silos.

Silos

In the early-afternoon vastness, twenty-five-metre monstrosities of production with no sky to hold them up. The three tiny girls walk perplexed heads turned towards the endless metal. Echoing voices. Horrendous heat. A barking Dog.

The Girl Are you sure there's no-one here?

A Little Girl They all sleep at siesta time.

The Younger Girl Tee Emm.

The Girl What?

The Younger Girl Tomasito Molina.

The Girl They're ginormous.

The Younger Girl Who's he?

The Girl They keep the seeds in them.

A Little Girl He's the owner.

The Younger Girl He owns all this?

The Girl Soy and sorghum in the summer.

A Little Girl Nearly the whole village.

The Girl Oats, barley and wheat in the winter.

The Younger Girl How do you know that?

The Girl Crops.

A Little Girl My mum works here.

The Younger Girl My hand's stinging.

The Girl They're different depending on the season.

A Little Girl Will I get some water?

The Girl How is she?

The Younger Girl Alive. I mean, fine.

A Little Girl Tomasito Molina.

The Girl My mum works here too.

The Younger Girl There's an echo.

The Girl Tomasito Molina.

A Little Girl Echo.

A Dog runs towards them. They try to speed up, gallop. Metal staircase, **A Little Girl** *scales a silo.* **The Girl** *follows, catches her up. Clumsy* **The Younger Girl** *advances, trips. A Dog bites her leg.* **The Younger Girl** *escapes, the Armadillo slips from her* *bloodstained belly. A Dog destroys the Armadillo. A bullet strikes A Dog, ricochets into* **The Younger Girl**'s *right thigh.*

A Little Girl *leaps from up high.* **The Girl** *treads on the head of* **The Younger Girl**, *climbs down carefully, runs to the disembowelled pieces of the Armadillo.* **The Younger Girl** *cries, her leg gushes blood. The shadow of a Fat Man who barks instead of talking approaches them warily. The girls run. They enter an enormous storehouse. They close the door. Complete darkness.*

The Girl   You dropped her.

A Little Girl   It bit you. Are you alright?

The Younger Girl   The bullet, it's bleeding, I can't see.

The Girl   How could you drop her?

A Little Girl   It looks really bad.

The Younger Girl   Are these stones?

The Girl   We need to go to the vet's.

A Little Girl   The vet's?

The Younger Girl   I think I've got a fever, I need water.

The Girl   We have to get the pieces and the dog and take them to the vet's, we can't leave them lying around like that.

A Little Girl   You need to go to hospital first.

The Younger Girl   It looks really bad. I can't feel the stones even though I'm sitting on them.

A Little Girl   Here, hold this.

The Younger Girl   They're so big.

The Girl   We have to leave.

A Little Girl   They're from a street they dug up, they stored them here.

The Girl   You're coming with us.

A Little Girl   I can't, I—

The Girl   You have to go, fetch the pieces of the armadillo and the dog, we'll go to the vet's and if they can't fix them, we have to hold a wake for them.

The Younger Girl   I can't breathe.

A Little Girl   We have to get out of here and take her to the doctor, she's losing a lot of blood.

The Girl   The dog's losing a lot of blood, too.

A Little Girl   But she's your sister.

The Girl She's not my sister.

A Little Girl Your cousin.

The Younger Girl Friend. I'm going to drink some water.

A Little Girl You're going to let your friend die?

The Girl She's not going to die.

A Little Girl What if she does die?

The Girl No-one dies that young.

The Fat Man barks and opens the huge door, his shadow floods in. **The Girl** *runs at The Fat Man.* **A Little Girl** *follows her, The Fat Man stops them, grabs them, one in each hand.* **The Younger Girl** *hurls a stone, strikes The Fat Man's head. It lands on the ground, The Fat Man falls flat on his face.*

The Girl You killed someone.

A Little Girl We have to get out of here.

The Girl He's dead, we'll be put in jail.

The Younger Girl Turn him over and let's go.

The Girl I can't touch him, look and see if he's still breathing.

The Younger Girl I don't feel well, turn him over and let's go.

A Little Girl Do as she says.

The Girl He's not breathing.

A Little Girl Open his mouth.

The Younger Girl No, he's not. Let's go.

The Path

The three walk in silence by the houses. They carry remains of the Armadillo and A Dog trailing blood just like **The Younger Girl**. *Five-o'clock church bells chime in the distance.* **The Girl** *filthy A Dog on her shoulder and hands stuffed with body parts of an animal that is no more.* **A Little Girl** *takes firm steps,* **The Younger Girl** *leans on her right shoulder blade, limps, woozy, close to collapse.*

The Younger Girl Look, a rabbit.

The Girl It's not a rabbit, it's a hare.

The Younger Girl It's the same.

A Little Girl They're similar.

The Girl No, they're different.

The Younger Girl   They run fast, they eat carrots.

The Girl   Hares don't eat carrots.

The Younger Girl   Yes they do.

The Girl   You've never seen one.

The Younger Girl   Yes I have.

The Girl   Where?

The Younger Girl   In a place.

The Girl   In what place?

The Younger Girl   In a zoo.

The Girl   They don't have hares in zoos.

The Younger Girl   Yes they do have hares in zoos.

The Girl   Hares are wild animals.

The Younger Girl   Exactly, they have wild animals in zoos too.

The Girl   You can't be wild in a zoo.

The Younger Girl   It's really bleeding.

The Girl   What must elephant blood be like?

The Younger Girl   How far is it to go?

A Little Girl   Far.

The Girl   I've never seen an elephant, they must be big.

A Little Girl   Elephants get frightened, they're scared of mice.

The Younger Girl   I'm scared of mice, they have poison in their tongues, if they bite you, you don't realise, they can be eating you while you sleep, and you won't realise they're eating you.

Barn owl wings spread wide, a sign of mystery, death or wisdom.

The Girl   That must be the best way to die, without realising, dying in your sleep, the people left behind suffer, but you don't notice.

The Younger Girl   How do you know you don't notice?

The Girl   Well, I don't know, but I imagine.

A cloud darkens.

The Girl   What are you scared of?

The Younger Girl   You know what.

The Girl   Well, what else?

The Younger Girl I don't know, this.

The Girl I'm scared of the infinite.

Cumulonimbus withdraws, dusk adorns thoughts and the tops of their heads.

The Girl Look, we're in a town.

A Little Girl A village.

The Girl A town.

A Little Girl A village.

The Girl Well, we're in a village, the village is in a town.

A Little Girl A province.

The Girl A town.

A Little Girl A province.

The Girl Well, we're in a village, the village is in a province, the province is in a country, the country is in a continent, the continent is in the world, the world is in the solar system, the solar system is in the universe, so where's the universe?

The Younger Girl In another universe?

The Girl I don't know, I don't know where it is, but it scares me.

A soccer pitch blocks their path. Boys playing football. They shout and insult each other. The three girls try to cross. **The Girl** *goes slowly,* **The Younger Girl** *much slower. The Boys jeer at the girls.* **A Little Girl** *approaches them, steals their ball, dribbles across the pitch, kicks it along as the Boys try to tackle her but fail.* **A Little Girl** *reaches the net, scores a tremendous goal. The Boys, angry, try to trip* **The Girl** *and* **The Younger Girl** *up.* **A Little Girl** *kicks the ball into one of their faces, The Tallest One of All. The Boys laugh and bow to the girls. They try to help them but the girls refuse, they don't need any boys in their story, for now.*

A Little Girl Now, after the football pitch.

The Younger Girl Burns unit.

The Girl Where's the vet's?

The Younger Girl You can't take animals in.

A Little Girl I don't think we're going to need it.

The Younger Girl Trinidad must be looking for us, and the fat man.

A Little Girl The fat creep?

The Younger Girl You know him?

A Little Girl The traffic inspector.

The Girl We thought he was a different fat man.

A Little Girl   There's lots of similar fat men.

The Younger Girl   They're chasing us.

The Girl   We went into Heartbreak Tango.

A Little Girl   You went into Heartbreak Tango?

The Girl   She was thirsty.

The Younger Girl   And she couldn't find anywhere better to find water.

The Girl   They left us locked inside.

The Younger Girl   But we broke out.

A Little Girl   The fat creep always comes to the hospital.

White Building

A Little Girl *and* **The Girl** *go inside.* **The Younger Girl** *waits outside, tries to hide the blood, the heat of the day. A dead Dog, the chill of the late afternoon, the scattered pieces of the Armadillo. They pass nurses, a pregnant woman smokes a cigarette, a lady in a wheelchair, a baby crawling and an old woman spitting green. Five motorbikes, a car, an ambulance arriving, thirty bicycles and the girls returning.*

The Girl   Your aunt.

A Little Girl   She's not here.

The Younger Girl   What do you mean she's not here?

The Girl   They say they can't see you because you're not from this town.

The Younger Girl   But a fat man shot me in the leg, they have to see me anyway.

The Girl   It's internal rules, they can't.

A Little Girl   We tried to convince them but nothing.

The Younger Girl   Did you tell them my aunt—?

The Girl   Yes, they didn't listen to us.

A Little Girl   They said to come back later.

The Younger Girl   Didn't they believe you?

A Little Girl   Yes, but they didn't care.

The Girl   Rules are rules.

The Younger Girl   But it hurts, it might get infected, seriously.

The Girl   I said the same to them, that they had to amputate your leg.

The Younger Girl   Didn't they care?

A Little Girl No.

The Girl They said we should go to the auction and buy you a wheelchair.

The Younger Girl Huh?

A Little Girl I think your aunt's there.

A motorbike pulls up, parks, from the helmet emerges the head of Trinidad who alights and enters the white building. **A Little Girl** *trots towards the motorbike, hotwires it and revs it up.* **The Girl** *puts* **The Younger Girl**, *A dead Dog, the pieces of the Armadillo on her shoulders. The three fly off on two wheels.*

The Girl You stole a tractor.

The Younger Girl We both did.

A Little Girl Was it stolen?

The Girl We stole a tractor, you let a dog kill the armadillo, a fat man killed a dog and you killed the fat man and we stole a motorbike. Now we are going to jail.

A Little Girl Juvenile jail.

The Younger Girl We have to get out of here.

The Girl And go where?

The Younger Girl Far away, where they won't find us, to another continent, on a boat.

A Little Girl There's no sea here.

The Girl I've never seen the sea.

The Younger Girl That's why we have to go to a place by the sea or a river or a stream, and where no-one knows us and we can change our clothes and our hair colour and we can buy sunglasses.

A Little Girl The police will still find you.

The Younger Girl Not if we go quickly. They won't know it was us.

A Little Girl You left your fingerprints on the tractor, on the stone you threw at the fat man's head, and now, on this motorbike.

The Girl She's right, plus it's impossible to leave, no-one ever leaves.

The auction microphone the sale. Hidden the three girls start to cry. They stop.

The Younger Girl We're not going in.

The Girl But you have to get treated.

A Little Girl You might get infected.

The Younger Girl I don't care, I don't want to go to jail.

The Girl But you might die.

The Younger Girl I know, but I don't want to die like that.

A Little Girl Like what?

The Younger Girl Aged fifteen, alone, in prison, with one leg.

The Girl You're not fifteen.

The Younger Girl That makes no difference.

The Girl Yes it does.

A Little Girl It doesn't matter, she's right, we can't go to jail for stealing.

The Girl That doesn't make sense.

The Younger Girl It doesn't make sense to get sent to jail for stealing to save yourself from being chased, that doesn't make sense.

A Little Girl I don't want to go to jail either, let's go.

The Girl But we killed a fat man.

The Younger Girl Fat men die every day, one more won't make any difference.

The Girl But we killed him.

A Little Girl And the fat man killed the dog and the dog killed the armadillo.

The Girl You're right.

The Younger Girl We have to bury them.

A Little Girl I know exactly where we have to go.

The Girl Not the cemetery, there's police there.

A Little Girl Don't worry, I'd never take you to a place where the police are.

The Girl What if you die?

The Younger Girl Sooner or later we're all gonna die.

Zooillogical Future

Rusted iron sculptures in animal shapes. **A Little Girl** *digs a hole with her hands.* **The Girl** *licks* **The Younger Girl**'s *wound. She rests her mouth on her palm, slides her tongue between her teeth, the tip extends, drools on everything. She runs it up and down the leg from side to side and goes on for a long time.* **The Younger Girl** *lets herself be licked. The earth flies, the cars pass a grassy roundabout.* **The Girl** *wipes her mouth with the back of her right hand.* **The Younger Girl** *pale, hurt, wounded, tired.*

The Girl Have you ever kissed anyone?

The Younger Girl Course I have.

A Little Girl   I haven't.

The Girl   Me neither.

The Younger Girl   Haven't you?

The Girl   No, I don't know how.

A Little Girl   I've never seen it.

The Younger Girl   Just a normal kiss.

The Girl   What do you mean normal?

The Younger Girl   Like normal, like a kiss on the mouth?

The Girl   With tongues.

A Little Girl   With spit?

The Younger Girl   Oh, yeah, course I have.

The Girl   Will you show us?

The Younger Girl   Me?

The Younger Girl *passes out.* **A Little Girl** *places A Dog and the remains of the Armadillo into the hole.* **The Girl** *tries to listen to the sound of* **The Younger Girl***'s heart, she doesn't hear anything or doesn't know how.* **A Little Girl** *does the same, shakes her head. Both girls cry. A police or ambulance siren approaches.*

A Little Girl   We have to get out of here.

The Girl   We can't leave her alone.

A Little Girl   We can't take her with us.

The Girl   We have to help her.

A Little Girl   She's dead, we can't help her.

The Girl *kisses* **The Younger Girl** *on the mouth, drags her to the hole, covers her quickly. The red and blue light comes closer.* **A Little Girl** *climbs onto the motorbike,* **The Girl** *follows her.*

The Girl   Where to?

A Little Girl   Anywhere close to the sea.

The Girl *holds on tight to* **A Little Girl***, the motorbike revs up and they disappear along the highway, in the falling night, amidst bats, truckers and nightbirds.*

SEQUEL

They hear the sirens singing.

The Road

Hot summer dust earth confinement. Night falls and the girls travel in search of the sea. They've never been, they've never seen it or wetted their fingers no jellyfish stings no fishing with lights to dazzle the fish no yemanyá goddess of the sea no pirates no mermaids. Faraway ambulance or police, the desperate yell of someone following tormenting. Night falls and the blue pink purple inferno fades into the early blackness. A cricket sings and **The Girl** *and* **A Little Girl** *stumble along on a clapped-out motorbike, dirty and hungry, they flee, they search for the sea. To keep their promise to see it.*

The Girl   I can't hear them any more.

A Little Girl   The armadillo, the dog, the dead fat man.

The Girl   I didn't kill a fat man.

A Little Girl   But you did kill her.

The Girl   No, I didn't kill her, she died, anyway you don't know, you don't know if she's dead.

A Little Girl   She stopped breathing, we buried her, she's dead.

The Girl   Are you a doctor?

A Little Girl   Did you hear that?

The Girl   You're not a doctor, so you don't know, don't say anything if you don't know, don't speak.

A Little Girl   It's sirens.

The Girl   Anyway she killed the fat man and now she's dead, we didn't do anything.

A Little Girl   I don't know if it's the police or the ambulance or both.

The Girl   I didn't do anything.

A Little Girl   Can you hear them?

The Girl   We're not to blame for something a dead person did.

A Little Girl   We have to give ourselves up, it's dangerous.

The Girl   What's dangerous is not keeping a promise you made to a dead person.

A Little Girl   What's dangerous is being put in jail.

The Girl   No-one's putting me in jail.

A Little Girl   How do you know?

The Girl   What have I done?

A Little Girl   You committed offences.

The Girl   Escaping from prostitution?

A Little Girl   Robbery and murder.

The Girl   It was self-defence.

A Little Girl   What's that?

The Girl   I don't know but they say it in films.

A Little Girl   Real life isn't a film.

The Girl   How do you know?

A Little Girl   You can't steal a tractor, start a fire and then run away.

The Girl   She said to us, you have to go to the sea.

A Little Girl   She's dead, she won't know if we went or not.

The Girl   Don't you believe in life after death?

A Little Girl   I think they'll kill us or put us in jail.

Livestock

The motorbike stops in the vastness. The fields lie in wait. Some two hundred cows cross the highway and the faraway sirens can now barely be heard. **The Girl** *and* **A Little Girl** *watch the herd pass, they rest.*

A Little Girl   How far is it to go?

The Girl   Not far.

A Little Girl   How not far?

The Girl   Kilometres.

A Little Girl   I think we lost them.

The Girl   Or they're resting.

A Little Girl   They'll be a long time, there's so many of them.

The Girl   What are you doing?

A Little Girl   I'm cold.

The Girl   They'll attack you.

A Little Girl   Cows don't attack people.

The Girl   All animals attack people if they annoy them.

A Little Girl   It's only a hug.

The Girl   I need to go to the toilet.

A Little Girl   Go behind a tree.

The Girl   I got my period.

A Little Girl   You're too young to get your period.

The Girl   You're too young to know what a period is.

A Little Girl   And you're too young to murder someone.

The Girl   Take your clothes off.

A Little Girl   What?

The Girl   Take them off.

A Little Girl   Get off me, what are you doing?

The Girl *takes* **A Little Girl***'s clothes and* **A Little Girl** *hits* **The Girl**, *the cows moo, they run about terrified.* **The Girl** *climbs on the motorbike and drives off.* **A Little Girl** *is left standing, she climbs onto one of the mammals and goes after* **The Girl** *who laughs at full speed.* **The Girl**, *the motorbike, the cow and* **A Little Girl** *disappear in the darkness of the tarmac.*

Heartbreak Tango

The clapped-out motorbike stops outside a crumbling dive bar, alcohol, police and prostitutes. **A Little Girl** *kisses the cow's mouth goodbye.* **The Girl** *complains and curses. Men and women dance the guaracha. La lluvia mojó by Sonido Cotopaxi plays and it starts to rain.*

The Girl   It's broken down.

A Little Girl   We'll have to pray or something.

The Girl   Or ask for help.

A Little Girl   We can't ask for help.

The Girl   It's the reserve.

A Little Girl   No, it's not the reserve, it's the valve.

The Girl   Go inside and ask for help, tell them we're going to visit my aunt in Dolores.

A Little Girl   Dolores is in the other direction.

The Girl   Fine, Cortinas then, it doesn't matter, they won't ask you.

A Little Girl   And what if they do?

The Girl   Make something up, start crying, ask to go to the toilet.

A Little Girl   I'm not asking to go to the toilet, it's a brothel, I might get disappeared.

The Girl   I wish you would disappear. That's not Trinidad.

A Little Girl   She's the same though.

The Girl   No, she's not the same.

A Little Girl   Yes she is, she's got that thing.

The Girl   What thing?

A Little Girl   She's neither one thing nor the other.

The Girl   What do you mean?

A Little Girl   Not a man or a woman.

The Girl   That's like saying all Chinese people are like Japanese people.

A Little Girl   Well they are.

The Girl   My aunt says you shouldn't say that.

A Little Girl   Who cares about your aunt?

The Girl   My aunt's gonna start a revolution and we're gonna go back and we're not going to jail.

A Little Girl   What's a revolution?

The Girl   An important thing in the street with women.

A Little Girl   A party?

The Girl   Yes, a party.

A Little Girl   What sort of party?

The Girl   Like one with dancing.

A Little Girl   Oh, like at Heartbreak Tango.

The tractor parks. A Young Man interrupts them. When A Young Man speaks, they hear a cock-crow coming from his mouth. **The Girl** *rips off the exhaust pipe and smashes the head of A Young Man who falls down flat with a thud. The music stops. From the window of Heartbreak Tango men and women watch* **The Girl** *and* **A Little Girl** *run like hares, climb into the tractor and drive away.*

A Little Girl   You killed another man.

The Girl   You don't know if he's dead.

A Little Girl   And you stole something again.

The Girl   We both did.

A Little Girl   And now the police, Trinidad, the fat man, men and women are all after us.

The Girl   We're going to jail.

A Little Girl   I'm not going to jail, I'm too young.

The Girl   We've got two options.

A Little Girl   I'll waste my whole life in a cell.

The Girl   Go to the sea and keep our promise.

A Little Girl   And get eaten by rats.

The Girl   Or go to the sea and keep our promise.

A Little Girl   And raped.

The Girl   All the girls in the village get raped.

A Little Girl   And the police will rape me.

The Girl   They rape all the girls.

A Little Girl   And I'll have to have an unwanted pregnancy.

The Girl   That's your fate if you're a girl in a village.

A Little Girl   And I'll give birth in jail.

The Girl   Be a girl who gets raped or die without ever seeing the sea.

A Little Girl   And I'll have to give my baby up for adoption.

The Girl   And we're going to see the sea.

A Little Girl   And when it grows up it won't recognise me.

The Girl   And no-one's going to rape us.

A Little Girl   And it won't love me because I had to abandon it when I was in prison.

The Girl   But we are going to die.

A Little Girl   I don't want to die, I'm too young to die.

The Girl   I'd rather die than go to jail.

A Little Girl   I want to choose.

The Girl   Village girls don't get to choose.

The Dune and the Sea

The Girl   They say there are lights in the heavens and in the sea and that in those countries it's always summer, there's sandstorms but no-one minds and it doesn't get in their clothes or their eyes because there's mountains of sunshine and the mirages make you forget the pain and the hunger and the sleepiness, and that in the oases they eat coconut and there's palm trees, the men are good and there's not many of them and the women are in the majority.

A Little Girl Are we there?

The Girl Not far now.

A Little Girl How far?

The Girl Kilometres.

A Little Girl Did we lose them?

The Girl Way back.

A Little Girl They won't put us in jail?

The Girl I don't think they can.

A Little Girl If we go to heaven will we find each other?

The Girl Maybe.

A Little Girl And if we keep the promise will they give us a present?

Suddenly the monstrous sea and silence. **The Girl** *and* **A Little Girl** *jump out of the tractor, sink into the sand and remove their clothes one by one. They walk to the mountain in a country with no mountains they walk through sand like rocks in formation. A volcano on the edge the tractor sets fire explosions far away. The soles of their feet burn but they don't walk faster. The only revolution they will know will be two natural disasters. Naked they reach the sea and wade in as if they were dressed and with stones in their pockets. They sink, hug, and kiss each other on the mouth. In the distance, sirens.*

END

Brief Glossary

Armadillo: The southern long-nosed armadillo, *mulita* in Spanish, is an endangered native species and folkloric symbol of Uruguay and South America.

Heartbreak Tango: A brothel in Trinidad, a town in Flores department, Uruguay. Also the title of a novel by the Argentine author Manuel Puig. In Spanish, *Boquitas Pintadas*, literally *Little Painted Mouths*.

La lluvia mojó: A song by Sonido Cotopaxi, literally *The Rain Wetted*.

Sol negro: A song by Sonido Caracol, literally *Black Sun*.

Sonido Caracol: A Uruguayan band, literally *Shell Sound*.

Sonido Cotopaxi: A Uruguayan band. Cotopaxi is a volcano in Ecuador.

Zooillogical Future: A sculpture park exhibiting iron sculptures of local animals and hunting tools created by Martín Arregui in Flores department, Uruguay.

Basic Principles for the Construction of Bridges

Jimena Márquez

Translated by Catherine Boyle

Nociones básicas para la construcción de puentes (*Basic Notions for the Construction of Bridges*) was written for the Comedia Nacional, the national theatre company of Uruguay, on the occasion of the centenary of the birth of Mario Benedetti. It premiered at the Teatro Solís, Montevideo, on 21 August 2020. It was directed by Jimena Márquez and performed by Leandro Ibero Núñez, Stefanie Neukirch, Fernando Vannet and Florencia Zabaleta. The four actors contributed their personal stories during the rehearsal process. The play was published by Editorial Fin de Siglo in 2021.

About the author and translator

Jimena Márquez is a standout figure in Uruguayan theatre. A professor of literature, playwright and theatre director, she has received numerous awards throughout her career. In 2022, she won the Florencio Award for Best Solo Performance by an Actress for her own play, *El desmontaje* (*The Deconstruction*). In 2019, she received the Uruguayan Ministry of Education and Culture National Literature Award for *La sospechosa puntualidad de la casualidad* (*The Suspicious Punctuality of Chance*) produced in 2017 by the Comedia Nacional. She has directed and written over 15 plays and represented Uruguay at numerous international festivals. She has directed plays on four occasions for the Comedia Nacional and has staged performances for the Montevideo Symphonic Band and for the Montevideo Philharmonic Orchestra. She has written for the Uruguay Carnival since 2008 and was voted as one of the Carnival's People of the Year in 2022. She has taught at numerous educational establishments and currently runs Teatro en el Aula (Theatre in the Classroom), a programme of theatre for young people run by the regional government of Montevideo. She is a columnist for the national newspaper, *La Diaria*.

Catherine Boyle is Professor of Latin American Cultural Studies at King's College London. She was a co-founder of the *Journal of Latin American Cultural Studies*. She is the director of the Ibero-American theatre and translation collective, Out of the Wings. She is a translator of Spanish and Spanish American theatre and poetry. Her translations have been performed internationally and she has published widely on questions of Latin American cultural and gender studies and translation. She is the Director of the Centre for Language Acts and Worldmaking which is dedicated to regenerating and transforming approaches to teaching and research in Modern Languages.

For my Luz.

"To cross
or not to cross
the bridge.
That is the question."

Mario Benedetti

Cast

Flor
Nando
Stefi
Lean

The actors enter. They dismantle the set. They set it up. They set it up fearfully, insecure, without wanting to, tense, in a space that is endlessly being set up.
The sound of different voices of people giving their opinions about Mario Benedetti.

Flor It's fine like that. That's it. It's fine like that.

Nando Hang on a minute.

Stefi Just a minute, no more.

Flor It's fine like that. That's it.

Lean It's not fine. It's not finished. It's never going to be finished.

Flor Please. That's enough. Leave it like that. It's fine. People are coming in. There are people here. People.

They stop everything. They stand in silence in front of the audience.

Flor I don't know who's going to explain. But somebody's got to. Now.

Nando Be quiet. If you're not speaking to explain, be quiet. This is when we explain. We enter, we set up and we explain. That's the plan.

Flor Whatever, but let's get on and do it, somebody, do it, please.

Stefi What's wrong with you?

Flor It annoys me. When things aren't what they should be, I get annoyed. I don't think it's right to put up with this. All the time we dedicated to th/

Lean We . . . are . . . municipal employees.

Stefi Don't say it like that.

Lean We are municipal employees.

Nando But first and foremost we're actors.

Flor That doesn't matter. Who cares about that? That's not what we have to explain. Get over it. Don't get caught up in that . . .

Lean No, I don't know if we're actors first and foremost.

Stefi You know what, you do actually know. We're actors. Actors in the National Theatre Company. It's a state company, that's right, we have a steady income, that's true, there's a competitive process to get in, we have regular hours and we'll be in this company until we retire, if everything works out right, today or tomorrow that will, effectively, be true, but, as our co-worker Fernando says, first and foremost we are actors. And actresses.

Lean No, I don't know if first and foremost, I don't know. Let's talk about the dark zo/

Stefi We are not going to talk about the dark zone. We don't need to.

Flor And anyway, it's not what matters now. It's not what people care about. People came to see a play and we haven't got one yet. It doesn't happen often, but it can happen.

Nando That's what we have to explain. That we haven't got a play.

Flor We came to do what we can, because that's what we're here for, to do what we can, but we didn't come to talk about ourselves, people didn't come to see the painful journeys of four employ/

Stefi Actors.

Lean Employees. Long-suffering municipal employees.

Nando Tell me something: when you do an interview, what do you say? I am an actor, or I am a municipal employee?

Flor Actress.

Stefi So you know/

Nando I didn't ask you/

Flor But I am omitting part of the information/

Nando I didn't ask you/

Stefi Omitting part of the information doesn't mean you're not an actress/

Nando What is it that makes you more of an actress than a municipal employee?

Flor Are you asking me?/

Nando Now I am/

Flor I didn't ask you/

Nando Don't act stupid/

Flor What's your problem?

Nando What's my problem? My problem . . .

They argue. Speaking on top of each other. Enraged. Deaf to each other. **Lean** *cuts through.*

Lean The problem is that I don't want to do this play.

Flor But you can't not do this play, you're a municipal employee.

Lean What do I care? I'll ask for a transfer to the planetarium, but I'm not going to do this play.

Discussion.

Nando Truce! Peace. I'll do this. Calm down. I'm here to do the explaining. I feel that I can do it. So, I'll explain. I think I can do that. Explain. I have a plan. That's a plan. I'll explain. That's a plan. We didn't manage to get the play done in time. We're going to share the log of our non-completion of the play we were commissioned to write.

Lean This play will be un-acted by Fernando Vannet. Thirty-nine years of age. From Montevideo. The most affectionate of the cast, the one who embraces the National

Theatre Company. Florencia Zabaleta, thirty-seven. Fernandina. Lawyer and divorcée. Give her a hug, Fernando, she needs one. Stefani Neukirch. Is that how you say it?

Stefi   No.

Lean   How do you say it?

Stefi   Neukirch.

Lean   Thirty-six years of age. German. A clear example of Germanic perfectionism. And though she looks very young, she is a mother. And me: Mario Orlando Hamlet Brenno Benedetti Farrugia.

Tension.

Nando   This is what we are going to explain later. Later. I can manage this. Stefani, please, the logbook.

Stefi   Day One. We are assigned the writing of a play for the celebration of the centenary of the birth of Mario Benedetti/

Flor   I still don't understand why we're not doing something for Idea Vilariño, who was born in the same year as Mario Benedetti.

Nando   Stefani is speaking. Stefani.

Stefi   Shall I start again or . . .?

Flor   Just carry on, for God's sake.

Stefi   Day One/

Flor   Shit/

Stefi   We are assigned a play for the celebration of the centenary of the birth of Mario Benedetti. The project raises certain doubts, we all liked Mario Benedetti at some point, but we're not sure if we still do. We're removed from his work, none of us reads Benedetti now. Benedetti holds a place that is especially difficult to define in young readers/ Uruguayans.

Flor   Young readers. We're almost forty.

Stefi   For us, his universe belongs more to the plane of nostalgia/

Flor   That's not what's important.

Stefi   They tell us that the play will go on tour. We're happy. We'll get out of our offices. We always work in three venues: the main auditorium of the Teatro Solís, its second theatre Sala Zavala Muniz, and Sala Verdi. The news that we'll tour is like opening wide our office windows. It fills us with light, it fills us with air/

Flor   But it doesn't matter anyway, people don't care about our happiness, what they care about is the play.

Nando   Our happiness has direct repercussions for the play.

Stefi   One colleague refuses to do the play we've been told to write.

Flor Names, give us names.

Stefi Leandro Núñez refuses to do the play we've been told to write.

Flor That is what matters.

Lean Who is Leandro Núñez?

Unease.

Nando We were asked to write a play for the centenary of the birth of Mario Benedetti. We had very little time for rehearsals/

Stefi That's what I was explaining/

Nando Mario Benedetti's work is vast. He published more than eighty titles, he wrote until his last days. So, we felt it was mission impossible.

Stefi I was going to say that/

Flor It's a question of rhythm, Stefani.

Nando This year there will be loads of works by Mario, about Mario and based on Mario and we didn't want to fall into what we suppose everyone else is going to do/

Flor But how do you know what everyone else is going to do?

Nando Leandro/

Lean Which Leandro?

Nando Leandro Núñez.

Lean Who is Leandro Núñez?

Flor Forget it. Forget it. Get on with the explanation.

Nando Now you want me to forget it! But didn't you want me to explain?

Flor It doesn't matter what you do, what I want is for you to get on with it.

Stefi Calm down. Please. Please. Let's have some order.

Lean I want to know who Leandro Núñez is. That's all.

Flor Nobody. Leandro Núñez is an idiot and because of him we're doing this piece of shit, or undoing it, who knows.

Nando OK. Like any story worth the name, this had a beginning. So, we'll start by telling how we began. Stefani.

Stefi Day Two. We got together. We shared our personal stories about Mario Benedetti, how he came into our lives, our opinions on his work. We discovered that we are far away, far away from him and far away from the years in which we read him. Far away from who we were when we were close to him. Far away from the most substantial worlds of his work/

Basic Principles for the Construction of Bridges 93

Flor It's not quite like that.

Stefi I am reading the log because I wrote it. We recognise an old attachment to Benedetti, we recognise also that we abandoned him. We exchange the reasons for our distance. We recommend reading his work until we begin the rehearsals. We get together to read. A long and hopeful period of reading starts.

They are all at the table except **Lean**. *They read. They read. They read and read.*

Lean I don't want to do this play.

Flor But you can't not do this play, you're a municipal employee.

Lean What do I care, I'll ask for a transfer to the botanical gardens.

Flor "I don't know if this has ever happened to you, but the botanical garden is a sleepy park in which one can feel like a tree or a local" . . .

Lean No, no. "Feel like a tree." I left that stage behind in drama school. I'll ask for a transfer to the zoo. I'll feed a monkey. I'll brush its back if it's really crawling. I really love animals. I'll feed the capybaras. I am not going to do this play. I don't want to be Mario Benedetti. I don't want to be born in Paso de los Toros. I don't want to be the child of Italians. I don't want to be the grandson of a chemist and to end up being a poet. I don't want to be the grandson of Brenno, son of Brenno and call myself Mario, I don't want to be the one who always breaks the branch of the family tree. I don't want to be the killjoy who tells his mother, "Dad and the neighbour are touching each other's legs under the table." I don't want to provoke endless months of marital silence. I don't want to be in the middle of my parents, receiving the "Tell your father . . .", "Tell your mother . . ." messages. I don't want then to write a story where I treat myself as if I were a stupid waste of a kid. I don't want death to come into my life through my grandmother Pastora/

Nando Bridge. Death came into my life when we were in Parque del Plata, with the death of my great-grandfather Alo.

Stefi Bridge. Death came into my life, when I was four years old when my maternal grandfather Eduardo died and my mother came back from the wake.

Flor Bridge. Death came into my life when I was sitting on my father's lap once listening to the radio and the obituaries came on and I thought, one day I am going to hear: "Florencia Zabaleta has died in the town of Maldonado . . ." And I realised that I wouldn't hear that.

Lean I don't want to go to the German School, I don't want to be forced to do the Nazi salute, but neither do I want them to send me to another school. I don't want to realise too late that the only other passenger on the tram that took me to the German School was none other than Juan Zorrilla de San Martín. I don't want never to have dared to talk to the man who would later become volume number one of the History of Uruguayan Literature. I don't want to be a municipal employee. I've said that from the start. I don't want to be number seven in a list of future deaths, nor to live, or imagine, or relive the moment that number six has just been disappeared, that they have taken Héctor away, that they've taken Zelmar away . . .

Stefi   We get it. We get it. We understand.

Lean   And above all, I don't want to be the one that is saved. I don't want to go into exile, I don't want to disexile myself, I don't want to invent the word "disexile" and I don't want to realise that nobody comes back from exile, that you don't come back from exile, that nobody bathes twice in the same Montevideo. And besides all that, I don't want to die. I don't want to die any more. I don't want to die at eighty-eight so that I don't hear them saying/

Nando   "Today we buried part of our history."

Lean   Part of our history. Do you realise the calibre of what I am being asked to do?

Nando   Then he said it.

Lean   I don't like Benedetti.

Pause.

Flor   Here. Read until you like him.

Lean   I tried.

Flor   You didn't try hard enough and it's not fair on us. We've been at this for two months/

Lean   If you multiply the number of pages he wrote by sixty, which is the number of meetings we had to put on the play, at one minute a page, it's not possible to read it all in two months. There is no way we can do this play.

Stefi   We don't have to read it all, we don't have to die to act dead.

Discussion.

Stefi   Day Seven. The discussions are interminable. Leandro can't find his way. He doesn't want to find it. He has drawn up all his bridges. Leandro is full of drawbridges. To get through this process, you have to be open/

Flor   For everything, Stefi, for every process, you have to be open.

Stefi   To go through the process you have to be prepared to go through the treachery of nostalgia. I repeat: the treachery of nostalgia. Benedetti is the nostalgia for Montevideo/

Lean   The nostalgia for a Montevideo that wasn't mine.

Stefi   The nostalgia for being present at a reading of a Montevideo that wasn't ours.

Lean   The Montevideo I read in him wasn't mine. I was not from the centre. I have nothing to do with it. I lived in Colón/

Nando   So did Mario.

Lean   In a humble house. With a yard, a tin roof.

Nando   So did Mario.

Lean OK, according to mister know-it-all here, maybe I do have something in common with him. The book I liked was *La borra del café*: *Coffee Dregs*. The descriptions of Capurro, more about the neighbourhood, more about the attics, not so many offices, more grass, not so much Palacio Salvo. In 2001, when I was in the second year of drama school, I went to see a show by the National Theatre Company, *Benedetti, Our Neighbour*, it was called, directed by Buscaglia, and I liked some of the stories about football, they really made me laugh, I liked them because it felt as if he hadn't written them . . .

> While I wind up my memory
> nostalgia forms a ball
> if I unravel nostalgia
> hope rolls itself into a ball.
> It's always the same thread.

He carries on speaking under the above song, "Ovillo" ("Ball").

Mario always seemed to me to be very like my father, the jacket, the shirt . . . I can't read him because Mario reminds me of my father. Bridge.

Nando We'll explain that later.

Stefi We couldn't stop investigating. We made ourselves read *Coffee Dregs* only because it was the Benedetti novel that Leandro liked most.

Flor I'd love to tell you the story of *Coffee Dregs*, but that would be another play.

Nando It was what we had to do to get closer. When they said that we four, the youngest group of actors in the National Theatre Company, were going to do a play on Mario, I thought that they were talking about Mario Bros.

Stefi Fernando, please.

Nando Why not? Why not do a play about Mario Bros? Completely representative of our generation. Did you not play Super Mario?

Flor Yes. At the same time that I was reading Benedetti, I was playing Super Mario. Bridge.

Nando You?

Stefi Of course.

Nando You?

Lean Who is Super Mario?

Tension.

Flor Let's have some order. Let's work on reviewing motives. This is the exercise that's done to understand the characters. Stefi, read what we agreed. What does the character Leandro need?

Stefi Leandro needs to be Mario Benedetti.

Flor What for?

Stefi So he won't lose his job.

Flor Why?

Stefi Because he's scared of economic instability.

Flor We started with a "what happens if . . ."

Stefi What happens if one day a municipal actor refuses to play a role they've been cast in?

Flor OK. Let's stick within the limits, please.

Lean But Leandro has other motives. (*Reads a paper*.) Sorry, it seems that Leandro left some things written down. "What does the character need? I need not to do the play about Mario Benedetti. What for? So as not to open old wounds. Why? Because I am afraid of suffering." It seems that these are Leandro's real motives.

Nando We'll review the motives later. End of the prologue. Zone One. Breath, Montevideo. Stefi.

Stefi Day Ten. We begin to find unexpected territories in Mario's poetry. We find the poem, "Sightseeing 1980". Sightseeing means tourism.

Nando And it had an epigraph.

Stefi "I would like to see what will be seen by those who are alive when Montevideo has one million inhabitants." Juan Zorrilla de San Martín.

Lean The number 36 tram
went to Punta Carretas
at quarter past six in the fragile morning
when the dew was lifting like mist
I took it every day to go to
the German School
in a street called soriano

It was a time of the day for stoics
which is why we were the only two passengers
me sitting up front at the little window
and way back a small and honourable old man
always in a dark suit and with a greying beard
who would read his newspaper and never look at me

Now I like to think of him
that regular passenger
certain that he took that groaning tram
in some vague corner of the nineteenth century
but at that time there was someone
my father

who said that is the national poet
that is don juan zorilla de sanmartín

The thing was
that the august name said nothing to me
so I went on considering him an old man
small and with his dark
wrinkled brow and his beard
one who every day shared with me
the number 36 on the commercial line
a little later he would die with all honours

I remember that one afternoon
when I was then an adolescent
I went into his house
which was no longer his house
but had recently become
the zorilla museum
and I had retrospective desire to speak to him
to sit with him
on the tram at quarter past six

In this half a century since
I have of course read
about his life and work
about his faith and talent

The tram carries on galloping in the mist
with him old and me a boy
with him alone and me alone

But I have never found out what he was doing so early
in the penultimate stage of his candid glory.

Nando Nostalgia for 29. Montevideo now. 1980. Sightseeing.

Flor Gentlemen and watches / children and fakes / ladies and fires
this is an excursion into the winters in summer
our country as you can see in the watercolour in front of you
has the form of a heart or perhaps bolas or a sack
later on we will dive into the semantic scruples and nuances
but in the meantime you might enjoy on your right
of the hill / our poor but honourable himalaya
with its colonial fort and its sealed prison cells
where creoles and bats learned to feel in the dark
if we had time
we would go there so that you
wouldn't be able to see even your hands and yet would hear

the moaning or versions or blasphemy of another time
so infinitely worse than now that it would make you happy
but since we don't have time what a port
also called docks or estuary or canal or bay
this is a free country you can call it what you want

in truth it is a jewel of a port through which always entered
the persecuted and the fulfilled with their saddlebags
of hope and wounded convictions
you have to agree that in the last decade
the exports of hope have greatly exceeded
the imports of help
which is considered a good indicator of commercial balance
here we have an old city although relatively new for europeans /
if we had time
I would show you a wall with a barely indelible stain
that looks like blood although it is blood
but since we don't have time
look at this beautiful banking unit
within the walls the cows become currency
let's say for example that today's price
is five dollars for a kilo of steak
independence square is of course a figure of speech
if we had time
I would speak to you about artigas
a naturalist who gathered stray dogs
but since we don't have time I encourage you to look at
this wide and spacious commercial avenue
it has a highly suggestive past
with trees demonstrations and carnivals
if we had time
we would stay for the carnivals
since the demonstrations and the trees have been cut back
but since we don't have time
here we have the square named in other times freedom
now it is simply a square which is logical
why give it obvious and hallucinogenic titles
that also sow and reap bewilderment
since there is elsewhere a closed-off place that has the same alias
as you can see this avenue is not only long but also monotonous
barely delimited by the national library
where mystic and not-so-mystic authors take a vow of enclosure
and by the enigmatic presence of what used to be the university
nowadays a marvellous museum of wax figures and desires
and so we move on towards the obelisk in daring
homage to the candour of the nineteenth century

if we had time
we would wait until it rained
because the rain gives it a splendid brilliance for agfacolor colour prints
but since we don't have time let's turn right into the boulevard
with its ever-present embassies and patrol cars
and pigeons and street walkers
and its nodding and reflective pine trees
that remember everything that we here forget
and now at last the river wide as the sea
where the sun polishes delicate feminine shoulders
and unisex scars
and snails rest in the sand
and the mutilated and the orphan children
and the mastiffs with their ears pricked up and curious as radars
might look every so often towards the horizon
it's difficult to know if the dolphins are coming or going
whereas the transatlantic ships are going
and the tugs for the ferries
the nitrate air is good for the soul and bad for asthma
perhaps that is why there is a considerable increase
in respiratory problems at national level and that there also exists
a certain unevenness between those who aspire and those who expire
but the happiness of the people is nevertheless well known
the sea as narrow as a river undaunted licks our rocks
unperturbed by time or titles
the sea as narrow as a river licks our wounds

I mean those that have wounds
not the sane and sound like you and me
the sea as narrow as a river ebbs and flows
and finally disorients us when in the end it becomes
a river as wide as the sea
so much so that you don't know
which is its labouring legal calm
and which is its clandestine breaking wave
I apologise for this hypochondriac parenthesis
and I invite you to lunge once more towards the landscape
which here and there has mansions and bicycles
see how blonde the girls are it feels like scandinavia
but don't go getting a fragmentary or false image
there are other neighbourhoods with girls
that are not so blonde and fewer bicycles
in reality more like the northeast of brazil
than stavanger or lund or björneborg
in the end a diaphanous sign of our famous diversity
since we have to say that lately

we do better in diversities than in universities
but it is all part of our transitory nature as you discovered
in different ways ecclesiastes and carlitos darwin and charles gardel
and that's enough history and ecology and anthropophagy
here we have our final goal our final lucid and ludic objective
the casino casino most casino of the southern seas
or perhaps of the rivers of the south as wide as the sea
I formally present to you, ungraspable phantasmal luck
fearful intrepid unconscious
squinty blind that god in a hood
quite frankly I don't know where that simile comes from
or rather gentlemen and clocks / children and fakes / ladies and fires
I formally present you to luck that idiot that sceptic
that improviser that chancer implacable
but let it be known that we do not leave nor will we leave luck to luck
but of course this is a mere play on words
and you are looking for a play on truth
but believe me truth is not always in the first dozen
or in the colour or in the odd numbers or in the line
at best luck is in each one of you
or close by you
or under you
if we had time
I would perhaps help you to unravel
that subterranean subcutaneous under-estimated
and under-developed truth
but since we don't have time and also
my domain is the most superficial surface
and not the subsolar underground
I simply say to you
gentlemen and watches / children and fakes / ladies and fires
it has been a real pleasure to accompany you
and leave you here beside luck
and one last piece of advice

learn it by rote
and win
if you are allowed
but if you are not allowed
learn it by rote
and win

Nando　I love it.

Stefi　I love it.

Flor   I love it.

Lean   Thank you. People don't usually go to those zones of my poetry. They don't usually speak to me about those poems.

Flor   Of course. They usually talk to you about your love poems, "Tactics and Strategy", for example.

Lean   Of course.

Nando   Bridge!

Nando's *story.*

All through primary school, I was in love with Inés, a classmate in the Norwegian School, the one with the rubber tree, the one with the big tree. We shared a few years together and others with her in the A stream and me in the B stream, or the other way round. Playtimes, afternoon teas, work, songs, the occasional dance, too. In fact, in the school choir we sang Mario's "I Love You", together.

Stefi *and* **Nando** *sing a fragment of "Te quiero" ("I Love You").*

Nando   In the last year, we were in the same group. We finished school together. I was eleven and she was more or less the same age. A friend, who knew about my love, decided on the last day of classes to tell her, so he went up and said to Inés that I "liked her".

Inés didn't come today, so you can imagine what her answer was . . . It was one of the first failures in love of my childhood . . . That day I threw myself into my bed and I didn't want to come out from under the covers.

In my house, when something like that happened, literature always appeared as a type of salvation, a way out, a rescue. From my mother's hand came poems written by her or by different authors; now that I think of it, not much Mario, she was militant about her love for Idea, she admired her, for her art and, also, because Idea had been her literature teacher. The thing is that, from the bunks I shared with my little brother, I looked up and there, on the wall of my bedroom, I saw drawings with sayings pinned up. Among them, there was one with a rabid sunrise, full of oranges and yellows that invaded the sea and palm trees that stretched across the middle of the drawing, a present from a girlfriend of my older brother. There were words signed by someone called Benedetti. The words, provided by Mario, appeared before me. That day, Mario, the grandfather of Montevideo, as someone called him, visited me. That Mario who didn't see so much, but who slept with me every night . . . visited me and whispered: "My strategy is that someday, I don't know how, nor do I know under what pretext, you will finally need me." That was my first bridge with Mario.

Lean   But why did your mother like Idea more?

Nando   In an interview, Idea Vilariño says:

Flor "Mario is a little inaccessible, that is to say, the rest of us have been more friendly with each other, closer as friends. Mario is more reserved, more difficult, you never feel that you are touching Mario, you can love and value him greatly, but this contact isn't what leads to friendship, and what you have with other people, with him, you can't reach him, there's no way in."

Nando And Mario in another interview says: "We always had a very good relationship, a friendly relationship and there has always been a sense of loyalty between us, we've helped each other, I've written about her and she's written about me, I think it's been a good relationship, which is not so easy with Idea, because it's not so easy for her to establish a close friendship, above all with a colleague and above all with her same generation."

Stefi That's the way things were with the Generation of '45.

Flor The same things that repeat in every generation.

Lean What did she have that I didn't have?

Stefi Letter from Idea Vilariño to Mario Benedetti: "I've been meaning to write to you since you left. But the thing is that it was a difficult letter. Because I said then that I would write about your book, and I don't know how to tell you that I didn't like it. It's not exactly that. Maybe I should start from the beginning. The thing is that we're at opposite extremes (or are all extremes opposite?). I don't know if you remember my book *No*? The last poem says: 'It's useless to say anything more. It's enough to name'. (**Lean** *says this with her.*) And that's where I've been for a while, more and more, prohibiting myself from—and not needing to—explain, develop. If that beautiful heptasyllable from your book had occurred to me, that verse would be the poem. I would have put it in *No*, naked, nothing else. It's full of meaning, there's no need to say anything else. Explaining it seems a prosaic procedure, it takes away its depth. And you have many lines like that, beautiful and full of meaning. I'd say the same about the last two verses of 'Love Letters'.

Lean / Flor / Nando A love letter is not love
but a report on absence.

Stefi Or the last four lines of 'The Sea' . . .

Lean / Flor / Nando what by chance is the sea?
why does the sea fascinate?
what is the meaning of that enigma
that remains
on this side and that of the horizon?

Stefi . . . In both cases the whole poem is in those lines."

Nando Maybe something like that. But that's not what's important.

Flor Of course it's not what's important. That drawing was always hung there, but you saw it when?

Nando I don't know. In December.

Flor When you needed it. When you let your bridge down. And look, isn't it curious how the wound hurt less because of a little drawing, cheap, mass-produced, with one of the most famous poems in the world, written in Uruguay and printed on an orange sunrise between two Hawaiian palm trees. You never know with pain. With poetry either. With marketing even less.

Nando Zone Two. Breath. Marketing. Stefi.

Stefi They call us. They threaten us. Maybe a centenary. Perhaps some cracks. Perhaps some forgetting. We can't do it. We can't get to Mario. We got late to Mario. We got there when Mario was a drawing was translation was an icon was an idol audio book CD meme publicity nostalgic postcard of Montevideo. We got to him when we had already sold him.

Flor When a Uruguayan poet lends his words for a background of Hawaiian palm trees something's happening. Something enormous is happening.

Stefi And it seems that Uruguayans, apologies for this, are not attuned to enormous things. And everything that rises from the hand loaded with the salted Montevidean air tends to fall, or be lowered, with its feet tied to a mysterious Uruguayan rejection of extreme popularity. Not in the sense of people, in the sense of success.

Nando "His capacity for communication implied a great professional success for Mario, his books are widely read, they sell a lot, others see in this a sin with no redemption."

Flor Eduardo Galeano.

Flor "A poet like Mario has created his own readership, which is very large, so perhaps, instead of feeling annoyed about this, we should be happy that someone has managed to make poetry so popular."

Nando Juan Gelman.

Stefi We're no longer the same people as when we read him. He said it:

Lean "To cross or not to cross the bridge. That is the question."

SONG: "BRIDGES LIKE HARES"

> The day that I finally understand everything
> I will finally understand that there is no forgetting
> I find myself in the street elbow to elbow
> with lives I have not lived and yet I know.
>
> Stories that embrace my story
> the marks of the marks of another wound
> with that contradictory sensation
> of they who remember what they forget.

> Broken hugs sudden smiles
> the joy of other lives I live in this one
> my heat in other fevers
> tying loose ends laying bridges
> bridges like hares.
>
> The day we wanted to be ourselves
> we entered through the revolving door
> we went in and came out as others
> in a forgetting full of memory.
>
> Sometimes the bolts of infinite indecipherable history
> slide open and then I discover
> the interminable chronology
> in other eyes.

Lean What same thread are we talking about? I don't have a thread, or a bridge, or nostalgia.

He stops on the spot. Something happens.

Flor Bridges appear when we least expect them.

Stefi Day Fifteen. The Benedetti dimension is swallowing Leandro up.

Nando I'll explain.

Stefi I'm explaining. Leandro insisted so much on the topic of the public employee. It seems that the bridge built itself. And . . . I don't know how to explain that.

Nando There's not much to explain.

Flor How lucky when something doesn't have an explanation.

The office unfolds.

Nando We more or less discovered that we run the very high risk that what is beyond us is a public office.

Stefi It depends on the quality of the drawbridge that each one has.

Flor Let's say that he saw what the other side could be if he insisted on this business about being a public employee. But we don't really know what he saw.

Stefi But something happened.

Nando Something happened.

Office.

Flor Good morning!

Mario I feel as if I'm looking for a certain Leandro Núñez. I found this piece of paper in his pocket. "I am Leandro Núñez. I am forty-one years old. I am an actor with the National Theatre Company."

Stefi An actor with the National Theatre Company? Wait a moment. Let me see . . . Alberto Candeau, Maruja Santullo, Dumas Lerena, Mingo Solari, Enrique Guarnero, there is no Leandro Núñez.

Mario What's your work?

Flor On this side of the threshold we write the history of what is happening on the other side.

Mario What?

Flor We send back out from here lives that come and go and repeat the same stories over and over. They re-edit history. We inventory other people's lives, we inventory unresolved issues and we send those unresolved issues out again to the other side, to see if someone, without eating or drinking the story, resolves them, once and for all, and so we go about eliminating paperwork. Sort of filling up the wastebasket, and when the file is empty and the wastebasket is full, we unwrinkle them and we return them to the filing cabinet and so it goes on, like that repeatedly, as we would expect from eternity.

Mario Are you telling me that eternity is a public office?

Stefi The republic is a public office. Eternity depends on each and every life.

Flor But since one person's life is everybody's, everything depends on the bridges that each one builds.

Mario I intuit a bridge. I need to find Leandro Núñez.

Nando He is Leandro Núñez, but he forgot that once he'd crossed the bridge. That's what the bridge does, it facilitates entry into the dimension of the material that calls us, it takes us to memory, but it provokes in us the forgetting of our own life. We take a holiday from the self for a perio/

Stefi If I may, Fernando . . . Day Twenty. Fernando discovers a spot in the centre of the stage. He discovers, also, that that spot is what we are calling a Universal Bridge. A connection with past dimensions. He discovers, too, that, depending on the precise needs of each person at that time, the bridge changes the direction of their present life towards the zone of the dimension that the person fears repeating/

Nando I would like to tell this bit, because I discovered it.

Stefi *carries on under* **Nando**, *in chorus with him but in third person.*

Nando I'm going to explain this! I stopped there by accident, one of the days when we were feeling most lost, and don't ask me what happened, but I saw everything. I saw my eternity. Absolutely related with the bridge we hadn't been able to build. I saw my fears. My panic. My fantasies of the past and the future. But I saw everything at the same time. I saw the unknown dimension of everything I know from somewhere, but I don't know where, or when.

Flor You're not making any sense.

Nando It's not so easy to explain. It's much easier to feel. I also discovered that, when I got back, I had forgotten some things about myself. I couldn't remember where I lived/

Stefi Good job I was there, and I know his house, I walked there with him so that he would learn the way again and we wrote the address down on a piece of paper.

Nando *takes a paper from his pocket, with his address written on it.*

Nando José Osorio 1345.

Stefi We wrote it down so that it wouldn't be forgotten.

Nando I never came back from that dimension. When I crossed back over from there to here, I was different.

Stefi You're the same to me.

Nando The same but different.

Flor That's not what matters. On you go.

Nando So, and I don't say this with any pride, we understood that if Leandro wasn't capable of building the bridge, we would have to build it for him. So, we stopped him directly on top of the spot. And we didn't let him come back for a few days. And when he came back, of course, he knew all about his fears, but couldn't remember anything about himself.

Flor Then we had a story. The story of the bridges, because we're bridges there and back, bridges of memory and forgetting. And acting is militancy and to fight is to commit completely. Bridge.

Nando Truce. Breath. Zone Three. Militancy. Florencia.

Flor Look, I'm speaking here because I want to, not because you make it possible.

Nando Get on with it, Flor.

Flor*'s story.*

Flor When I was sixteen, I had my first real relationship, although I had had boyfriends at school. But at sixteen I fell in love. And he fell in love. And we started going out. We were in the struggle together. My first Benedetti text was a present from him. The novel *Andamios: Scaffolding*. We were in fifth grade, and we realised that two years later we'd have to move to Montevideo to study. And so we set up a commission to decentralise the University. And we managed it. But not in time, so we had to come here in any case.

As well as theatre, I studied law, because I had inherited that fear, imposed on us, that I wouldn't be able to live from art. Of course, we took up our militancy in the union and one day we decided to declare certain personalities *honoris causa* members. I proposed Mario. I'm not sure why. I remember my nerves on that day. My job was to meet him, make him feel comfortable, take him to his seat in the auditorium. He recited his poem "Defence of Happiness". But I don't remember much else.

I bumped into him once in the street. I spoke a bit to him. Something about spending some months here and some in Spain. A bit about his health. I also remember when his wife died. She was his companion for his whole life, and I don't know why that death particularly affected me. I felt that he wasn't going to survive for long. Then he died. I was in rehearsals for a play in the Prado. His lying-in-state was in the Palacio Legislativo. I passed by that day on my way to the rehearsal. But I didn't go into the lying-in-state.

I feel that Mario invented words and phrases and appropriated others. Like "desexilio": disexile. Exile. Parenthesis. Office. Nostalgia. Truce. Feet of clay. Crepuscule. Ball. Insomnia. Forgetting. Memory.

Nando   Please, Stefani.

Stefi   I prefer not to read today. I feel uncomfortable.

Flor   Don't complicate things.

Stefi   Day Twenty-Five. The Generation of '45 seeps into our discussions. Mario Benedetti belonged to that generation.

Flor   As did Idea Vilariño.

Stefi   Yes. And many others, who later lived through the dictatorship. And spoke about the dictatorship with more authority than us. We realised that the word "dictatorship" generates tension. And differences. We found a significant bridge that connected all of us: we were all born in dictatorship. With the exception that I was not born in the country. I was born in Germany/

Flor   That is developed later.

Stefi   All four of us belong to a generation born in dictatorship, we lived the dictatorship, but we carry on living as if we hadn't lived it. They even call us "the children of the dictatorship". That's why it's always been difficult for us to discuss that topic, it's uncomfortable, it's like a topic that's . . . alien . . . to us. I don't know, as if someone else should say it. I don't feel as if I can speak about this. Let someone who was here do that.

Flor   It's as if it's not right for us to talk about it. The Generation of '45 should. But not the generation of '80. As if 1980 wasn't a year of dictatorship. We carry the weight of the Generation of '45. More than once, when I've talked about that, I've been told/

Nando   "You don't know because you didn't live it."

Flor   Speaking about the terror, no? I'm lucky not to have lived through that. But it doesn't silence me. I was there. Many people close to me were there, and it stays in me in a certain way. We live with that, and it even feels disrespectful to talk about that. As if we didn't have enough moral authority to express ourselves in that respect/

Stefi   If you can try not to dwell too much on that . . . (**Stefi** *goes on under* **Flor**.) It's not up to us to speak about this because we didn't live it.

Flor So, you're saying that I must be shipwrecked or even drown to do a play about shipwrecks.

Stefi I'm simply saying that we can save ourselves the commentary. Let the parents of our generation/

Flor If they're here/

Stefi Let the Generation of '45 speak. It's not up to us to speak about this. Let's not be presumptuous. (**Stefi** *goes on speaking under* **Flor**.)

Flor The second generation is a generation directly affected, perhaps, luckily, not in their bodies, but yes in their psyche and their daily life, by the violence that affected their parents or siblings or unknown people.

Nando *tries to stop* **Flor** *talking.*

That is my opinion and I'm going to express it! At that time, their suffering was made invisible and there was a denial of the consequences. They even found it difficult to speak, to tell the story. And we need to repair that failing, we need to build that bridge. We are carrying a drawbridge on our backs, a huge bridge of respectful silence.

Nando To '45 what belongs to '45. Let's breathe. Zone Four. Exile.

Flor I don't think we've resolved what we were talking about.

Nando That's how we live, with things that aren't resolved, we're not going to die because of a drawbridge. Exile. Stefi.

Lean Apologies for butting in where I shouldn't. Apologies for this sudden intergenerational bridge.

But it seems to me and I know
I never forget it
that my fertile voluntary destiny
is to become mouths eyes hands
for other hands mouths and eyes
let the bridge down and keep it down
let in love and hate and voices and shouts
let there come sadness with its open arms
and illusion with its new shoes
let there come embryonic and honest cold and
summer with its calcined anguish
let there come rancour with its mist
and the farewells with their tearful bread
let there come the dead and above all the living
and the old smell of melancholy
let the bridge down and keep it down

let in rage and its dark expression
let in good and evil

and what mediates
between one and the other
that is
truth that pendulum

let in the dogs
the sons of bitches
the midwives and the gravediggers
the angels if there any
and if there are not
let in the moon with its cold child
let the bridge down and keep it down
let in they who know what we don't know
and knead bread
or make revolutions
and they who cannot make them
they who close their eyes
in the end
so that nobody is called to confusion
let in my unbearable neighbour
so strong and fragile
so necessary
the one with doubts shadow face blood
and life to the end
that welcome one
let the only one to stay outside be
the one in charge
of raising the bridge

by this time
it can't be a secret
for anybody
that I am against drawbridges.

Stefi Day Thirty. I build my bridge. Exile. We talk about the strong presence of the sea in Mario's work. Of the painful pilgrimage of crossing the sea.

Because it is so insipid
the sea is immense
it has no heart or way through
like the saliva of an inexplicable god
it comes and goes
giving us nothing

Flor the transparent or opaque sea
ebbs and flows in the bed in its depths
the lord of the shipwrecks leaves bodies
in the islands that await his legacy

Nando   its sunless waves are not moved
even by the loyal mermaid in
Copenhagen the sea is not a dagger
it is a thousand daggers
that finish off the old fishermen

Lean   it does not know how to pardon its timeless law
that the bigger fish must eat the smaller
we will pass
but the sea

Stefi   The sea was the witness to various changes in my life. House moves, all sorts of moves, of country, culture, language, social class. I could go on. I was born in Bonn, Germany, then we moved to Montevideo, from there to San Salvador, back to Germany, Guatemala, New York and finally Montevideo. It was in Guatemala that I laid my first bridge with Mario, through the Spanish textbook that had one of his poems "Defence of happiness". That phrase, "defending happiness", later became the cover of one of my personal diaries.

I wrote diaries for a long time. At home I have a huge trunk full of diaries. From the ages of eleven to twenty-three I have every day of my life written in a secret diary, and now, if you don't mind, I'm going to share—not a fragment of a diary because that might not be very interesting—but a poem I wrote when I was studying in New York City. It says:

New—York new—life.
City of suburbs
and trams that have very little to do with desire.
The pedestrians seem like suffering souls
unhappy men beside women who are
frivolous
cold
as the streets at dawn.

New York and its skyscrapers
its inhabitants like fake ants
and a girl—a foreigner—under the umbrella
ignored by others who do not see
suicide in her face.

New York and Broadway and the Empire State Building
and Fifth Avenue and sex and the smell of marihuana
—which is absolutely prohibited—
and hugs earned
and sheets static with so much starch.

And me in New York
wearing my necklace of illusions
blinded by the mist of my dream.

Me in this impersonal immensity
covering the artery to deception
so that it does not rebel in spurting bursts
looking as if ill
the smell of dried wood
the dense breeze of summer days
your true embrace
that is consumed midst looks of steel
and soaked shoes.

New York, February 2003.

Lean   Bridge. I was in New York. I was alone. And I also wrote a poem there.

Everyone walks
I too walk

It is Monday and we come with bitter saliva
better put
they come

in the shadow of I don't know how many floors
millions of jaws
chewing their gum
but yet they are people of this world
with a whole heart under their jackets

I breathe and I feel myself breathe
that is good
I am thirsty and it costs
ten cents of a dollar
to get another fruit juice

that tastes of Guatemala

this birthday
is not
my true birthday
because this environment
is not
my true environment
I will celebrate my birthday later
in February or March
with the eyes that always looked at me
the words that are always said to me
with a sky from yesterday on my shoulders and
my stubborn ragged heart

I will celebrate later
or I will not celebrate
but this is not my true birthday

that sky
has never been so far away
and so small
a cloudy isosceles triangle that
is not even a whole cloud

I have the kitsch painful
desire
to see a bit of sea
to feel how it rains in the Andes and in Colonia

but it is also good
to feel at times a bit of tenderness
towards this enormous stream
this powerful
defenceless stream
of humanity docilely rushing
with the cross of comfort on their forehead
a little unexpected rootless tenderness
let's say for example for a certain mother
who yesterday in the zoo in Central Park
was saying to her son with beautiful nostalgia
look Johnny this is a cow
because of course
there are no cows among the skyscrapers
but everything is clear
and it is sweeter
more useful
above all sweeter
to recognise that time is passing
that time is passing and making a fuss
and feel for once and for all
forgotten and calm
like a waste of space.

New York, 14 September 1959.

Bridge.

Nando   "Exile is not a journey to Europe, or Mexico, or Africa, but to the Self."

Flor   Daniel Viglietti.

Nando   1976. "Another principle for the nation".

Flor It is abundantly clear that we have grown
since we have invaded the four points of the map
in venezuela there are about thirty thousand
including forty footballers

Stefi in sydney, oceania
there is a bookshop
called oriental
with uruguayan authors
to the great surprise of the australians
they are not confucius or lin yu tang

Nando but onetti

Flor vilariño

Stefi arregui

Lean espínola

Nando in barcelona there is a café petit montevideo
and another place called el quilombo

Lean a noun that means something to people from the river plate
but not a lot to the catalans

Stefi in buenos aires seven hundred thousand, so there's no room for any more

Flor the same thing in mexico, new york, porto alegre, havana

Nando panama, quito, algiers, stockholm, paris

Lean lisbon, maracaibo, lima, amsterdam, madrid

Stefi rome, xalapa, pau, caracas, san francisco, montreal

Nando bogota

Stefi london

Lean merida

Flor gothenburg

Lean moscow

All arriving from everywhere

Nando envelopes full of nostalgia
recounting how you have to start from zero

Flor navigate languages that are barely tributaries

Lean build something somewhere

Stefi sometimes

Flor lovely times

Nando with hands lent in solidarity

Stefi and other times

Flor bitter times

Stefi receiving the xenophobic gaze in the neck

All arriving from everywhere

Lean serenity

All arriving from everywhere

Lean despair

Nando dark silences in a broken voice

Flor one in every thousand resigns themself to be different

Lean and even so we are privileged

Nando we can see the night without bars

Stefi own a talisman

Flor or if not a dog

Lean yawn

Nando spit

Flor weep

Stefi dream

Lean sigh

Flor confuse

Nando be hungry

Flor work

Nando permit

Lean curse

Stefi play

Flor discover

Nando caress

Lean   without the vigilant watchful eye

Stefi   with this rabid melancholy
this nomadic rootedness

Nando   this courage stewed in sadness
this disorder this not knowing

Flor   this absence in pieces
these bones that demand their bed

Lean   with all this mysterious collapse
this whole cabinet of pain

All   we are privileged

Nando   the little country is there
and it is a certainty
perhaps now it is raining
on the earth there

Flor   long may it last
the watering is good for it

Lean   it's good if we have rain in my torrential land
wherever we might be
there

Nando   or anywhere else

Flor   patient fury

Stefi   rain

Lean   wrathful silence

Nando   there and everywhere

Flor   with such a heavy downpour
that the iron dictatorship
will finally rust

Lean   and victory will slowly grow

All   like victories have always grown.

Flor   Mario Benedetti, 1976. We had to talk about this to talk about him.

Nando   Truce. Zone Five. Desexilio. Breath. Who is going to talk about that?

Lean   I'm going to talk about that. I found this letter.

Nando   Who from?

Lean   Leandro Núñez.

Nando   Who to?

Lean   Me.

Letter from **Lean** *to Mario, in which he gives the reasons why he can't or won't read him.*

Mario, this letter is for you.

I want to tell you that you reminded me a lot of my father, the way you looked, the way he looked, that look of an urbane man, of the city, the office-worker, the suit, the tie, the moustache. The descriptions in your writing, your world, was his world. I related it all to my father. And above all anything that had to do with exile, with disexile. My parents were political exiles, like you. They had to leave from one day to the next because my mother was being hunted by the military. They went to look for her twice outside the lecture theatre in the Law Faculty and they didn't find her. The next day, my parents left for Buenos Aires along with a group of three or four more comrades. They lived for a month or two in a very precarious state, until one day, my father goes to the football and plays the pools and won the first prize when he got all that day's results right. They became rich and lived a life of complete abandonment and pleasure. In which they began to be part of another social circle, to have lots of friends, lots of influences. All of that put the military off their scent.

I'll tell you a few anecdotes so that you can paint the picture. With the money my parents won, they bought a flat in Buenos Aires, in cash, of course, because they couldn't be registered anywhere. They bought a two-berth van, a Jeep, a huge thing. They didn't know how to drive, they didn't have their licence, they couldn't get a licence, so they had two drivers, full time. Well . . . they went everywhere in that van. They kept their money in the house, they obviously couldn't open a bank account, would you believe that they kept it in two huge clay pots and the flat was always full of friends, if you have money, you have friends. My mother and father used to say, if anyone needs money lift the lid of the pot, and of course everybody lifted the lid of the pot. And in short, one example, so that you get the idea, my father bought a hot air balloon.

At last, and with my birth, came disexile, the return to Montevideo. The money ran out, they were left with absolutely nothing. When my mother was pregnant with me, my father spent the last money they had on tickets for the 1978 World Cup. (I guess he had earned it, that's how he won the money and with that he finished enjoying it.) They came back with nothing, and we lived in a neighbourhood on the outskirts of the city, far from the centre.

You'll understand me, Mario. Your father also got rich gambling and then he lost it all. And you will also understand this: when I was about eleven years old, my father left home. He disappeared without a trace. He left one night and we didn't know anything about him for a long time. (A new exile, a new disexile.)

With time, we, that is to say my mother, my siblings and I, learned that he simply did not want a family life. He wanted to live like he'd lived in Buenos Aires.

You reminded me a lot of him, and that's why I couldn't read you.

Leandro Núñez.

I am Leandro Núñez. This is eternity.

SONG

Memories of the song of songs
calmly warn that the future is this
we carry on watching football crossing seas
like the faded writing of a palimpsest.
We seek in the desperate ashes
the faces of the parents we did not have
we walk around always confused always nauseous
crossing Montevideo disconsolate.

We sing to the memory that gives us refuge
we look in the ocean for alphabets
a centenary is celebrated everywhere
we are short of time, short of hours.
Some costumes are ironed in each siesta
no matter how bitter the grey letters sound to us
we carry on so modestly ruining the party
we dream of an old idea of fatherland.

You shift a memorial a shade to the left
boots spring the broken corner
blessed be the windows of the office
the lofts of the broken love affair with the neighbour.
Certain when you wake up
you will know
that death made a mockery of eternity.

Blackout.

Poems and songs by Mario Benedetti cited in the play

1929 Tram (Tranvía de 1929)
Sightseeing 1980
Tactic and Strategy (Táctica y estrategia)
I love you (Te quiero)
On Love Letters (Sobre cartas de amor)
The Sea (El mar)
Bridges Like Hares (Puentes como liebres)
Defence of Happiness (Defensa de la alegría)
Against Drawbridges (Contra los puentes levadizos)
Birthday in Manhattan (Cumpleaños en Manhattan)
Another Notion of the Fatherland (Otra noción de patria)

Prelude to Anne

Sandra Massera

Translated by Rachel Toogood

Preludio de Ana (*Prelude to Anne*) premiered on 12 May 2017 at the Teatro Solís, Montevideo. It was directed by Sandra Massera and performed by Norma Berriolo, Lucía Calisto, Ximena Echevarría, Roberto Foliatti and Agustina Vázquez Paz. The play was published by Estuario Editora in 2018.

About the author and translator

Sandra Massera is an actor, playwright, educator, and theatre director. She has directed numerous plays and one opera: *Rashomon*. The writer of 32 plays and the libretti for four operas, she has been the recipient of Uruguay's major playwriting awards including the Florencio Award for Best Playwright on a number of occasions, the Ministry of Education and Culture National Literature Awards, the Juan Carlos Onetti Literary Awards, the COFONTE (National Theatre Foundation Commission) Award, the Museo Vivo del Títere (Living Puppet Museum) Award, the Centro Cultural de España (Cultural Centre of Spain) Award, and the FEFCA (Fund for the Promotion of Artistic Creation and Training) Award for Artistic Excellence. Her plays have been produced, translated and published in countries including Brazil, Argentina, Costa Rica, Mexico, Peru and France. She is the founder, director and producer of the theatre company Teatro del Umbral, a team of artists who for over 25 years have represented Uruguay at international festivals, round tables, and masterclasses in several countries in Europe and the Americas.

Rachel Toogood is a freelance producer and translator. She has translated two plays by Laura Rubio Galletero: *Shopping Centre Paradise* was featured at the 2021 Out of the Wings festival (Omnibus Theatre, London) and later published by Inti Press; *The Glass Ceiling: Anne & Sylvia* was published by Estreno Contemporary Spanish Plays (Pace University, USA). Her other translations include *La Distancia* for the theatre company La Société de la Mouffette (Spain) and, forthcoming, a Cuban reimagining of *The Bacchae* by Raquel Carrió and Flora Lauten. Her other translation projects include working with Manchester International Festival and Jewish Book Week, and translating the lyrics of the Cuban singer and dancer Omara Portuondo. She is the co-translator of *Rongo, The Forgotten Story of Easter Island* by Patricia Štambuk. As a producer Rachel has worked on several translation projects for theatre companies such as the Royal Court, Foreign Affairs, Modern Culture and Performing International Plays. She is a member of the Ibero-American theatre and translation collective, Out of the Wings.

Characters

Anne
Elena, *the playwright*
Iona, *the actress*
Fernando, *the director*
Silvia, *the producer*

Scene 1

Music. Four or five rows of wooden seats at the back of the stage. The seats are laid out in ascending rows, making it look like rows in the stalls of a theatre. The last row of seats is close to the back curtain. **Silvia**, *holding some folders, is seated in the first row.* **Fernando**, *standing close to* **Silvia**, *is listening to a reading by a very young girl standing opposite them. He is completely absorbed by* **Iona**'s *reading. Before they are all fully lit* **Iona**'s *voice can be heard.*

Iona (*in a slightly nervous voice, reading a text she is holding in her hands*)   I can't trust you. Why is everything that Margot says right? And everything that I do is wrong? Dad doesn't think so. Why do you?

The music gradually disappears. The stage is fully lit.

However much I tr . . . y it's useless. You don't trust me. I can understand the most complicated things, about incomprehensible subjects I read about. You won't achieve anything by stopping me reading what I want to read. Ever since . . . we've been here I . . .

Silvia (*to* **Iona**)   Sorry . . . Would you mind starting again please?

Iona   From the beginning?

Fernando   Yes, that would be great. Take your time.

Iona   Yes, of course. (*Reading.*) I can't trust you. Why is everything that Margot says right? And everything that I do is wrong? Dad doesn't think so. Why do you? However much I try it's useless. You don't trust me. I can understand the most complicated things, about incomprehensible subjects I read about. You won't achieve anything by stopping me reading what I want to read. I've changed since we've been in here, but you don't see it. You'll never understand! I'm going to be a writer and to do that I have to be able to read a lot, whatever falls into my hands. And I'm going to sign everything I write with my own name. I'm not going to use a pseudonym like some women do. Everything will be by Anne Frank. I'm going stand on my own two feet and I'm not going to follow in your footsteps and educate my children like you have . . . If I could . . .

Silvia (*interrupting*)   Good, good. Has anyone ever mentioned you have a bit of a lisp?

Iona   Ah . . . Yes. I'm seeing a speech therapist. Well, I saw one once. She gave me exercises.

Silvia   Do you do them?

Iona   Yes, quite a lot.

Fernando   Come over here, sit down if you like . . . What do you think about the relationship between Anne and her mother?

Iona   Troubled, without a doubt. Very different to the one with her father.

Fernando Totally.

Iona I kind of think it's a bit oversimplified in the text.

Fernando Well, maybe, yes. But in theatre sometimes you have to be concise, don't you think?

Iona Yes.

Silvia Other nuances can come through acting . . .

Iona Yes, yes, of course. But I don't know, maybe the adults in the play . . . If they had a few more speeches . . . Sorry, I don't want to judge the play . . . I'm not the one who . . .

Fernando Don't worry, it's interesting what you're saying. It's great to hear your thoughts. (*Looking in a folder*.) I see here that . . . you're twenty-two?

Iona Only just.

Silvia The call was for up to twenty-one.

Iona Yes, sorry. It's just I don't look my age. Everyone says so.

Silvia You didn't mention it to me.

Iona Not to you. But I told the lady with short dark hair . . .

Fernando (*looking at* **Silvia**) Elena. (*To* **Iona**.) That's fine, let's carry on, don't worry.

Iona I really love Anne Frank, I've read everything about her.

Silvia You've read . . . everything?

Iona Yes, articles by the people who knew her, her Diary . . . Well . . . her Diaries, accounts, by her friend Hanneli for example, Miep Gies' book, her father's secretary who protected them whilst they were in hiding.

Fernando A very special woman.

Iona She made a great impression on me. I read the book she wrote afterwards, *Anne Frank Remembered*. I found it very moving that Miep travelled kilometres and kilometres by bike to find food for them all. And after they were captured, she was brave enough to go to the Gestapo's offices to ask for news about the Franks and challenge the Nazis with questions.

Silvia What is it that interests you about her?

Iona Anne?

Silvia Yes.

Iona The independence of mind she had. The maturity. And the play, I love the play.

She suddenly falls silent. Pause.

Fernando Anything else? Something no-one but you would say?

Iona The contradiction between the child and the woman . . .

Fernando Something no-one but you would say.

Iona (*after a pause*) Anger.

Fernando Anger?

Iona Yes, anger because they don't let her be herself and because nobody, not even her father, realised she had changed so much. And her repressed sexual desire, which she didn't even realise herself.

Silvia I think she realised.

Iona Yes. She realised a bit, but not that her feelings towards Peter van Pels were sexual, for example.

Fernando Maybe . . . Probably, yes. Good . . . Choose an extract from one of her speeches, any one of them, at least six sentences long and come with it memorised. Is that OK?

Iona Yes, of course. Thank you. On the eleventh right?

Silvia At five.

Iona Great. I'll be here on the eleventh at five. Thank you. And have a good afternoon.

Fernando Goodbye.

Silvia Goodbye, have a good day. Was there anyone else outside when you came in?

Iona No.

Silvia OK, tell them to let you out and to lock up.

Iona OK, bye.

Silvia Bye.

Iona *leaves.*

Silvia (*to* **Fernando**) Where did she come from? She's the first one that's read anything. That knows a little bit.

Fernando A little bit? She seems to know a lot. What do you think?

Silvia I don't know. She's got a kind of repressed joy that could work well, but I don't know. Did you notice she didn't have great pronunciation? Why is it so hard to find people who speak well!

Fernando It's not that bad. She sounds good, she makes sense of the text, the punctuation is right. That's the most difficult thing. That's it for today, right?

Silvia Yes.

Fernando And don't you think she kind of looked like . . .?

Silvia Yes, without a doubt. That's why I let the thing about her age go.

Fernando I don't know how many people we're going to find that look any younger. She easily passes for fifteen.

Silvia Maybe . . . She also has to play thirteen.

Fernando Well, thirteen. It's more or less the same.

Silva Thirteen and fifteen really aren't the same thing.

Fernando That kid could do it.

Silvia I don't know . . .

Fernando She could. And if not, as I said before, let's lower the age and . . .

Silvia No, no, no way. And have to deal with all the permissions and everything? No. I prefer them to have some kind of training. Some experience.

Fernando Me too. We know we can't really work with someone who's thirteen, I don't know why we're even talking about it. Where did you say she studied?

Silvia (*looking in a folder*) With Susana Pampín, in Buenos Aires.

Fernando I think she's the best so far. We'll have to see what Elena says.

Silvia Yes, I don't know.

Fernando How many have we got tomorrow?

Silvia Ten, if they all come.

Music 2, quietly at first, then gradually increasing in volume, mixing with the voices. **Fernando** *and* **Silvia** *leave the stage, but their voices are still heard until they are lost because they are so far away.*

Fernando They're the last ones, right?

Silvia Yes, let's see . . . Because if none of them fits exactly . . .

Fernando We could still go for that kid.

Silvia Or do another casting call. There must be someone. There are loads of people studying theatre. Everyone wants to do theatre and just when you need . . .

Fernando Ah, but there's one thing studying theatre and another thing finding someone responsible, who fits, and is that young . . .

Silvia Well yes, that's the question. That's why I said . . .

Total blackout. Music 2 increases in volume. A few seconds pass.

Scene 2

Music 3. Softer lighting than in Scene 1. In the same place. In front of the first row of seats, very close to them, a woman of about fifty-five is lying down on the floor, with her clothes in a mess and a strand of hair over her face. Her posture is somewhat unusual, as if she had been struck by a sudden bolt of lightning that made her fall haphazardly to the floor. She has one hand resting close to her throat and the other open hand appears to have suddenly let go of a stack of papers and other objects that lie scattered across the floor, close to her body. She has her eyes open, looking without seeing, towards a fixed point in the distance.

Short moment of calm. The figure of a young woman, almost a child, appears on one side of the stage. Approaching the woman lying on the floor, she looks at her intently. Music 3 starts to decrease in volume.

Anne   What happened to you Ma'am?

The woman focuses her gaze towards the young girl with difficulty and only moves her lips.

Elena   What happened to me?

Anne   I don't know.

Elena   Where have you . . .?

Anne   I . . .

Elena   I don't think I can move.

Anne   What are you going to do?

Elena   Let someone know. My coat is hanging on the coat hook. It's blue, it's most likely the only one hanging there. My phone's in the pocket. Bring it to me please.

Anne (*looking all around her*)   I can't see it.

Elena   It's by the door. There's also a phone on a desk, did you see it?

Anne   I haven't seen anything yet. This is the first thing I've seen.

Elena   When you got here, I mean. What time is it? Did you get here early? Are you waiting for someone?

Anne   No. I don't know what time it is. I've no idea.

Elena   Me neither. But . . . what are you doing here then kid?

Anne   This sometimes happens to me.

Elena   It looks like it's already dark, is it?

Anne   From the light it looks like it is.

Elena   But why are you here now? We're closed already.

Anne So sorry. I didn't mean to bother you.

Elena Well, it's better if you come back tomorrow. Pass me the phone. Or even better, call them yourself. I'll tell you the number . . .

Anne I don't think I can.

Music 3 disappears completely.

Elena What . . .? Please, tell me who you are and what you're doing here.

Anne I'm Anne Frank.

Elena (*with a visibly unsettled look but without being able to move any other part of her body*) Anne Frank? What . . .?

Anne Don't you recognise me? Many people have seen photos of me.

Elena Anne Frank!

Anne Am I that different? It makes me sad to have changed so much.

Elena (*trying to sit up, she manages to lean on an elbow. She breathes with difficulty*) OK, sorry but you can't just turn up like this. How did you get in? It's all closed. I remember I closed up . . . I think . . . Who let you in? Did you see anyone in the hall?

Anne I didn't see anybody.

Elena I left it open. Again! Look, in any case if you want to, come back tomorrow between nine and twelve and speak to Ms Silvia who can put you down on the list. Is that OK? But seeing as you're here, could you help me up?

Anne Put me on the list for what?

Elena For the audition. See if you can help me sit up. I'm stiff. But nothing hurts, which is strange. I must have fainted.

Anne I'm not here for any . . . the thing you said.

Elena That's enough! What do you want then kiddo? You're scaring me. Stop messing around, you see me here on the floor and you're not even able to . . . (*She stops and looks at her intently.*) You do look a bit like . . . And that frightful thing that you've got on reminds me . . . It's very good, it seems real.

Elena *realises that the young girl is wearing a tunic that looks like the uniform from a Nazi concentration camp and that she has very short hair, almost shaved, covered by a scarf. Her shoes are very broken and too big for her. The young girl's skin is pale and dirty.*

Anne It's what they made me wear.

Elena Stop messing with me. What's happened to you? You can't just show up here like this and in costume. You have to respect office hours. And the auditions aren't in costume. Do you understand?

Anne I don't want to be like this. I'd like to be how I was before they took me away. But I can't be. This is how I am. I'm telling you that I'm Anne Frank. But if you don't want to believe me then don't, it doesn't bother me.

Anne *moves away from the woman and walks around the place, looking everywhere with curiosity.*

Elena (*talking to herself*) I'm almost certain that I closed up. (*She goes back to talking to the young girl, more and more surprised.*) How did you find out? Do you know Fernando and Silvia? Are you on their list?

Anne No.

Elena Ah . . . So you came here and got into the building at this time of night and that's that. Does that seem normal to you?

Anne I didn't come here. I arrived, I'm not sure how. It's always like this.

Elena (*more and more disconcerted*) Always? How did you get here . . . ? I can't see you very well where you are. Can you come a bit closer please?

Anne *comes closer, bending down a little to look at the woman inquisitively.*

Anne Can you see me better now?

Elena More or less. The lighting must be bad.

Anne Sometimes I can't be seen very clearly. It's nothing to do with you.

Elena (*speaking as if playing along with the game*) Oh of course . . . Supposing you were Anne Frank, I wouldn't really recognise you as you are now. Although I've seen many photos of her, naturally.

Anne My father took them. He loved to photograph us, Margot and me.

Elena (*trying fruitlessly to raise her arm*) What's happening? What's going on? I can't move.

Anne I don't know. I just got here and I saw you lying on the floor. Do you feel ill?

Elena (*speaking to herself*) I don't feel ill. It's strange. I drank too much wine . . . It must be that . . . No! I haven't drunk anything for days. My new medicine, that's it! The anti-inflammatory. It said so in the leaflet . . . I worked more than I should have done. And just when I had a quiet moment to keep writing . . . Why am I like this? I want to wake up!

Her breathing becomes agitated. Her body becomes completely horizontal again. She tries to shake her head and can hardly do it. The girl sits down gently on the floor, next to the woman, and looks at her inquisitively.

Anne Your clothes look strange to me. Do women wear trousers?

Elena Of course they do. Could you call an ambulance? I've just remembered! My phone is in my trousers! Could you get it for me?

Anne I don't think so.

Elena Why?

Anne Sorry. I can't do that.

Elena Aren't you going to help me?

Anne I would if I could. You've already seen. I can't.

Elena Why not? What's happened to you? This is all very strange . . . Seriously, why are you like this?

Anne Like what?

Elena Dressed like that . . . And your hair . . . (*The woman's face has a sudden look of terror on it. Her lips grow tight.*) You look like she would have done when she was in . . .

Anne Yes, that's why you don't recognise me. Hardly anyone saw me like this, thankfully. I'm really angry about my hair.

Elena I want to make it clear that I could never have seen you in person in any way. It would be impossible. I was born in 1963.

Anne That's interesting, now I understand why you're dressed like that.

Elena Like what?

Anne Differently to when I was . . .

Elena Oh my god! This situation can only be explained by . . . Am I dead?

Anne Maybe, probably. I'm not sure. Were you thinking about me before you ended up on the floor?

Elena Yes, I think I was thinking about you then . . . I think it could have been a while ago that I fell over. I don't remember what happened to me . . .

Anne *goes over to the seats and leans gently on one of the armrests.*

Anne What were you thinking about me?

Elena Well, I'm a playwright. I write for the theatre. My name is Elena. I can't greet you with a kiss, or shake your hand, as you can see . . .

Anne It doesn't matter. We've met now. Why were you thinking about me?

Elena I'm . . . I'm trying to write a play about you, well, about Anne Frank, about her life, what happened to her . . . Well really I've written it already, but I'm not all that happy with how it turned out.

Anne Ah of course. I've been written about before.

Elena You know that. If you were really Anne Frank you wouldn't know that.

Anne Sometimes I can see what is happening. It's as if a fog clears and everything that's happening in the world appears before my eyes, I also see things repeated from my life. It's very disconcerting, I see myself in the world, as if I were still there.

Elena What's that like?

Anne I'm calm for a moment and sometimes I see scenes from my life, things from the past and sometimes, but very rarely, things from now. They are always to do with me. I even saw a very stupid actress play me in the theatre.

Elena I agree with you. Some actresses who have played you were very stupid. You must think me pretty impertinent trying to write about you . . . That's to say . . . What am I saying? If indeed you really are her. I'm not sure I have a clear head right now . . .

Taking a deep breath, **Elena**, *surprising herself somewhat, manages to get up slowly and stand up in the same spot that she was lying in.*

Anne You're better now.

Elena (*looking around as if she doesn't recognise the place*)   I don't know . . .

Anne It doesn't bother me that you're writing about me, it's good that you write. You've read my Diaries I imagine . . .

Elena Yes, but I don't want to make a play only based on the Diary . . . I want to show other things, more than anything that you wanted to be a writer. I . . . read quite a bit about your life.

Anne It wasn't just one Diary, there were lots of them. And that's right, I wanted to be a writer, and journalist.

Elena Anne . . . So, sorry for asking . . . I'm really scared right now . . .

Anne Scared of me?

Elena No, how could I be scared of you? I read your Diary when I was the same age as you when you wrote it. I'm scared of what's happening to me, that I can hardly move and I wanted to ask you . . . I don't know how to ask you without offending you Anne, but . . . are you a ghost?

Anne (*getting up and moving towards the audience*)   I don't think so. I don't have anything to do in the world any more. They say ghosts only appear in the world of the living when they have things left undone. I read it in a novel. But I don't have anything left undone. But despite this I still keep coming here again and again. I come against my will. I didn't mean to scare you.

Elena Do you believe in ghosts?

Anne Of course I don't. That's why I told you I'm not one. Ghosts only appear in books.

Elena I don't believe in ghosts either or anything else I can't see. So, if you're not a ghost . . . and you're talking to me . . . I . . .?

Anne You what?

Elena (*trying to convince herself*) I'm OK. A while ago I saw a film where an actress appeared in a theatre unexpectedly, in costume to impress the director and get the part.

Anne I'm not here to play a part. These were the last clothes I wore and I think this is how I'll stay. Have you ever thought about how many dresses you had from when you were born until now? I had lots when I was a girl. But when we were in hiding I could hardly change my clothes and they started to get too small for me.

Music 4 starts to be played very softly.

Once Miep gave me some red heeled shoes as a gift. They were the only heels I ever had. She bought them for me and gave them to me in hiding. She said she was scared they wouldn't fit me, but they were perfect.

Music 4 increases in volume. **Anne**, *as if she is remembering the moment, pretends to walk like a woman with heels on, she takes a few steps and then spins around a few times as if she were dancing.*

Elena (*as music 4 decreases in volume*) I've never thought about the dresses I once had. But sometimes I remember a special one . . . a red one for instance . . . to wear to all the parties when you turn fifteen . . .

Anne (*stops dancing, whilst* **Elena** *starts to dance with timid steps*) Red, like my shoes. I like red, but they always dressed us girls in light colours.

Music 4 disappears.

I also think about the number of hands that have touched me, from the ones that picked me up when I was a new born, to the ones that threw my bones away at the end. There must have been so many of them, despite the brevity of my life. Many hands.

Elena You think about things . . . In day-to-day life we're not used to thinking about things like that.

Anne In life I suppose we're too busy living. Now I think I exist in the thoughts that surround me. They don't seem to come from me, but surround me.

Elena I'm trying to understand you . . . I'm dreaming you're saying all this to me . . . but it feels so clear . . . I hear my voice. In your dreams you don't hear your own voice so clearly.

Anne *stretches out her arm towards* **Elena** *but it seems to pass through her without touching her.* **Elena** *shivers.*

Anne You see, I can't touch you, or help you. Not to mention be able to make a phone call for you. Now do you believe me?

Elena This must be a very special dream. (*She opens and closes her eyes forcefully.*) I can't wake up yet. Whatever this is, it's an incredible privilege for me that you're here. Who knows how many writers in the world are thinking about you right now, but you came to me. I don't know why but I want to believe you. There's something making me believe you.

Anne I'm sorry to disappoint you but I didn't choose to come. I came here and that's that. I've not been able to choose much since I've been . . . in this state.

Elena What's it like to be dead?

Anne It's like being still, suddenly seeing things and arriving in places, different places. It doesn't hurt at all, it doesn't weigh anything, there's no wind, nor heat, nor cold, the ground feels soft because it hardly needs to support me, light hardly exists because it slides over me. It's being where everything fades, it's thinking when everything dissolves.

Elena I don't feel any of that. I know this is not being very sympathetic towards you, but I'm glad I don't feel the same. It means I'm still alive.

Anne I'm happy for you, I really am.

Elena But, you don't seem blurry, or delicate, or fragile to me. You seem very real.

Anne I still don't understand what it is that surrounds me, what protects my thoughts. At times when I'm alone I feel like I'm in an indescribable place, like a far-off shore without any sea, or horizon, or anything that feels real. It's difficult to explain. There's silence and a strange emptiness. But it's not the silence and emptiness we know in the real world. It's a silence and emptiness that stops you in your tracks. And without seeing anything, without knowing how, everything changes and I suddenly find myself in an ordinary place, like now.

Elena Will we all feel like this when we die? It doesn't seem too bad. Although I'd like to stay a bit longer in this world in any case. There's always time to die. There's still so much for me to do . . . I'm a bit dizzy . . .

Anne Sure, you can always die. And you're right, it's not that bad.

Elena Fate was unfair to you. I say fate so's not to mention God. I don't believe in any kind of god, I'm not religious. I know you were.

Anne Yes of course I was. Now I'm just me. There's just my thoughts and what I see each time. For example, right now there's just you and me here talking.

Elena There's so much I'd like to say to you, I don't know where to start. I know a lot about what happened to you.

Anne No, you don't know. Or if you think you know, you don't really know. It's impossible to explain what it was like. I don't want to talk about it. Do you have children?

Elena A daughter.

Anne I'll never know what it's like to have a sexual encounter.

Elena I don't remember what it was like not to have had a sexual encounter. It's not easy to put into words.

Anne It doesn't bother me too much. I think now I feel all that it's possible to feel.

Anne *starts to move away from* **Elena** *and moves around the seats in the small stalls area.*

Elena I'm pretty bold to think that I could write about you. If someone had told me this was going to happen, I wouldn't have believed them.

Anne I like you, I like your sincerity. I don't know if you're a good writer or not. But carry on.

Anne *moves quickly about the place, curious. She turns around and appears behind the last row of seats.*

Elena Thank you. I'm feeling better now. But I still have a tightness in my chest. I've been working really long hours, eating badly and not sleeping. It must be that. Anne, seeing as you're here and neither one of us really knows what is going on, I wanted to tell you that I'm so pleased to have met you, that I thought I knew you well, but seeing you here like this has had an impact on me . . . I don't really know what to say . . . Your voice, it sounds so much like it could be hers. It must be just my imagination, but I want to believe it.

Anne (*interrupting her, from right up behind the last row of seats*) Where are we? What is this place?

Elena Well, it's basic because it's just recently opened. That's why we're all pretty exhausted. We've been looking for a place for years and we found this . . . It's not really in the centre but . . .

Anne Is it a theatre or a cinema? . . . I mean because of the seats.

Elena Ah yes, of course, it's a theatre. There won't be that many seats in the beginning, but we'd like to make it bigger.

Anne What country?

Elena Sorry?

Anne What country are we in?

Elena Oh right, well . . . Uruguay, we're in Montevideo, the capital, a small, unassuming place, I don't know if . . . Why am I explaining this to you?

Anne The continent?

Elena Ah yes. The continent.

Anne Which continent?

Elena American. America. South America.

Anne What country did you say?

Elena Uruguay. On the ocean . . .

Anne Next to Argentina, to the south of Brazil.

Elena You know it.

Anne I studied it. Whilst we were in hiding Miep brought us a beautiful book about geography and an atlas. We studied a lot, a little of everything. It's not so small your country. The Netherlands is pretty small too.

Elena Yes, of course, there are lots of countries that are smaller than Uruguay . . .

A bell is heard in the distance. **Elena** *is startled and tries to move but something is stopping her. It looks as if her body is gently colliding with an invisible wall.*

Anne I used to like the cinema more than the theatre. Have you written a lot of plays?

Elena A few. Not many. I need to go and see who it is. (*She tries to go towards the door to the street but something invisible stops her.*) Maybe Silvia forgot something or left her keys behind.

Anne Could it be someone important for you?

Elena I don't think so. Everyone at home knew I was staying late tonight. The group that rehearses here . . . they weren't coming today . . .

The bell rings again. **Elena** *looks at* **Anne** *uncertainly and takes two steps forwards, but is stopped again.*

Elena It looks like I'm not going to be able to go and see anyway . . . and I imagine that neither are you . . .

Anne So you can carry on talking to me.

Elena (*with her mind on the door still*)   I think they've gone. What was I saying? . . . I want to open the theatre with a play about you, if you would let me . . . that is . . . if you could let me . . . I hope it seems like a good idea to you.

Anne Yes, why not? I never imagined I would be known here, in so many places. I'm pleased to have met you too. I wanted to be a cinema actress back then. How stupid!

Elena You had dreams just like all girls do. It's not stupid at all.

Anne When you write about me don't forget to put that I liked the cinema. I didn't like the theatre as much. It made me nervous.

Elena Why?

Anne Because in theatre you can't go back. When I went to the theatre I had the feeling that the actors could forget their lines at any moment, that they were going to get it wrong in front of everyone. I remember one time when an actor fell over and hurt himself. I wanted the play to stop so that the audience could leave and the actor could clean up his knees.

Elena   That's exactly why I like the theatre: because you can't go back.

Anne (*coming down from the stalls and getting closer to* **Elena**)   But the cinema is perfect. The actors are always OK.

Elena   But theatre is always alive and the cinema is always a little dead, don't you think?

Anne   No, not at all. The actors stay alive on the screen. The same with photos.

Elena   That's true. There are photos of you that I like a lot, like the one of you sitting at a desk, writing. Every time I see it, I think you're looking at me.

Anne   You see? People on screen and in photos are alive, in their own way. Do you have any photos to show me? Photos from when you were my age . . .

Elena (*trying with difficulty to tidy up her hair and clothes, although her movements seem to be suspended half way through doing them*)   Not here. I don't like you seeing me like this. It's as if an iron corset is stopping me from moving normally and keeping me stood in one place.

Anne   It's strange . . . You should be able to move better.

Elena (*pensive and scared*)   Did the same thing happen to you? Were you still at first?

Anne   It's so long ago that I don't remember. I think so. I remember seeing Margot fall from the bunk and I knew straight away that she was dead. I could still hear the shouts from the German guards, but getting further and further away. After that I decided to stay very still, so's not to waste any energy. Then . . . I don't really know what happened. The only thing I know is a long time afterwards I was standing up and I felt fine, but I didn't see things like I had seen them before, it was all messy. It's hard to explain.

Anne, *with a gesture of fear as if remembering the presence of the guards, starts to collapse until she is lying down completely on the floor. She covers her face and moans.*

Elena   Anne, I don't know what to say. You and I here together . . . Whatever is happening, I don't think it matters knowing what it is for now. There's something in the air. Something I've never felt before. A feeling of heaviness.

Anne   Miep said the same thing when we spoke.

Elena   Miep?

Anne   Yes. I spoke to her once. I appeared in her office. At first the same thing happened to her as to you. She was confused. She was very scared. But then she believed me. We spoke for a while, I've no idea how long for, until I felt that she was leaving me. I couldn't stop it.

Elena Was she OK?

Anne Yes, she was OK.

Elena She wasn't dead.

Anne No. At that moment she wasn't dead.

Elena (*turning her body a little, with relief*) Ah . . . OK.

Anne Tell me a little about the play that you're writing.

Elena Ah, I don't want you to think I'm being stupid, but I can't seem to decide on the focus of the play. I finished it more than a year ago. But there's something that's not quite right and I want to do something about it. The thing is Silvia . . . the producer, is putting pressure on us to open as soon as possible. They've been auditioning actresses from the casting call I told you about over the past few days. Early tomorrow morning we'll have a meeting with the director and producer. And me here feeling so strange!

Anne Who did you put in the play? Which characters?

Elena Several. Well, you of course . . . your parents, your sister Margot, the three van Pels, Fritz, the eight people in hiding in Prinsengracht that is. But I just can't find the key to the first scene. It's not going to be a play that only shows scenes from when you were in hiding. There are other things: your thirteenth birthday, moments with your friends, with Hanneli. An imaginary meeting between you and Petr Ginz in Auschwitz . . . I don't know if you two ever met or spoke, but I read his Diary and I was very moved by it. I liked to imagine you had met at some point.

Anne I suppose that's part of the job of a writer. To imagine. But no, I don't know who he was.

Elena He was from Prague. He wrote a Diary about what was happening during those awful years. Just like you. Later, when he was fourteen, they took him to Theresienstadt. He was there for two years, then they put him on the train to Auschwitz.

Anne I would have liked to have known him.

Elena He was in Auschwitz in the same month in 1944 that you were there. He died at the end of September that year.

Anne Before me.

Elena Yes. There's a sentence in his Diary that I found very moving. A note at the beginning of 1942. It was while he was still in Prague, during the Nazi occupation. He said, "Jews can no longer take the tram, nor walk on the pavement, nor walk along the banks of the river. What now seems completely ordinary, would have caused outrage in normal times."

Anne He wrote that? He realised. Not everyone realised.

Elena His younger sister writes about when she said goodbye to him for the last time. She was also sent to Theresienstadt. She wrote about the day that the train arrived to take him away and how she could still reach her brother's hand through the bars in the train's window to give him food. Then she writes, "Now Petr isn't here and the only thing that remains of him is his empty bed."

Anne What happened to his sister?

Elena She survived. It was her who found his Diary.

Anne She survived. Like my father. After the war he was alone. I've seen him. But that wasn't the last time terrible things happened, was it? Sometimes, during those special moments when I see things, I've felt like the world is still in a bit of a mess.

Elena Awful things also happened around here not that long ago. When I was a child.

Anne Did they kill people?

Elena Yes. And many people disappeared without us knowing what happened to them.

Anne I only had a very short time in the world. It's important that you write about everything you're feeling.

Elena Yes, I'm trying to. I want to write about you in a different way. A lot of plays based on your Diaries have already been written. Still, it worries me that someone will come to claim the rights. There will be people who believe it's about your Diary. (*Smiles sarcastically.*) Imagine the situation if that were to happen. I could say to them, "Don't worry, I spoke to Anne Frank myself and it was fine with her." (*Interrupts herself suddenly, downhearted.*) Don't be so stupid! Why am I worrying about the bloody rights issue? I have a much more urgent problem right now! I can hardly move!

Anne (*sitting down*) Put me in your play.

Elena Of course, you're the lead!

Anne I mean how you see me now.

Elena How . . . ?

Anne The play could start with me seeing the world of the living.

Elena But the audience . . . How will they make sense of this?

Anne Because they will see me as I am now. Miep could be there too. I think she died very recently, very old. I felt her death and I saw her when she was very still too. In your play perhaps she and I could meet. We could talk and reminisce about the others in our memories. What the audience would see would be what we see, from the twilit earth we're always in, with no horizon.

Elena Maybe . . . I'd have to change the beginning. It would change the focus of the play. But I could try it. I don't know . . . The character herself giving the writer an idea!

Anne (*getting up and moving away as if offended*)   I'm not a character. I'm a real woman. I'm fifteen years old, I'm already a woman.

Elena   I meant the person who inspired a "future character" in a play that is not yet finished. I want to get better to finish it. But giving a voice to someone who is dead . . . (*Interrupts herself, uncomfortable.*) Sorry for calling you dead. It's more thoughtful to call you a spirit, I know. Or a soul . . . What should I call you?

Anne   Anne.

Elena   Of course. Anne. I wouldn't like to be called a dead person. It makes me anxious to think that I already am.

Anne   The only thing we know is that we are here and this is a theatre. I like your theatre a lot, it's small, but it feels nice. Now I want to go.

Elena   It's not a bad idea, really. Miep, the woman who protected you in hiding, at the age when she died . . . at a hundred years old . . . We'd have to find a very old actress or someone who could play that age. It wouldn't be easy.

Anne   And a young Miep could appear too when she went to see us in hiding. Then you could see the same character when they're young and when they're dead. I used to give Peter ideas when he wanted to be a screenwriter.

Elena   Yes, the character of young Miep is already in the play. But to add her in after she's dead . . . I like it . . . She could see herself amongst the living, she could remember when she was young. And how would the actress dressed as a prisoner represent the two Annes?

Anne   It would be two actresses, who look like each other. One representing Anne's soul and the other Anne in real life.

Elena   More casting problems! But it might be possible. So, two of them would be dead and then all the others.

Anne   It's an idea.

Elena   It's an idea . . .

Anne   Once I thought I saw my father.

Elena   You knew he survived. That after the war he was alone, without you all.

Anne   Yes, but I mean after that. I saw him afterwards as well. I'm almost certain that it was him.

Elena   Where did you see him?

Anne   In the same place I'm almost always in that's so difficult to describe. He was standing up, alone. Suddenly I saw him from behind, still, with the same shirt as always and his waistcoat. He looked rather old. I walked towards him and he didn't move. Eventually I was standing in front of him. What happened was very strange. I couldn't recognise the face as his, but also couldn't say it wasn't. He had very blurry eyes and he didn't look at me. Suddenly he turned around and left. (*Long pause.*) Why do you want to write about the time when I was alive if awful things also happened in your lifetime too, like you said, right here?

Elena I've already written about what happened here. Now I want to write about what happened to you. I can't get some of the images from the war out of my head. And when I saw the film *The Pianist* . . . Are you going?

Anne *starts to slowly move away.*

Anne We'll see each other again, some other time . . .

Elena Anne, wait! I'd like to talk to you about so many things. This is the most incredible dream. Meeting you. From one side of time to another. Anne!

Anne You already know too much about me. And what you don't know, I don't want you to know. No film could show what it was like. Goodbye Elena. You have a beautiful name. My real name is Annelies.

She keeps walking away and the shadows start to envelop her.

Elena Yes, Annelies. Of course, sorry. The films, the photos . . . they're not anything compared to . . . What are you doing now? Where are you going?

Anne Those are useless questions. (*Stops for a moment and looks at* **Elena** *again.*) There's one person who touched me that I don't want to remember. One of the hands that touched me in my life. If I had to count the hands that touched me, I wouldn't want to count that hand.

Elena Anne . . .

Anne The guard's hand that led us to the huts the night we arrived in that horrendous place. We were in single file, all the women. Not all of us, some had been taken away when we arrived. I was with Mum and Margot. They had already separated us from the men, from Dad . . .

Elena Don't tell me if you don't want to, please Anne . . .

Anne (*looking into the distance, without paying attention to* **Elena**) Suddenly a hand grabbed me forcefully by the arm and separated me from the group. He shouted something I didn't understand. I was so scared I didn't say anything. Mum and Margot tried to run towards me. But they forced them to stay in the line. I felt his hand, which dug into me like a hot iron, was dragging me away from them, until another man shouted something to the one taking me away, which made him take me back to the line. I won't ever forget the look he gave me. He looked at me like a wolf who is made to let go of his prey. He didn't want to let go of me. He led me to the line again but his hand stayed nailed to my arm. Despite the thick coat I had on, I felt every one of his fingers sink into my skin to the bone. Eventually he let go of me, looking at me with rage. That night and the days that followed, I carried on feeling the imprint of his hand on my skin, as if he was still holding on to me. I wish I could forget it. I would like to forget it. I don't have things left undone Elena. Life, for me, was left undone. I'm going. Good luck with your play.

Elena Thanks Anne, my play doesn't matter any more.

Anne It has to matter. Elena . . . It has to matter.

Music. **Anne** *disappears completely.* **Elena** *tries to raise a hand towards where* **Anne** *left, but she can't manage it. Her expression is of deep distress. After a long inhale, she lets her head fall again, as well as her arms alongside her body and she begins to slowly fall to the ground remaining completely motionless again, in the same place and in the same position as at the start of the scene. A few seconds of complete stillness pass. Suddenly she starts shaking, takes an enormous mouthful of air, like a drowned person starting to breathe again and sits up abruptly, remaining seated on the floor. The music stops.*

Elena (*looking feverishly all around her*) Oh my god! What was that? I've woken up! What happened to me? It was crazy! I should get to a doctor . . . How did I fall? . . . I must have hit my head . . . What time is it? (*Pause.*) What an idea! I've got to write down everything right now before I forget. I can't let it disappear, it's the key to whole play. (*She jumps to her feet and starts gesticulating energetically.*) It wasn't Anne Frank, it was me! It was my mind . . . From thinking so much about the problem. I'm not dead! I wasn't dead! How crazy was that? Ghosts don't exist. That's lucky! (*Pause, looking towards where* **Anne** *went.*) But she seemed so real. It must be the tablets. I won't take them any more. (*She touches her throat and her head disconcertedly, she looks around her and starts to pick up papers, her jacket, a pen and a mobile phone, that had been left strewn across the floor. She tidies the papers and sits down on one of the seats in the first row, she takes the pen and starts to write, talking to herself.*) Scene Zero. That's what I'm going to call the scene at the beginning. Scene Zero. The best ideas come when you're dreaming. Just as you're waking up, they come. If you're lucky enough to remember them. (*She interrupts herself and stands up. She takes her mobile phone out of her trouser pocket. She looks at it.*) It's run out of battery. What time is it? (*She takes two or three steps forwards as if leaving the place, but then thinks better of it and sits down again to prepare to write.*) It doesn't matter. Let's see, before I forget the idea. I'll write down the most important things and I'll go home. Or even better, I'll write it straight away. First, the description of the place Anne's ghost is in. And the description of Anne as I saw her just now: light, with her arms floating at the side of her body, with a serene look . . . Yes . . . And then the arrival of old Miep, who has just died. What they say to each other when they see each other in the land of the dead and then they start to see scenes from the real world. They can see moments from the world of the living, watching them from the other side of the shore . . . (*It looks as if something is suddenly bothering her in her chest, she puts her hand there, breathes deeply for a moment and carries on making notes.*) I'll make an appointment tomorrow. They won't give me one for at least a month, it's always the same. And they'll get cross with me, like the last time. They'll give me an ECG reluctantly, because they have to . . . It's nothing, they'll say. Don't get so stressed. It's probably just tiredness?

Some music starts very quietly.

Anne tells Miep she can see everyone again from where she is, as if time were a roll of film that sometimes stretches and sometimes goes back on itself, over and over again. The dead see the living, but the living don't see them, of course . . . That's a good writing device. The audience knows more than some of the characters. The audience loves that!

The music gets louder. **Elena** *keeps writing feverishly whilst the light fades until it disappears. The light fades completely and the music carries on at a high volume.*

Scene 3

After a few seconds of blackout, the lights come back on. The music stops completely. The same place, but without anybody there. **Fernando** *enters and moves pensively about the space near to the seating.* **Silvia** *enters soon afterwards carrying a folder.*

Silvia　All ready. Shall I tell them to come in?

Fernando　Yes. I hope it goes better today.

Silvia　I don't know. I told you it wouldn't be easy. I told you having two Annes was going to be more difficult than the older actress.

Fernando　Of course. We should have waited a bit.

Silvia　And cancel again?

Fernando　Yes . . . To gather ourselves. Take some time.

Silvia　Things don't work like that. People are waiting for us to open and there are so many costs . . .

Fernando (*resigned, goes to sit down in the centre of the first row of seats*)　I know, I know.

Silvia　If we don't open in three months from now, we've lost the whole season.

Fernando　OK, tell them to come in. Let's see if we can sort it all out today.

Silvia　Don't think I'm disrespectful, but that idea made everything more complicated. The play was perfect as it was. All those last-minute changes . . .

Fernando　It's great as it is now. It's going to be a great play. The complication with the casting doesn't bother me.

Silvia　It's not just that. It's more actors, more costume, more cost.

Fernando　More interesting. And what she wanted. I don't want to keep talking about it. We already discussed it.

Silvia *exits, seemingly resigned.* **Fernando** *whispers to himself.*

Fernando　I'm not going to be intimidated. We'll manage to fund this. We've got to do this play, now more than ever.

Elena enters from the back of the stalls and listens to what **Fernando** *says.* **Silvia** *comes back carrying a sheet of paper with the names of the hopefuls printed out on it. She hands it to* **Fernando**.

Silvia   They'll start to arrive in five. First off we should ask for their availability, especially those playing Anne, both of them. They've got lots of scenes together.

Fernando   Of course.

Quiet music. **Anne** *enters.*

Elena (*to* **Anne**)   They're about to start.

Anne   I hope someone turns up.

Elena   You didn't come yesterday. They auditioned about twenty people. There was one really good one, I think. But now they have to find someone who looks like her.

Anne (*pointing to* **Silvia**)   That woman looks anxious.

Elena (*amused*)   She's not very happy with the finished text. It made the production more complicated for her.

Anne   Poor thing. People get so bothered about things like that.

Elena   But they think the play is good. They're going to do it. Can you believe it?

Whilst this dialogue is going on between **Anne** *and* **Elena**, **Fernando** *and* **Silvia**, *who seem to neither hear nor see the two women, carry on talking. They say the first few sentences quietly, in a secondary scene.*

Silvia (*showing* **Fernando** *the list*)   We should cross this one out. She let us know she wasn't coming. Here are the details of the ones for today, the last ones.

Fernando   Great. How old does it say here?

Silvia   Twenty-one. They're in order. But I'm still worried about the other stuff. More people to employ . . .

When the conversation between **Anne** *and* **Elena** *finishes, the conversation between* **Silvia** *and* **Fernando** *takes centre stage and the music stops.*

Silvia (*continuing*)   And we're going to have to cut some of the set costs, we have to make some budget savings somewhere.

Fernando   We can make it much simpler, yes. Elena didn't like complicated sets anyway.

Silvia   Just as well. Because if the set were to get as complicated as the number of characters, I don't know what we'd do . . .

Fernando (*standing up, starting to lose patience*)   Do you not want to do the play? It's better that you say so now.

Silvia   Yes, I do want to. More than that, we have a moral obligation to do it . . .

Fernando I'm not doing it out of obligation. I'm directing the play because it's good. And of course I think that's the best tribute to Elena. But if the play were bad, I wouldn't do it, you know that.

Silvia (*trying to appease him*) Of course, of course . . . Let's talk about it later. We're going to have to talk at some point.

Fernando About what?

Elena *silently climbs the platform and sits down in the last row of seats.*

Silvia You're upset with me. I should have kept trying or called you. Especially when she didn't answer.

Fernando Oh Silvia! Not this again.

Silvia I should have kept trying when she didn't answer and let you know. But I went home.

Fernando It's not your fault at all. You weren't to know that . . .

Silvia If they'd got here in time . . .

Fernando As they said, there might have been nothing they could do. You can't keep thinking that.

Silvia I can't get it out of my head.

Fernando (*making* **Silvia** *sit down*) Silvia, let's see . . . Listen to me for a minute. We're all tired. Anyone could forget their key. The light could have been left on with nobody here. You're not to blame at all, you weren't to know, it was an unfortunate tragedy. Do you hear me? An unfortunate tragedy. Elena wasn't doing great anyway. I'm not upset with you. Your stubbornness drives me mad though.

Silvia (*trying to recompose herself*) Let's talk later. Here's the girl with the strange name.

Fernando Which one?

Silvia The one that was too old. She got here first today.

Fernando Ah . . . Yes.

From where she is, **Elena** *signals to* **Anne** *to come closer to her.* **Anne** *climbs the stairs to where* **Elena** *is and sits in a chair in the last row.* **Iona** *enters, hesitantly.*

Iona Sorry. We were told to come in . . .

Fernando Yes, come in. Hi. (*Consulting a list.*) You are . . .

Iona Iona Xenidis. It's Greek. Although everyone calls me Aline.

Fernando OK, great. So Iona . . . did you chose a speech?

Iona Yes.

Silvia   OK, I think we're ready.

Iona   Shall I start?

Silvia   Yes, please. (*Pointing to the seats.*) Leave your things there if you like. If you could go a little further back . . . so we can see you properly.

Iona (*taking off her jacket and rucksack*)   Yes, yes, of course.

Fernando   Do you want to read it first?

Iona   No. I know it.

Silvia   OK . . . When you're ready.

Iona   I chose the section from the end of the first meeting with Miep in the land of the dead, when Anne tells her how she feels.

Silvia   The end of Scene One.

Iona   Not Scene One. It's Scene Zero.

Silvia   The first scene.

Fernando (*looking at* **Silvia** *impatiently*)   That's fine. What does she say to her?

Iona   It's when Miep wants to say goodbye to Anne to carry on exploring the world of the dead and try to find her husband Jan, who died many years before. Anne asks her where she is going and she replies, "I want to see what there is on the other side." And Anne says to her . . .

Iona *breathes slowly, she looks at a point in the distance and starts to speak in a clear voice. As she's speaking, her body and her voice change a little. Leaning slightly forwards, with her arms a little separated from her body, she transmits a kind of melancholy, like being old and very young at the same time. At the back,* **Elena** *and* **Anne** *watch.*

There is no other side, this is the other side . . . The place full of mist, the place full of silence, where nobody wants to go. The place full of shadows, the place full of emptiness, where everybody will go. The wind is delicate here, because it doesn't exist, the faces are blurred, because they don't see us. The ground is soft, because it doesn't support us, the light is elusive, because it doesn't reflect us. Who knows if you will ever find Jan. And even if you find him you might not recognise him, nor him recognise you. Look at me, how long have I been here for? I can't sense time any more. I'm here, but the wind doesn't touch me, the ground doesn't support me, the light doesn't reflect me and the faces don't see me. I am here and yet I think, I see the light, I see the faces, my body shakes. Where everything fades, I am here and I think. Where everything dissolves, the remains of me stay. What membrane still surrounds me? What empty shell protects me? Where are my notebooks? My Diaries . . . The pages must be drying out and be as fragile as my hands. Surely the ink on their pages no longer shines and the paper no longer smells of saffron. Where is everyone? Why have they left me all alone? Why?

Iona *stops and remains standing, very still. Long pause.* **Fernando** *and* **Silvia** *look at each other in silence and look at the girl.* **Anne** *sits up in her seat in the stalls and looks at* **Iona** *and* **Elena**.

Silvia (*to* **Iona**)   Thank you. We'll put up who was successful on the theatre's billboard on Thursday.

Iona   That's all then?

Silvia   Yes, thank you.

Fernando   Thank you Iona.

Iona   Shall I tell the other girls to come in?

Fernando (*pensive*)   Why did you choose that speech?

Iona   Because it describes how Anne feels in the land of the dead really well. And it felt a little strange to me. It conveys that strangeness.

Fernando   Do you like the character of dead Anne more than the other Anne?

Iona   More than the living Anne? Yes, of course. When I was sent the new version I couldn't believe it. I loved it. I had already chosen the speech that I was going to give, I'd even learnt it too, but when I read what Anne says in the other world I liked it a lot more. . . so I spent almost the whole night studying . . . (*She stops herself with a worried expression.*) But if you think I would be better as the other Anne that's not a problem. That is . . . Sorry, if you think I could be either of them.

Silvia (*getting up, nervous, moving around papers*)   So, if you want to pass by on Thursday . . .

Iona   Yes of course. Shall I tell the next person to come in?

Silvia   Yes.

Fernando   No, don't. Off you go. We'll let you know.

Iona   OK. Goodbye.

Iona, *a little flustered, gets her things and leaves.* **Elena** *stands up and carries on watching what happens with interest.*

Fernando (*to* **Silvia**)   We don't have to see anyone else. It's her.

Silvia   But there are other people waiting outside . . .

Fernando   Silvia, it's her.

Silvia   I think so. Well, yes. (*She starts to smile.*)

Music. **Silvia** *becomes impatient again. She goes over to* **Fernando**, *who doesn't seem to hear her. She sits down next to him.*

Silvia   What do I say to the others waiting outside? They've been there a while. We've got to say something to them, they've come all the way here . . . Look at the list, there's still all of these to go . . . I think we should probably go out there, we'll have to explain something to them . . . Fernando! . . .

Silvia *remains focused on* **Fernando**, *in a secondary scene. Meanwhile the final dialogue can clearly be heard between* **Anne** *and* **Elena**, *who are still at the back, behind* **Fernando** *and* **Silvia**. *The music gets quieter.*

Anne (*to* **Elena**)   Everything that you made me say . . . Did you come up with that? After we spoke that day?

Elena   Yes.

Anne   I liked it.

Elena   Thank you.

Anne   You made me say things that are very . . . I don't know how. I think I like it.

Elena (*smiling*)   Not you, the character.

Anne   Of course, the character. Not me. I'm not a character. I'm real.

The light fades. The music becomes louder. **Fernando** *looks into the distance, with an expression of intense concentration. You can hardly hear what* **Silvia** *is saying.*

Blackout.

I Will Give You Verses, Not Children
(Delmira Agustini - A Life)

Marianella Morena

Translated by Kate Eaton

No daré hijos, daré versos (*I Will Give You Verses, Not Children*) premiered in October 2014 at the Teatro Solís, Montevideo. It was directed by Marianella Morena and performed by Sofía Etcheverry, Mané Pérez, Mariano Prince, Alfonso Tort, Lucía Trentini, and Agustín Urrutia. The play was published by Criatura Editora in 2019.

About the author and translator

Marianella Morena is one of Uruguay's most internationally successful theatre artists, whose work has been produced throughout Latin America and Europe. Her many international awards include the Premio Molière (awarded by the French Embassy in Uruguay), the Centro Cultural de España (Cultural Centre of Spain) Award, and the University of Buenos Aires Award (Argentina). Writer of over 30 plays to date, her works include *Don Juan, El lugar del beso* (*Don Juan, The Place of the Kiss*), *Las Julietas* (*The Juliets*), *Antígona Oriental* (*Eastern Antigone*, staged with an on-stage chorus of 20 former political prisoners), *No daré hijos, daré versos* (*I Will Give You Verses, Not Children*), *Ella sobre Ella* (*Her on Her*), *Bicentenaria* (*Bicentenary*, an intervention staged by 200 women in the public square in Lima, Peru), and *Naturaleza Trans* (*Trans Nature*, a documentary piece featuring trans women from the Uruguay-Brazil border). Published in several countries, she was in March 2024 the first-ever Latin American artist to direct at the Suomen Kansallisteatteri (Finnish National Theatre, Helsinki). As an artivist, she stages performative interventions in public spaces to call out social injustices in relation to the environment, femicide, and the sexual exploitation of minors.

Kate Eaton is a UK-based literary translator, theatre practitioner and researcher. She has been a member of the Ibero-American theatre and translation collective, Out of the Wings, since 2016, and has translated a wide variety of plays from Cuba, Mexico, Argentina, and Spain amongst other countries, including multiple works by the renowned twentieth-century Cuban playwright Virgilio Piñera. She holds an MA in Literary Translation from the University of East Anglia and a PhD in Collaborative Translation Practices and Cuban Theatre from Queen Mary, University of London. She participated as a translator on the 2022-24 Royal Court-Autonomous University of Mexico new playwriting project, and is currently co-editing an anthology of Cuban and diasporic adaptations of Ancient Greek theatre.

Characters

First Act

Three Delmiras
Three Reyes

Second Act

Delmira
Reyes
Mother
Father
Brother
Maid-Stage Manager

Third Act

Three Contemporary Couples

The actors work with a poetic accumulation and each new character incorporates the previous one.

First Act

THE DEATH
Towards Life

Characters

Three Delmiras
Three Reyes

6 July 1914, 1206 Andes Street, the city of Montevideo; a bedroom in carnage as though war had broken out. Two bodies lie on the floor. **Delmira Agustini** *has two gunshot wounds. In his death throes* **Reyes** *is saying her name: "Delmira."*

The furniture and objects are destroyed. Nothing gives an indication as to time, era or place. Nothing.

The actors and actresses lie tumbled together on a bed. Their clothes are muddled up and do not necessarily correspond to their genders. There are traces of both the past and the contemporary in their costumes and in the stage set.

Their movements are disjointed. The texts and narratives are fragmented too.

SONG

There are wars that are just for one person.
The bullet crossed the city
crossed the sky
like a whip of fire.
It entered.
The bullet returned and killed me once more;
two shots, Reyes fired two shots at me.
I am Delmira
Delmira Agustini
That gunned-down woman is me.
That woman I see; that you see,
that the press saw, the police saw,
that my parents saw,
that history saw.
That same woman is me.
Delmira.
The dead woman.
The murdered, murdered,
murdered woman.

The texts are not divided up. Each actor is **Reyes** *and each actress is* **Delmira**. *They say the lines sometimes in unison and sometimes not. The dialogue overlaps, lines are* *spoken over each other, repeated. One actress, three actors. One actor, three actresses. A soundscape is created that is, at times, chaotic. During rehearsals the how and why of what is heard can be decided in order to achieve a symphony of parts. Garments are changed and exchanged. There is no visual distinction as to the gender of each actor.*

Delmira *Bang, bang, bang.* Know what the headlines say? "Jealous husband kills wife and then kills himself." Or: "Ex-husband kills ex-wife and current lover and then takes own life with same gun", *bang, bang, bang,* fall to the ground for goodness' sake, come on, let's play horsey, *bang.*

She plays and he interrupts her.

Reyes Wait, not now. We can't play all the time.

Delmira You're so stupid. You understand nothing.

Reyes No, I know nothing. I understand nothing. Talk to me. Explain.

Delmira There's nothing to explain.

Reyes I don't love you anymore.

Delmira You can't.

Reyes You'll see that I can.

Delmira I'm not interested in talking.

Reyes But we're talking now . . .

Delmira I'm rehearsing.

Reyes Am I a character to you?

Delmira Life isn't lived, life lives us.

He gets violent with her. Then becomes despondent. Suffers, repents.

Reyes Yesterday I auctioned off a lot made up of shoes. It caught my attention. They're like those strange things you write, I don't know why I made that link. I'm not sure how I connect one thing with another or why, but there were all these shoes mixed up, men's and women's, all jumbled together. That image stayed in my head; it made me think about their owners . . .

Delmira What's interesting?

Reyes About what? The shoes or me?

Delmira I don't want to talk. I don't want to answer every question. It isn't interesting to have conversations all the time. Why should I have to answer? I don't want to; you know how I am.

Reyes What's a man supposed to do when his wife speaks to him like that?

Delmira Nothing.

Reyes Nothing? You walk through life with that historical air as though you were the last queen standing after the revolution.

Delmira You haven't got the imagination to insult me, Reyes. You are vulgar. Vulgar and soft.

Reyes Soft? What does that mean? Everything is poetry to you from Swiss chard to the shit in the toilet. There's a practical world out there. But of course, she doesn't do practical.

Delmira You always interrupt me. You interrupt me. You interrupt my thoughts. I don't want to talk, at least not with those words.

Reyes Idiotic child. Useless. You're rehearsing? What did you say?

Delmira I want a divorce. I'm leaving. I can't stand so much vulgarity.

Reyes We got married a month and twenty-two days ago.

Delmira Yes, maybe, and?

Reyes Maybe? No, we did. Do you know what your mother said to me on the night of our wedding? Do you know or not? That you wear the face of a consumptive angel? That you wouldn't be able to get pregnant. That you would devote yourself to your poetry not to me. You've got a screw loose! There's no place for you in this house, not in my bed, not in my heart. You can't talk? What happened, what happened to the lady of Uruguayan letters?

Delmira What do you want from me? Always digging. There's nothing more. Or rather what there was for you is over now. What are you looking for? I want to leave, Reyes, let me leave.

Reyes Soft?

Delmira I don't want to hear anything. I want to wake up alone in my bed without anybody telling me what the day will be like, what the next week will be like. I don't want it; I don't like it. Let me leave.

Reyes Am I a character to you? You're cooking something up, you have no shame, nothing matters to you, you have no idea of my pain. How dare you speak of vulgarity? The only vulgar person here is you.

Delmira You understand nothing, you never understood anything, what is sex to you?

Reyes Oh, so you're experienced now are you? You stopped being a lady to become mistress of the bed.

Delmira You sell other people's lives for a few pesos.

Reyes Shut your mouth, shut it because I'm going to shove all your books up your cunt and down your throat, I'm going to fill up all your holes, you'll be stuffed full of your own overheated little verses. You don't look at me when I get home, your nose is always glued to the window or stuck in your papers. Look at me when I speak to you.

Delmira The macho-man puts his cards on the table. In case anyone forgets who wears the trousers. You don't listen. I told you I want to leave; I'm bored of this discussion. So you just sit there all quiet and sweaty like a man from the labouring classes? Well, you know what? Men from the labouring classes know how to fuck their brides and you weren't capable of that, which is why I call you soft . . . Auction it off, Reyes, auction it off, come on, I want to hear how you auction off the engagement, the wedding, the bride's virginity, the useless lover that you are, only ever getting it semi-hard . . . Auction it off, Reyes, and auction it off for pennies because nothing is worth nothing. Not you, not this bed, not this erotic life you made me wait so long for and for what? To give me what? What do you give me? Why did you make me wait so long? Speak! You're as silent as the thunderous silence of the wood when the gavel falls and that broken voice says: "Sold."

Reyes Leave, Delmira, get out of my life, leave, but really leave. Don't write me letters, don't cry, don't beg, don't grovel, leave, and leave me alone with the little I have, with this piece of nothing that I am. Leave, leave, I don't want to stay here and for you to see me, I don't want that . . . Leave, Delmira, leave, get ill and die please. Just finally do it and take your mother, both of you. No, even better, take the whole family. Stand out in the rain the whole lot of you so that you all catch pneumonia and die, and I'll be there watching you through the windowpane like you watch me when I come home, and you don't even touch me . . .

Delmira When it stops raining I'll go.

Reyes Now, now. I don't want you in my house anymore. Take your crap with you.

Delmira Tomorrow the sun will come out and I'll leave.

Reyes Can you repeat the things you said to me?

Delmira So that you can note them down? Ah, why don't we do a scene now? Which one would you prefer?

Reyes Whichever one you like . . . Soft?

Delmira We could do the erotic scene we didn't do before we were married.

Reyes No, I don't want to.

Delmira You don't understand, that's what's happening.

Reyes No.

Delmira Sometimes I'd like to be a man . . .

Reyes And sometimes I'd like to forget I'm a man. I don't like my work; I don't want to be an auctioneer.

Delmira And what would you like to be?

Reyes I'd like to be brave.

Delmira Would you like to be a revolutionary?

Reyes If I could . . .

Delmira What's the first thing you'd do?

Reyes I don't know.

Delmira Come on, Reyes. We're playing, why do you change like that? You're my character, remember . . .

Reyes Because it's late and I have to get up early tomorrow.

Delmira Shall I go, or shall I stay?

Reyes If the sun comes out, you go.

Delmira The sun won't come out, my love.

Reyes Sleep with me the whole week.

Delmira Yes, leave your work. Don't go. I don't like you being an auctioneer.

Reyes I can't.

Delmira See, you don't love me like you said you did!

Reyes Don't play with me anymore. I'm a serious man, I did what I had to do. I love you. I don't have eyes for anyone else.

Delmira Broaden the conversation.

Reyes I don't understand.

Delmira You're stupid, you're stubborn. Don't get radical. It doesn't suit you. Let's think of something else.

Reyes Like what?

Delmira Fantasies.

Reyes You have fantasies?

Delmira We all have them, you too. The whole world has them.

Reyes Tell me yours.

Delmira That we get divorced and become lovers . . .

Reyes What?

Delmira No, that's for public consumption, we play with that, we fool people. I can't stand this life. I'm not a domesticated animal, I don't want to live like this. It bores me.

Reyes Don't start again.

Delmira I hadn't finished.

Reyes I can't, Delmira. Please, please, I can't Delmira. I'm not like that, I'm not.

Delmira Let's make a plan: we tell everyone that we're separating, and I divorce you, but we continue seeing each other as lovers.

Reyes   And what do I gain from that?

Delmira   It's not a competition, Reyes.

Reyes   I don't understand, what do you want?

Delmira   It's a game with equal conditions.

Reyes   And what are the conditions?

Delmira   Freedom.

Reyes   Go to hell, get out of my house, now, leave now, I don't want to see you, leave, I'm throwing you out.

Delmira   It's raining.

Reyes   Yes, and it won't stop. It's never going to stop raining.

Reyes *kisses* **Delmira**, *he throttles her.* **Delmira** *struggles.*

Three Reyes (*text shared between the three actors according to the staging criteria*)   I bought it. I went and bought it. Many months passed before I decided to kill her. Many months passed before I decided to buy the gun. First, the auctioning of the body. Mentally I auctioned it. I split it up into lots like you do in a big auction. I spent a lot of time thinking about where the first shot would be, which day to do it, how . . . Before or after? In the front or in the back? First in the head. The first gavel blow . . . How much is the head of Delmira Agustini worth? Who wants it, who will bid more? Sold to the gentleman. A Monday. I went and bought the gun. The day after signing the divorce papers. Who'd have thought that someone could leave after a month and a half of marriage? Forty-five days exactly. I got up and I bought it. She had spoken to me twice: six words. I got up, I went and bought it.

Even so I feel nothing
when I kill.
I kill and I die when I kill.
I feel nothing, I think it, I feel nothing.
I say it, I feel nothing.
I am certain: nothing.
I say nothing, there is nothing to say when they let me speak.
And when I speak, I lie
and if I don't kill, I kill dying so as not to speak.
I don't know what to say.
I do it, I feel nothing, and I blow her head off.
I blow it off.
Whore.
Just the gun and the two of us.
She knows and she looks me in the eyes.
It's not alright, I can shoot you and I did it.
I want more, a little more
and to go back to my house with you.
I want you to love me forever and not die.

I am Reyes and I'm already dead.
We're all dead.
My lover who used to be my wife and before that, my bride.
I only want Delmira to love me.
Sons of bitches.
Why do you look at me like that?
Why do you look at me with pity?
Why do you look at me with hate?
There are also wars for just one woman and one man.

SONG

There are wars for many, millions, thousands
for continents, countries, tribes
ethnic minorities, religious minorities
political minorities
military minorities
and there are wars that are just for one person.
The man who in the night takes the gun he has bought
the man who walks towards the meeting with the lover who used to be his wife
is a man with war upon him
he has missiles in his retinas
he sleeps with grenades
embraces the FN P90 submachine gun
dreams of a .45 calibre pistol or a Magnum 500.
There are also wars for two.
Wars for just one woman and one man.

Three Delmiras (*text shared between the three actresses according to the staging criteria.*)   I want to write. I want to write like a murderer wants to kill. A murderer comes back, always comes back. I don't know how long he waits, but he always comes back. There's always something left to do. After death the bodies are buried, they rot, the books go back to the library, nobody reads them. But murderers return, Reyes comes back for more Delmira. Did you see him? I'm not scared, I don't want to be scared, I was never scared, the others never knew or wouldn't know if I was scared. I also didn't know or wouldn't know if I was scared: in order to be scared you have to allow it. Scared to open my legs like ballet dancers who point their toes to the ends of the earth and opposite, the neighbour opposite, from the pavement opposite, from the window of his house watches the black hole expand over the pavement to the street until it reaches the door of his house. Is that girl scared? No, no she's not, because she dances and stretches her legs out like nobody else. My legs are crossed, closed and over them I have various layers of cloth: cotton, polyester, linen, flannel, silk, gabardine, lace, tulle, wool, hessian, felt, suede, velvet, corduroy, calico, poplin, muslin. No-one knows what my crotch really looks like. Reyes will come tomorrow. His hand gives no relief. His hand tires and pleads. Every so often he returns. I saw him running down the street, he is desperate to see me. The two of us are dead on the floor. Reyes survived and comes back for an hour, a day more, a minute more, a year more.

SONG

>There are wars that are for everyone.
>For many, for thousands,
>Muslims against Christians
>Jews against Palestinians
>urban tribes
>mafiosi
>police and criminals
>criminals against criminals
>politicians against politicians
>capitalists against communists.
>And there are wars that are for just one person.

Delmira I don't know. I don't know if I can touch myself nor what the moans of love are like when you are penetrated. I don't know if my parents fuck. Do people fuck after marrying and having children? I think about the male member and its vigour; if it can enter my mouth or just lie there inside a pair of trousers. I think about my brother's member when I see him sitting by the window, and I think about my hand which goes down below. I don't know if you can think these things or if people touch themselves like that when they're together or alone. Reyes won't let me touch it, not even to plunge his flesh between my buttocks, he doesn't like it, why doesn't he like it if he loves me? I don't understand men. I die of heat every night and I want to get under my brother's sheet and soothe myself. He also wants to try and doesn't have anyone to do it with. The fruit is soft. Sweet and red. Reyes' hands are not for my skirt which gets lifted up by the wind in the square. Why don't you look at me if everyone else looks at me? Why don't you take what's yours, Reyes?

Reyes Whore. She's a whore. No, no I can't think that. But she lifts up her skirt and she shows me her crotch without underwear, and she begs me. Enough! I need to stop thinking. It's her mother's fault, she lets her hear the nighttime groans. She doesn't close the bedroom door in the summer and it's common knowledge that the brother sleeps with the maid. Shit, I must think about something else. I need to occupy my mind. Can she love me? I don't know; that wildness in her, her strange obsession with getting undressed, eating strawberries, and hiding them under her panties, can that be normal? I shouldn't think any more.

Delmira I don't know why I say those things that shouldn't be said. My mouth is full, and my crotch is empty. I eat and I soothe myself a bit. I don't know what the weather's like outside, I can't go out, it's nighttime, men go out with their trousers bulging, they go towards the edge of the city, which isn't my bed. I would like to put on other clothes, men's clothes and go out whoring. Go to the lowest brothel in the city and sleep with all kinds of anatomies. Not possible, it's already late.

Reyes I see her, I don't just see her, she's behind the glass, crouched down. I arrive and I kiss her, she doesn't react, I go, and she stays behind the glass. Some hours pass and I return, wretched, I kiss her, many times. She still doesn't react. We almost attempt an absurd dialogue. The family look at me with suspicion. As though I were a thief in disguise. She stays behind the window. I think so many things . . . Kiss and hit, kiss, and hit, kiss and hit, enough! I have to get rid of some thoughts that haunt me, they haunt me from when I open my eyes in the morning, and they haunt me when I see you in the evening and I dream of you at night. I am lying on the floor, and I cannot drag myself over to your white and red feet. Why are your feet red? Open your mouth to tell me what I want to hear, open it and I will be able to auction calmly. A lot made up of useless things awaits me, as you say, but they're important to somebody. Sometimes I think that I'm no more than a vulgar auctioneer and a little bit of death clings to me with each gavel blow that sinks into the wood like a coffin. Burials are different. I know that she's not making fun of my work, but I can't manage to shed the misery of the days when I hug her, and I know that she senses it and sometimes she asks strange questions like: "Did you auction off the bedding of a widow woman?" Or: "Was it a lot made up of knives you were selling this week?" I never answer her, it isn't right to talk about my work, not with her. But the moment always disarms me and when she breaks the silence it's always to say things I don't understand. I don't know why you're laughing.

Delmira   Because you understand nothing! I'm burning, I've been burning for days and months. My hand is red, I showed it to Reyes, and he slapped me and then he kissed me, and I slapped him, and I kissed him. We stayed there with our cheeks red, and our legs entwined. He pushed me but he didn't throw himself on me or shove me up against anything. He stayed there as if frozen in time.

Reyes   Delmira, Delmira, Delmira, where are you? Delmira, answer me. She never answers me when I call her. She's always somewhere else, which isn't here, even though she's at my side, she's somewhere else, she doesn't answer me. I woke up in the early hours and my hands were stained, my head split half open. But I got up and . . . everything had disappeared, I don't know. It must be a recurring nightmare. The bedroom in carnage as though a war had broken out. Delmira, are you looking at me now? No, don't come, I don't want you to, I'm ashamed, Delmira, I don't know what to do with what's happening to me. She showed me a gun. She showed it to me and ran away, damned whore. I can't think about these things, she is my love, the only one I can love. Don't go! I don't know why I think you will leave me one day, if you are the one I love most in this world. Come, even though you are dead, come.

Second Act

THE FAMILY
Towards Realism

Characters

Delmira
Reyes
Mother
Father
Brother
Maid-Stage Manager

The actors and actresses reassemble the space using the same elements that were there during the previous act. They try to reconstruct a dining room from the 1900s, but they never manage to do it. The **Maid-Stage Manager** *will tell them how they ought to behave and dress. The costumes which have been allocated in a disorganised, anachronistic way, and not according to relationships and gender, will now be distributed in line with era and character. Like a sergeant and her troops they change roles.*

SONG

    Come On! Let's Go!
    We must make order!
    Skirts for the women,
    trousers for the men,
    hair tied back,
    give yourselves names,
    we must make order.

    It should look like a real room.
    A table, a tablecloth, a vase.
    Somewhere to sit.
    Order.

    The women with make-up,
    the men with their hair slicked back,
    and listen, it's very important that Delmira's father has grey hair.
    We must reconstruct a realistic picture of the 1900s,
    and we must remember that a family functions through order,

and good theatre as well.
No hint of poetic fragments, strange things that nobody understands.
Eyes to the horizon, the fourth wall is imposed
and nobody here thinks of death.

Maid-Stage Manager   Very good. Character preparation. Delmira's character, step forward please. Delmira's character is going to perform Delmira's mannerisms. One, two, three, go.

Delmira *performs a gesture, the* **Maid-Stage Manager** *imitates her, this repeats.*

Maid-Stage Manager   Good, now another of Delmira's mannerisms, one, two, three, go. Write . . . "I die strangely, life doesn't kill me, death doesn't kill me." Delmira's mannerisms! One, two, three, go. Very good, very good. The Mother, Delmira's mother, step forward please. Very good. Madam, Delmira's mother was sturdier . . . sturdier . . . fat! Fat! Delmira Agustini's mother was fat. Good, the Mother's mannerisms. One, two, three, go.

The **Mother** *faints repeatedly until she lies on the floor unconscious.*

Maid-Stage Manager   Another, another mannerism for the Mother . . . Middle-class maladies . . . One, two, three, go! Madam, the Mother's mannerisms, mannerisms! One, two, three, go. Good. The Father. Delmira Agustini's father, a gentleman of the 1900s. Gather yourself, please, Sir. The Father's mannerisms, one, two, three, go!

The **Father** *performs a gesture, the* **Maid-Stage Manager** *imitates him.*

Maid-Stage Manager   Very good, very good. Another mannerism for the Father, one, two, three, go. And he says: "But it's always me who has to maintain order in this house!" Father's mannerisms, one two, three, go. Excellent! Excellent! The Brother.

The **Father** *picks the* **Mother** *up and carries her off.*

Maid-Stage Manager   The character of the Brother step forward please . . . Gather yourself, the Brother please, gather yourself.

Brother   But I don't know what to do.

Maid-Stage Manager   The Brother's mannerisms, one, two, three, go.

Brother   I don't have any mannerisms.

Maid-Stage Manager   He has a body-language, he must have a body-language, yes. The Brother's mannerisms, one, two, three, go.

The **Brother** *argues with the* **Father** *because he doesn't have any mannerisms.*

Maid-Stage Manager   Good, good, say, you say: "This notion of masculinity exasperates me; women are so privileged after all." Repeat . . . Good, off, off. Reyes! The character of Reyes please . . . In position . . .

Reyes *appears fleeing from* **Delmira**. **Delmira** *embraces him from behind, touches him, puts her hand down his trousers.*

Maid-Stage Manager Reyes' mannerisms, one, two, three, go . . .

Reyes *tries to conceal the fact* **Delmira** *is touching him.*

Maid-Stage Manager Very good, and say: "My love, I have brought you the photos from home, an anticipation of our happiness." Reyes' mannerisms . . .

The Maid-Stage Manager *realises that* **Delmira** *has her hand down* **Reyes'** *trousers and attempts to conceal them both from public view.*

Maid-Stage Manager The family, the family please! The whole family. Family in position. The family sits. Good. The Agustini family, Reyes, Maid-Stage Manager, second act.

Family photograph from the 1900s, in the living room of a house.

Mother Put that vase there, it looks much better. I don't know, cut flowers depress me a little, but they're necessary.

Father Why?

Mother A home with flowers has something more, people who know how to appreciate beauty.

Father I hadn't thought of that.

Mother We can have paintings of flowers.

Father Yes we can. Where's the girl?

Mother A young girl like her shouldn't get married. She marries, produces children, loses her looks. Sweetheart, fetch some flowers from the garden.

Brother Where does this go?

Maid-Stage Manager Over here.

Mother I don't know, it's all a disaster. It looks like an earthquake. Did people die?

Father People always die, people die everywhere. There are even people who die whilst still alive.

Mother It doesn't matter. Tidy your hair.

Delmira Yes.

Mother And change your clothes.

Delmira I have a foreboding.

Mother A foreboding of what?

Delmira / Maid-Stage Manager "I die strangely, life doesn't kill me, death doesn't kill me. . ."

Mother I slept a bit.

Delmira It's daytime.

Mother It doesn't matter. The sun does you good.

Brother I'm tired of all this.

Mother Hurry up.

Father I was asking where the girl is . . .

Mother She went into the garden for a while. I need fresh flowers, ah no, she went for a nap. We need to tidy up. We must put things in order.

Delmira Mother.

Mother What? Have a little lie down.

Delmira Mother!

Mother What?

Maid-Stage Manager Father, Father.

Delmira Nothing. Come here Father. Help me with this. No, Father, not you . . .

Father Sweetheart . . .

Brother Ah, and me?

Mother Wait, you're always in a hurry. Why are you in such a hurry?

Brother They're waiting for me.

Mother Who is waiting for you?

Brother My friends.

Mother And? What do you have to do out there that you can't do in here?

Brother I'm a man, Mother . . .

Mother Yes, I know. Go.

Brother No, now I want to see.

Father What do you want to see? You are so lacking in judgement! Men don't give up so easily.

Brother Nothing. I like the landscape of the home. There is so much written about the domestic setting, the tranquil gazes, women like shadows and us men giving orders. I have to be much more intelligent outside than in here, I circulate more freely in here. And anyway, this family is somewhat different.

Father How little you have inherited from me! Take control of your time, feminism hasn't arrived yet, how can you have these types of thoughts? Do you want to show me up? Let's see now who can tell me how to put things in order here . . . No, there's nobody. When one needs help one is always left alone in the middle of nowhere shouting like a raving lunatic. Does this go here? I don't know. Would someone like to tell me? Where do things go? Miss?

They try to reconstruct the room in the style of the 1900s, but elements are missing and there is no corresponding aesthetic. It's like a jigsaw puzzle with missing pieces.

Maid-Stage Manager   Good. Everything needs to be put in order. The tablecloth must go on the table, the flowers in the vase and the vase on the shelf. The family must sit at the table to eat. The plates must be piled high with tasteful food and the women must keep their legs shut until marriage. Clothes must be ironed, the rumours about the wardrobe should be correct. Posture must be rigid, conversation must be agreeable, and people should speak dialogue that is coherent and not in poetic fragments. The setting must seem as real as life itself in 1900. It's important that the room should be well lit in order to make out detail. We need to reconstruct the picture; we need to make an effort. Dialogue needs to be appropriate. We must keep calm and remember that families function best with order and good theatre as well. The bullet, the bullets are not here at the moment. Nobody is thinking about that. Let's continue please.

Father   You are not answering my question, Miss. That's to say I ask you one thing, and you give me a hundred answers. How does one do a reconstruction? Does it go slowly, quickly, does one speak or is it done in silence? Is there an archaeology of memory, a museum of poetry, a theatre of the lost? What a load of academic claptrap! We are trying to put the family in order here and it's pure anarchy. Starting with you . . . (*He looks at the* **Mother**.) That bovine appearance of yours, go to the countryside and they'd mistake you for the first cow that wanders into view. Such a loss of elegance, there's nothing to be done.

Mother   Let's take a look at the original photo. We've been whizzing about like tops in a storm for a while now. Nobody knows anything. We'll have an attack of poetry and that'll be the end of realism. We need to put the table back where it goes, the food on the table, have everyone sitting at the table, let those who have something to say speak, everyone else should be quiet and we ladies will listen as corresponds to our status. That girl (*she points to the* **Maid-Stage Manager**) who is in charge of organising the realism of 1900 needs to bring us the information and feed us our lines at the right moment and in a way that is in keeping with her role. Otherwise we'll anticipate revolution and it's not time for her to rise up against the bosses yet. What's more she's so ignorant she doesn't know her own rights and worries more about ours . . .

The **Mother** *faints.*

Delmira   And me, Mother?

Mother   You, write, take advantage of the silence that the social order imposes upon you and write. Look, despite everything, you have benefitted, you have a huge advantage, because it's not an easy task to walk around weighed down by ideological speeches, playing the simpleton is much more advantageous. You're no danger to anyone, make the most of it, child, make the most of it. Think about the benefits of silence, the possibilities for introspection, it's stupendous, it's a strategy that shouldn't be lost through strange, modern ideas. Keep on with the silence.

Brother That's exactly what I was saying. Keep on with the silence. You who can, those of you who can, the women. Nobody demands that you should be intelligent. Not like us men. We have to walk around the whole time, demonstrating mental acumen, verbal acumen. That's why masculinity exasperates me.

Mother / Father In short, what are we reconstructing? The room, the house of the married couple or the parents' house?

Maid-Stage Manager We must reconstruct a house from the 1900s in Montevideo. The room where the family spend most of their time together. Where they eat and receive visitors. And listen . . . listen . . . because it's also the place where Delmira is seen with that faraway look in her eyes, enraptured by who knows what. The family is organised and very well-mannered. We can look at this photo for example.

Brother That's not us.

Maid-Stage Manager We can look at the photo. The flowers always go on the sideboard with the porcelain figures. And sometimes, due to carelessness, there are petals on the floor. A poetic carelessness, of course. Let's continue please.

Mother I don't understand. Why can't you just explain everything? Be more detailed and more precise. That way you'll fulfil both your roles.

Brother I understand nothing. There is no sideboard, there are no petals nor anything else here.

Maid-Stage Manager There will be no explanations for now. For now you each need to take charge of your mannerisms. The way we do this has been established. For example, family: Delmira's mannerisms. One, two, three. Now.

They all make the same gesture.

Maid-Stage Manager Weak, weak . . . Mannerisms for a father from the 1900s in Montevideo. Delmira's father's mannerisms: Mr Agustini. One, two, three, go.

They all make the same gesture.

Maid-Stage Manager Weak, weak, weak. Mannerisms for the whole family. Greetings, social attitudes. Ladies and gentlemen. Intimacy is not on display; those things are not written. First the outward appearance of the family is reconstructed, the image they convey. Then the inner life of the family is reconstructed. And, lastly, the inner life of each family member. Temperament and behaviour. Let's continue please.

Brother You're such an idiot.

Maid-Stage Manager You, why are you insulting me like that?

Brother Idiot no, stupid, stupid, stupid, stupid woman, like all of them . . . Stupid, silly little woman, knows nothing, has an opinion, and knows nothing, go outside into the street and get acquainted with how, where and why things happen and then come back and tell us how we should behave.

Maid-Stage Manager   Two! Two, ladies and gentlemen! Two instances of attempted rape. Do you know what you are? An embittered failure and a dead cat. A dead cat!

Brother   Oh, the poor little thing, the typical victim of capitalism and exploitation. She's waiting for the Marxists to come and liberate her. Well they'd better come quickly, before they forget about her.

Maid-Stage Manager   I can anticipate history and reveal facts.

Brother   I'm trembling, shaken by an earthquake! Beware the anticipation of ideology. This house is brimming with anticipation!

Delmira   This reconstruction of a life we're doing is complete shit!

Mother   Be quiet.

Brother   I won't be quiet. Why should I be quiet? Do you have all the speeches? Are you the only one assigned to say what's new, to reveal mysteries?

Mother   What are you talking about? I said be quiet to your sister, not you.

Brother   Ah, sorry, Mother.

Maid-Stage Manager   Embittered, failure, dead cat. Dead cat!

Brother   Ahhhh, such verbal audacity. That's not in the reconstruction, off, off, off, bitch, off.

Father   Enough! Each person knows what they have to do. So just do it. So much discussion! Talking is overrated. To your tasks. Immediately.

Brother   It's the music, Daddio.

Father   Daddio, no. Don't speak to me like that.

Brother   Am I disrespecting you? Sorry.

Father   This isn't my son. You are not my son. You don't resemble my son in the slightest. No, my son wouldn't speak like that. My son wouldn't speak like that, and he wouldn't wear those clothes. Not that gesture nor that behaviour nor that way of speaking. My son is a gentleman with verbal acumen. Get out of my sight, I am waiting for my son. You're not fit to wipe the shoes on his feet. Aren't you ashamed that the star of this house is your sister Delmira?

Brother   Ah, and what's he like? You who know everything and know nothing about me. What do you know about Delmira's brother, your son? What's he like?

Father   He wears a different shirt, he sits differently, he's accepting, he has an ease of movement, his way of going through the door, his way of sitting in the chair and looking out of the window. When my son enters a room, everything lights up. When you enter, everything goes dark. How he grips the fork before plunging it into the meat. Authentic, discerning, purebred. An alpha male, a product of his genes and of his country.

Maid-Stage Manager   Embittered, a failure, a dead cat.

Father No a forgotten faggot who doesn't even know how to treat women. An affront to biology.

Brother Ah. Whose biology?

Father My daughter your sister Delmira's. Look at her. And be quiet, I would like a little bit of decency, a little bit of intelligence in this house. Listen everyone. Look at this photo. The family does not smile. Nobody smiles in that era, that's the context. Basic stuff. It's always me who has to stay on top of everything. I don't know what would become of this family without my constant vigilance. And you, behave yourself for once.

Mother Are we going to continue reorganising?

Delmira And could we have a little bit of silence?

Brother Why?

Delmira To listen for the things that are missing . . . Now is not a time of happiness, not the hour nor the moment. Happiness comes later. Happiness does not always bring happiness, sometimes it brings misfortune. We are standing at the river's edge waiting for another place in history, but it won't be because of country, because of continent or because of gender. Nobody will be transcendent. There is no need to hurry or to worry. That's for the losers. We are more foolish than the losers and the orphans. It doesn't suit us to laugh. It distracts us. We need to concentrate on the concrete image of a concrete family that is waiting for something to happen or is hoping that something will happen. That faraway look they say I have, is, in reality, the concentration needed for the photo not to freeze us into a moment of opportunistic comedy. We must anticipate a heavenly melancholy. We can see progress. We can smell it, the flesh in repose brings the scent of politics, the scent of revolution. No need to get ahead of ourselves.

Reyes Delmira. I have brought the photos from home. The images of the house. I have them here. For you. They are anticipations, my love.

Delmira Anticipations of what? Everyone here talks of anticipations. It's an abuse of language.

Reyes They are anticipations of happiness.

Delmira The only anticipations that exist are the verses yet to come.

Reyes Look. I brought these photos . . . Flowers! I brought you flowers.

Reyes *gives an empty vase to* **Delmira**.

Delmira No.

Reyes I won't auction off anything you don't want me to.

Delmira This conversation doesn't interest me.

Reyes Why?

Delmira Don't say anything.

Reyes But you like these things.

Delmira I like silence.

Reyes You are my little creature.

Delmira I wanted to be your fire, and you turn me into a pet rabbit.

Delmira *tries to jump on* **Reyes**, *but he flees. As they run around the stage, the* **Father**, **Mother** *and* **Brother** *read and pretend to ignore them. The* **Maid-Stage Manager** *tries to keep calm.*

Reyes Not now, Delmira, not now.

Delmira Not now, when then? No-one can hear us. You are the cause of my nocturnal afflictions. I can't talk. I have a knot that grows and strangles me. Why don't you kidnap me and carry me far away? You are a miserable, dogmatic Catholic.

Reyes One cannot, one cannot do what one cannot do, you . . .

Delmira You see nothing beyond the act of raising and lowering your eyes, the brow, the morals that oppress us.

Reyes Enough, Delmira.

Delmira You're a weak man. Men are strong and provide for women. In all senses of the word.

Reyes In all?

Delmira In life and in death.

Reyes I offer you everything.

Delmira What death can you offer me? Say it once and for all. Speak, use that tongue, and give a speech to the family, something lovely. It's time for the bridegroom to shine. If not now, then when? When do you think you might shine?

Reyes It's not appropriate.

Delmira You are not appropriate for me.

Maid-Stage Manager Family . . . Family . . .

Reyes Family, we have some news for you. Lovely news. Delmira and I are very happy. We are going to get married.

Delmira Because we have no choice, because if it were up to me we would just go to bed and have done with it. I always pictured riding naked with you through the countryside, but you only have hands for that gavel that rises and falls, the only part of your body that does rise and fall, Mr Auctioneer. But as you love anticipations, I'm going to anticipate something for you: before getting married I will change my mind. Even so I will say yes, and afterwards I will write about it, but we haven't got to that part yet . . .

Mother That's enough, too much chat, let's have a little something to eat.

Delmira There's nothing to eat, Mother.

Mother Well, let's cook. Delmira, prepare something.

Delmira I don't know how to prepare anything, Mother.

Mother How you like to improvise. What a nightmare. A poet doesn't walk around scattering flowers. A poet wears flowers on their chest.

Brother Do you know something? I could also be someone's husband, but here I am waiting for somebody to pass my window so that I can say I love you and that I can be a good husband. Oh but no. In this house everything is upside down.

Father Not one of you can just sit in the right place and say the right words. Could that happen just once in the life of this family?

Mother We have to reorder everything from the beginning. We'll begin. Let's begin.
Good day.
Good day.
Good day.
Good day.

Delmira I don't live; I write. You live, you get up and have breakfast. You get up, get dressed, you make the accustomed movements for getting dressed. The expected movements. You live because the body ordains and commands it and you make decisions for just a few minutes every day. I wait for those minutes anxiously from the moment I arise. I don't wait for anything else. They see me, but they don't know who I am. Not even when they read me . . . You live and in life people cross your path.

SONG

>   I look
>   I walk
>   I eat
>   I sleep
>   and nothing happens then.
>   Life happens and I do not choose how to live.
>   I push against the hours,
>   the hours.
>   You live and let some things in.
>   I open the door, I look at the afternoon,
>   I walk in the garden; I go back to my single bed.
>   The bed that swallows me night after night,
>   afterwards comes the double bed.
>   Life isn't lived. Life lives us.

Father After greeting each other, we sit down to breakfast. Now comes your remark about the flowers and Delmira goes to fetch some from the garden. Our son talks like a Chekhovian character wandering about among ghosts . . . He wanted to be a writer, but genetics betrayed him.

Brother I never wanted to be a writer.

Father Shut your trap, nobody cares, you understand nothing. What's important is knowing that we are constructing society from this point onwards, we are advancing towards the future, progress begins here. You can smell it. Come on, make the effort with me. Progress begins with the family. Decline is upon us; women are meant to care for the family and bring up children. I say this now: if we don't control it we face chaos; God help us all. Let us pray. Now Reyes will start. His turn. Make yourself at home.

Reyes I see you here. Here, sitting by my side. I see you here. Here, in our little nest. I see you here. I see you there. There with me, I see you with me. Always and forever.

Delmira Always, yes, forever near-sightedly, nothing further than the horizon. Never an untrammelled sightedness, an exaggerated sightedness. No, nothing, nobody, the steppe, the arid land that is not our land, well, he brings it all closer with his poverty of expression.

Reyes Don't forget that I'm here . . .

Delmira Be aware that you are not here, just for once in your life, contribute something that isn't an excess of realism. Contribute, be still and contribute.

Reyes I don't understand what you want, Delmira.

Delmira I want, very simply, for you to be still and to contribute something that isn't about living out the wretched daily routine. Contribute, be silent, I'm talking about you. I'm criticising you, in front of you, I'm conversing with my father, with my mother, you realise that you are not here, that you're not listening, or you are listening, and you don't care. I'm giving you three options, choose.

Reyes I choose not to listen. I will think about other things. I will choose some beautiful images. One that I saw one afternoon at the auction house. Another from a painting.

Delmira That is your inner world. You don't have to tell me everything, life isn't like that, each person has their own private life, relationships don't cross over, nobody mixes them up or travels from one to the other. I make a complete distinction between each relationship, each thing I that have, there's no need to give details. For once, just for once you could accept this situation, accept it, and live it, or act it.

Reyes I act it.

Delmira And what is the difference between living it and acting it?

Reyes I invent something that I don't feel, and I show it on my face.

Delmira You're a young lady then.

Reyes No, I'm an actor who's playing the part of Reyes at the moment he realises that he doesn't listen when Delmira criticises him.

Delmira You're getting worse.

Reyes No.

Delmira You haven't got the aptitude, gender or talent needed to act.

Reyes I act, yes, I act.

Delmira Are you trying to steal my limelight? I act socially.

Reyes You don't talk, which is different.

Delmira I don't talk to you.

Mother Well, we'll start again, you need to go off and then come back after a moment.

Reyes I'll look as though I'm not listening, or something, or I don't see, I don't hear.

Mother Then we'll do the same as before and criticise you.

Delmira But you can't move or do anything.

Reyes Alright, I won't do anything.

Reyes Did you hear that?

Brother *and* **Father** Yes. *bang, bang*, long pause, and *bang*.

Reyes *Bang, bang*, long pause and another *bang*, silence.

Mother They're coming from the heavens. My God, it's a disaster.

Father You don't say it like that. It's a foreboding. But in this house there's no room for tragedies. Now we'll have a drink and listen to music.

Brother We've just had breakfast. How come we're already going to have a drink?

Father Do I have to explain it all to you again? We started, we stopped, we went back and when we resumed we went forwards. Realism is like that. It plays with our emotions. Life outside continues and we are trying to reconstruct this disaster. It's as though someone has gone crazy outside of time. It's not about madness or the disaster of the tragedy, it's about a bedroom in carnage and the bodies inside it. How can you rebuild a life after that? Is there room for anything after that? We need to put things in order, because if we don't, we can understand nothing. We need to put the pieces together. It's a way of mitigating the pain. There will be no answers, but the actions will deceive the heart.

Reyes Of course, I can hear the church bells. We're about to get married.

Father Don't be so negative. Open your eyes a little, we have set the scene for you, and we all are complicit in the unfolding disaster. Idiots all of us. Reyes isn't the only imbecile in this story.

Mother What are you talking about? I'm not responsible for what's coming, for what happened, I can't know anything, I don't see anything.

Father Exactly, you wouldn't see an elephant in front of your nose. You are not in the habit of seeing, you are in the habit of finding solutions, like all mothers. But we could have avoided it.

Mother What?

Brother What?

Father You could have avoided making disagreeable remarks about motherhood and what to do so as not to have children.

Mother You're getting ahead of yourself again.

Father Because I'm the only visionary in this house, the only one who anticipates tragedies, but nobody, nobody, nobody in this house pays me any heed. Everyone is in a state of inertia, lacking in anger. Anger being the masculine marker and hysteria the feminine one. Have some self-awareness. Remember the education you gave your daughter, you, and your middle-class maladies, never reacting appropriately and therefore what has to happen happens, what the heavens anticipate, and nobody wants to see: the tragedy.

Brother Father is right.

Father Shut your trap, I'm not talking to you. I'm talking for the world, for those who are raising children now and don't know what to do, I speak for those little ones.

Mother Stop getting worked up, you also agreed that Delmira couldn't have children. Don't blame me.

Father When it happens, when you speak, when it occurs, when there is no way back, you will come crawling, beating your chest, bleeding from the knees, and I will be sitting there, waiting for you in order to say: "I told you so."

Reyes Delmira, you make me nervous.

Delmira Dogs obey.

Reyes When we get married, Delmira, when we get married as God intended.

Delmira Take me away, don't leave me in this normality. Save me, Reyes, save me. If you love me, save me. Someone save me!

Reyes Conduct yourself like a young lady, I have to go, let go of me, let go of me, Delmira, You mustn't behave like that. You are in your parents' house.

Delmira You say that to me now, but in time you will beg me, you will drag yourself across the city. Like a puppy you will come, licking at my heels, pawing at my skirt, at my non-surrender, my non-opening, my non-silence . . . You will come, Reyes, with your blood inflamed, looking for blood. You will come like the wind on Andes Street, with blood in your retinas, like hunters with their prey reflected in their irises, there I will be, your little pet rabbit, your sweet little girl, waiting for you as a lover, not as a wife, you will come as a man not as a husband, to fulfil your role in bed, which is where men should fulfil women, without worrying about papers or weddings or rings or photos. And if you don't know how to fulfil that role then the whole city will know how little a man you are for this Delmira on fire. "There is no tornado more intense than a night without bed, and a bed without a man who makes you understand why you were born."

Reyes *destroys some of her papers.*

Delmira No! Those are my originals. No! You are killing me!

Reyes Do you want me to kill you? I really am going to kill you. Spell it out, one thing at a time, I am sure I can bring it home to you.

Delmira It's my life. It's my life. It's my life.

Reyes Look, I didn't know that you were pulsating. Always dead in life. You are going to be dead in death. Not this shitty life you live, that you lived with me, that you filled with death for me. I gave you my love, and you, unmoving, absent, without giving me even so much as a moan, a sound, something, even if it was of pain.

Delmira Calm down. Things are as they are. Calm down, please, calm down. My body yes, my papers no. Don't touch my papers, do what you like with me, do it to this body, here, look at me . . . I am nobody, do what you like, but my papers no. I am drowning, Reyes, Reyes.

Reyes Why aren't you normal, like everyone else? All women want the same things and do the same things to get what they want. They seduce men, they make themselves beautiful to have a husband and afterwards, afterwards, and listen to what I'm saying, their point of interest is the husband, the house, the family. What makes you different to other women? Do you think you're superior? Delmira Agustini is better than all the mortal women in the world? Better than me? Do you think that? Stop snivelling like a sparrow, you are not some mystic with the air of a captive Russian princess. You are here, with me, you write me letters, you tell me that you love me, that life makes no sense if I'm not in your arms. What are these things, words? Are they just rehearsals to see if you can write better? Are you rehearsing with me? Did you fall in love in order to write better?

Delmira What should I explain to you? You're a repressed individual, you're not even primitive, you lost. That's the difference between you and me.

Reyes You are incapable of giving life.

Delmira Ah, of course, because the only way I'm capable of giving life is through motherhood, the other lives that come out of me mean nothing.

Reyes What lives?

Delmira Stupid and vulgar.

Reyes Me?

Delmira More vulgar than stupid.

Reyes Do you want to see the acts of vulgarity in all their splendour?

Delmira Yes, I do, show me.

Reyes Is there anything more vulgar than being a Uruguayan woman?

Delmira Yes, being the wife of a Uruguayan man.

Reyes And what do you expect of your beloved nation?

Delmira Except for the flesh and the organs, there is no difference between men and women, so why do men have rights that women don't?

Reyes I thought you were more intelligent than that but you're a just a silly little woman . . . the same as all of them: sentimental, displaying emotion towards people and things. Life is practical and the realm of men.

Delmira Impotent.

Delmira *hits him without stopping, she grabs his crotch,* **Reyes** *does not defend himself.*

Delmira Useless lump of flesh.

Reyes You are nobody, you will never be anyone, history won't remember you, nobody will read you, people spoil you because you're a pretty young lady who's entertaining, they find you charming, nothing more.

Delmira *collapses, cries.*

Delmira I can't, I can't, I don't choose, it isn't my will, it's my destiny. Writing chooses me, it isn't my will, it's my destiny. Destiny entered into me, took over my body and I live to write. I am nobody, nobody, nobody, lost in the last word, in the last step I make so that the poem permits me, I am nobody, nobody, nobody until I write a phrase a day, before that I wander about in fragile thoughts, unfinished, and I see you, I need to see you, I need to stand there with my heart beating fast when you are near me and you look at me, you touch me and I realise again that I have a body that lives for these things. Don't leave me. I love you. I love you with all my heart.

Reyes My love, I will never leave you, never, never, never, never. I can repeat it until infinity, until exhaustion sets in. I don't know what infinity is. Will there be something after the end? Together, without anybody telling us what is good or bad.

SONG

> I can get to my feet now,
> with blood dripping from my eyes when I see you,
> dripping from my fingers,
> nothing can freeze,
> no heat can resist.
> I get to my feet, look I'm on my feet,
> I bleed and I'm on my feet.

Kneeling and on my feet.
Stupid, uncultured, clumsy, and loving you on my feet.
Bleeding and shot.
On my feet.
Step by step
with details.
Like making an inventory.
That's it, an inventory.
And I will auction it all off.
The high gavel comes down on the wood.
Wham.
That's it, a blow, then another and another,
Like the bullets, *bang, bang, bang.*
The gavel blows, before or after?
After the death will come other deaths.
Until everything ends.

Third Act

THE DELMIRA LOT

Hyperrealism

Characters

Female Office Worker
Male Office Worker
Policeman One
Policeman Two
Female Journalist One
Female Journalist Two

The auction begins. Clothes, belongings, furniture and other objects are placed with their corresponding labels. The actors wear contemporary street clothes. They perform as though they were giving testimonials to camera. The fourth wall is broken. General lighting state.

All During the month of July 2010, at a well-known auction house in the Old Town, an auctioneer presents the Delmira Lot. The event proceeds completely unnoticed. At that time Montevideo is living through the intensity of the football World Cup. There is nothing in the press, nobody is aware of it. Not the public institutions nor the custodians of national heritage. We six were the privileged ones who could attend the auction and acquire some of the objects, among them the gun with which Reyes shot Delmira, the correspondence between Delmira and Manuel Ugarte, a personal diary and a recording with a confession. What stays in my mind though is not only the image of the auctioneer's gavel hitting the wood, but also the constant cry of "What am I bid, what am I bid, what am I bid?", "How much for the last writings of the poetess, what am I bid, what am I bid?", "How much for the blood-stained slip, how much for the family furniture?" To this day no-one knows what happened to the rest of the belongings, the things that people weren't interested in. Here are our testimonies, third act.

Female Office Worker In 2010 we went to an auction in the Old Town. We weren't looking for anything in particular. We like auctions and every so often we go. As spectators. I don't know why, but I really like that moment when the auctioneer brings down the gavel and concludes the bid. My blood pressure goes up, I don't know, it gives me a thrill, I love it. It's something that doesn't happen to me with other things. Actually, I go quite often, not looking for anything, just to experience that moment, and I try to not make myself obvious or not to be noticed. I don't want anybody else to see my excitement either. It embarrasses me, but I can't help it and each time I experience it more intensely. One day I invited him saying there was something that would interest us both. I lied. Or rather I lied about that in particular. We went and it was at that auction that the auctioneer suddenly suspends the action, pauses, and says: "Well, we have something exceptional here. It is part of what is listed as the Delmira Lot." In it were various things of hers, but one of them really grabbed our attention and the auctioneer goes on: "It's an old recording, well, from quite a few years ago. There's a confession from the woman who rented out the apartment where Reyes killed Delmira." It turns out that this woman told her daughter once that she knew everything and one day the daughter decided to record her. Actually the recording is the daughter's not the woman's. It's a recording from the 70s.

Male Office Worker And I thought she had brought me there for that. So I made a bid, and I bought it. On the way home we didn't say anything. We were silent. We got back and had supper without saying a word. The tape recorder remained untouched. We couldn't bring ourselves to listen to it.

Female Office Worker The days passed, and we just moved it around the place. One day I decided to put it in my handbag. I said to him, "Let's go", and we went out together. We stopped at 1206 Andes Street and there we sat, by the building, on the pavement and we listened to it for the first time.

The following text is heard as a recording.

Recorded Voice We rented the apartment to Reyes; he was our friend. At first he didn't say anything to us, and we didn't ask either, he was a recently separated man. We thought he would use it for his man's business, poor thing. He looked very sad, very subdued, he was so happy with his marriage, poor thing, it lasted such a short time. The rumour going around was that he couldn't perform as a man and that she, resentful, had left him. So, if he was renting to be with a woman, it seemed quite alright to us. His honour was tarnished. How could he find a bride with that stain on his character? A man who can't perform is considered a poof by everyone. He would just lower his gaze, squeeze the edge of his jacket, it was very wrinkled, and murmur softly: "I love her more than I love myself."

One night my husband invited him in for a few drinks and he started to cry. He didn't stop for hours. The poor thing didn't say a word. My husband asked him what had provoked the rumour, and he left. He never answered us.

That's why, the thought that he might be with someone was also for us a way to help him and to start the rumour, true this time: Enrique Reyes is very manly and knows how to satisfy women.

The first time that an encounter took place for definite, we didn't know who she was, but the third time we were astounded to see that she was his wife, well, his ex. We became a bit more stand-offish after that. We started to get the feeling that this wasn't going to end well.

Policeman One *and* **Policeman Two** (*text divided between them both*) We didn't know who Delmira was. Well actually, we did know something, but we weren't steeped in her personal history. I had read one of her poems in high school, but nothing more than that, and knew that her husband had killed her. Well, her ex. We love auctions. People's memories are contained in the objects that marked their lives.

But that was a special day. It was in 2010 at a well-known auction in the Old Town. We don't always go, but we're regular customers, they know us and there's an auctioneer friend who calls us every so often to tell us about things that might interest us. He called us and told us: "There's a gem. A Delmira Lot and in it is the gun with which Reyes killed his ex-wife: Delmira Agustini."

We didn't believe it, but we went just the same. It was winter and we happened to be off that day, so we took advantage. The auctioneer was there. We ended up with the gun. Since that day, we've made an in-depth study of her story.

What's more we found out where Reyes bought the gun, what the day was like. Winter, sunny.

He bought the gun the day after she abandoned the house they both shared. But he used it a year later. He hesitated. We like that detail. It makes us think about all the times he would have had it in his hand before using it. We like to try and picture him. Sitting on the bed, semi-naked wearing a white shirt, braces dangling, with the gun, cleaning it. Yes, that image is the one we like most. It seems that after the murder it lay abandoned for a while at the police station. Nobody claimed it. Until his sister came and took it away.

It's not known how it ended up in the Delmira Lot.

I don't see it as strange or wrong. Every family has their own way of recounting their stories. My great-grandfather, my grandfather and my father were all police officers. We would like to create a department within the institute that houses these kinds of objects that tell a story. Objects that tell violent stories that is. It wouldn't be a museum or anything like that, but it might change the stereotyped view people have of us. There's a few of us trying to make it happen. We're very excited about the idea.

Female Journalist One *and* **Female Journalist Two** *(they have correspondence, photos, poems, press-cuttings, the personal diary)*   The lot is called "personal items". They are letters, the diary, some unpublished poems. I came because of my own personal research into these materials. I'm a journalist. We are journalists. I have been working for five years on the profile of the female artist as an historical precursor to feminism. We are centring on Delmira. We have developed our own way of looking at the history of women free from the gaze of the male writer. As well as the well-known letter written by Delmira to Manuel Ugarte, which is also published, we found some unpublished correspondence between the two of them. We shall read these letters out to you.

Letter from Delmira to Ugarte:

"Do you think that those two words, that I could wittingly say to you the day after meeting you, should have died on my lips, if not in my soul? To be completely truthful, I had to say them; I had to tell you that you made my wedding night and my absurd honeymoon a torment. What could have been a long humorous novel was turned into a tragedy. What I suffered that night, I can never, ever tell you. I entered the living room as though it were a sepulchre the only comfort being that of thinking I

would see you. Whilst they were dressing me I cannot tell you how many times I asked if you had arrived. I could describe to you all of my mannerisms from that night. The only gaze I was conscious of, the only inopportune greeting I gave, both were for you. I had a lightning-flash of happiness. It seemed to me for a moment that you were looking at me and that you understood me. That your spirit was right beside mine in the midst of all those awful people. Afterwards, in-between kisses and greetings, the only thing I hoped for was your hand. The only thing I desired was to have you close for a moment. The moment of the photograph. And afterwards to suffer, to suffer until I said goodbye to you. And after that to suffer more, to suffer the unspeakable.
Me, Her, and The Girl."

"My Dearest Delmira:
Only the angels and the infernos that inhabit me know the true suffering that I endured on the night of your wedding. That night where you were the only moon, with that wolf that gazed at you from the depths, lurking. Let me profess to you, on my knees, my admiration, a bold brave woman is a rarity in this country plagued by young ladies who only value complacency. You come from another world to light up mine. Do not stop, not for me, not for anyone, even though you might have to tread on my bones, do it, shun piety and seize life, of my life I have no need to tell you, because I am already in your hands and between your legs.
Manuel Ugarte."

"My Dearest Manuel:
If tragedy should come upon me unexpectedly. I want to be remembered in the manner of common people who circulate and live according to their impulses. I do not want pedestals, or windowpanes, or books, or studies, or critiques. I want to be in a garden by the sea, with the wind blowing so that the pages of the book are always open, as my legs have been with nobody between them.
Your Little Girl."

"My Dearest Delmira:
I will personally take charge of fulfilling all your wishes, even after we are taken to the great hereafter. I shall leave testaments on all continents so that your will may be respected. Nobody shall ever leave you in a place far from the daily conflicts that signify what it is to love and to hope. Life should always be messy and never ordered as though it were a notebook. Do not worry, you are in my hands.
Manuel Ugarte."

"My Eternal Manuel:
There are no roses after the thorns. Just thorns in the heart and in my eyes that cannot see you. Where are you? Leave everything and come to me. There is no time, God will come and not let me see you, touch you or smell you. And you cannot see me, penetrate me, or have me. I do not hold on to your perfume, it has gone and abandoned me with the thorns. Nobody could conceive of this fire that consumes me when you are not inside me. Swim across the river. I will be your port.

Your Little Girl."

"My Dearest Delmira:
I promise as a citizen, as a patriot, as a South American and as a revolutionary, that on the 8th of July I will be there inside you.
Yours always,
Manuel Ugarte."

We have taken a decision that may not be seen favourably by this country's institutions: we are not thinking of officially depositing these documents. We have a position in regards to this and we consider that these types of materials need a place of poetry that has its own dynamic, which re-signifies the work and places it in dialogue with the here and now, inviting people not only to become familiar with it, but also to reflect on the role of art. An artist like Delmira cannot be encapsulated within a bureaucratic setting. That would be anti-poetical. The institutional format insults the revolutionary ideal. The first revolution was in poetry.

SONG

There are wars that are just for one person.
The bullet crossed the city
crossed the sky
like a whip of fire.
It entered.
The bullet returned and killed me once more;
two shots, Reyes fired two shots at me.
I am Delmira.
Delmira Agustini.
That gunned-down woman is me.
That woman I see, and you see,
that the press saw, the police saw,
that my parents saw,
that history saw.
That same woman is me.
Delmira.
The dead woman.
The murdered, murdered,
murdered woman.

END

Emotional Terror

Josefina Trías

Translated by Sophie Stevens

Terrorismo emocional (*Emotional Terror*) premiered on 4 May 2018 at the Teatro Alianza, Montevideo. It was directed by Bruno Contenti and performed by Josefina Trías. The play was published by Salvadora Editora in 2020.

About the author and translator

Josefina Trías is an actor and playwright. She trained as an actor at the Instituto de Actuación de Montevideo (Montevideo Institute of Acting) and has performed in more than 25 plays. She is Programme Manager of the Las Piedras Cultural Centre in Comuna Canaria. Her play *Terrorismo emocional* (*Emotional Terror*) has had over 124 performances in Uruguay, Argentina, and Chile. In 2020, the script won the Uruguayan Ministry of Education and Culture National Literature Award. In 2018, she received the Florencio Award for Best Solo Performance for her role as the protagonist, Clara. In 2021, she premiered *Llamaste a Walter* (*You Called Walter*), a prequel to *Terrorismo emocional* which won third prize in the 2022 Uruguayan Ministry of Education and Culture National Literature Awards. Her work as a screenwriter includes the short film *El mundo se ha terminado* (*The World Has Ended*) supported by the audiovisual production fund of the Instituto Nacional de Artes Escénicas (National Performing Arts Institute), *Tiempo de Amigas* (*Time for Friends*) and, as co-writer, the second season of *Encierro Demente* (*Crazy Lockdown*).

Sophie Stevens is Lecturer in Latin American and Caribbean Studies at the Institute of Languages, Cultures and Societies, University of London, where she specialises in Latin American theatre, performance, activism and translation. She has previously worked at the University of East Anglia in collaboration with the British Centre for Literary Translation, where she held a prestigious Leverhulme Fellowship, and King's College London where she also completed her PhD. Her book *Uruguayan Theatre in Translation: Theory and Practice* was published in 2022 by Legenda and includes three stage-ready translations alongside chapters of analysis. Her translations have been published by *The Mercurian: A Theatrical Translation Review* and Inti Press. She is a member of the Ibero-American theatre and translation collective, Out of the Wings, and her translations have been presented in London at the Royal Court Theatre (2024), Barons Court Theatre (2022, 2023, 2024), Omnibus Theatre (2019, 2021, 2022, 2023), Cervantes Theatre (2017) and Southwark Playhouse (2017).

For my mother and father.

Characters

Clara, *f*
Dad

The character of **Dad** *does not appear on stage. His voice is heard at certain points in the play, either as a recording during a phone call or when Clara is impersonating him.*

Waiting

Clara *is in her room. She writes.*

Clara Words were everything to us, so I think it's only fitting to end this in writing.
This email isn't a contract for you to sign.
If you're going to walk out of my life today, I just need to feel I did everything I could.
This is our story.
Day one
we talked about books
obviously
some American writer whose name began with H
I wish I could remember who.
I knew as soon as I got on the bus.
The second, third day, just the same
meeting at the same place at the same time, but without arranging it
meeting, as if it were a sentence
as if to test it somehow
or as it said on that magnet I ended up with:
Meeting to get to know one another.
To start everything.
Your trip
emails
full of lines from Cabrera's songs
your return
your presents
you came to meet me at uni
you picked me up
as if I was light as a feather
it was a bit awkward.
Ice creams at the station
a kiss, not yet
take it slowly
I got on the bus and read your first letter.
Then that was it
first official date
and from that moment onwards, the world was at our feet
that's how it feels.
Do you know what that's like?
To have the world at your feet?
To start to really understand who you are
who I am with you
just where I should be.
Creating our own language
a secret code
creating a bubble

a bubble which will never burst.
Acting like tourists in our own city
spending our money on going out as if it were cheap
as if money multiplied in our pockets
talking about films but never agreeing
sending a text to say I love you
smiling constantly
expanding our worlds
meeting our families
learning about our differences
secret nights away
studying all night
living life like a glowing zombie
sending each other lines from Cerati's songs.
Staying at yours four nights a week
moving in together
our two moves
our non-sexy nicknames
a notebook with Klimt on the cover that you bought me in Buenos Aires
your handwriting in block letters
googling how to revive a petunia
holding one another in the sweltering summer heat
arguing over air conditioning or a fan
because you always were the best pillow
your smell
spending the weekends in our pyjamas
your singing out loud for no-one.
Push the hot water bottle over to my side when I come back late at night.
Cherries frozen in the fridge
the one joint we smoked and your kisses felt like suction
your moments in front of the mirror
being naked together.
My love for Idea Vilariño's verses.
Your love for Juan Carlos Onetti's writing.
Your exceptional reviews of plays you don't want to see.
The photo on the fridge from our trip to the beach at El Pinar
texting poems to one another
holding up notes to the bus window for each other
writing about you.

SUMMER

It's Over

Clara   They say you always know
the exact moment when you pronounce the word "death" and then everything
becomes clear.
I never knew
I never knew when "we" ceased to exist
I never knew.
I don't know.
Are you still here?
Are you coming back?
Sometimes I feel like you'll come walking through that door at any moment now
because, well, you are here
you're like Hamlet's father.
Not a day goes by without my mum mentioning you or missing you
or my dad lovingly insulting you (and missing you).
Both of them invoke you
everyone invokes you
we invoke you.

It happens to some people, doesn't it?
Getting back together after a time apart.

The same people but also not.
Somehow, they get over being so stupid
somehow, they get over being so broken and bruised
because that's why we break up
why couples separate
there's no other reason apart from the fact that
we are so lost
that we'd rather go through all that again.
It's exhausting.
I just want a blowout
to meet someone
hold back the hysteria
mine and theirs
wait for him to make up his mind
make up our minds
fall in love
grow jealous
to end up suffering again
and end it again

instead of leaving, you rebuild everything again with the love of your life and you are happy.

Rebuilding is tiring.

Pause.

So is being happy.

Pause.

That goal ruins our lives.
Happiness.
As if life were just like a Coca-Cola advert
one where some young, freckly, red-haired kids are on a rooftop somewhere with the rays from the warm evening sun bathing their faces.

Dad One

Clara *hides under a quilt. Her phone rings. A hand emerges from beneath the quilt. She picks up her phone and answers.*

Clara   Gustavo . . . No, I don't want any, thanks . . . I know it's delicious. It always is the way you make it. I mean, I have tasted it before. No. I'm fine in my room. Dad, just leave me in peace on a Sunday, would you! Isn't it enough that I'm back in the room two feet from yours?

She gets tired of holding the phone and puts her dad on speakerphone.

I'm sad. I've just been through a break-up. I want nothing more than to come downstairs and stuff myself with pizza with you, but no, I've changed my outlook, I took the millennial pill, and I went out to get laid. Dad! I'm trying to break up with lots of things here!

Dad   This pizza is really good.

Clara   I need you to give me a bit of space.

Dad   No way. I'm your dad and I love you and I'm always going to be here, whether you like it or not. Christmas and New Year, at home, my home, forever. And I don't really care if your boyfriend doesn't like it, you and your brother should be here at home; that's the only thing I ask.

Clara   Dad.

Dad   What?

Clara   I don't have a boyfriend anymore.

Dad   Yes, right.

Clara   And besides, it makes no difference if I come over the day after.

Dad   Don't be mean.

Clara   That time I spent New Year in Valizas with my friends, I missed you all like crazy. I felt crap. It's not fair.

Dad   It's because you should have been here. God was punishing you.

Clara   Gustavo, you're an atheist!

Dad   Am I?

Clara   I'm weak. What will I do when you're not around anymore? I'm like a big ball of your homemade pizza dough and when I feel crap, I think to myself: at least Dad's here.

Dad   That's nice.

Clara   More like pathetic.

Dad   Well, it's because you're an artist and so it would be much better for your material if I were a terrible father.

Clara   That's not what I'm talking about.

Dad   Write it Clara, stop messing about, you can't experience everything. Why don't you start writing? Why are you going to therapy? Is that psychoanalyst really any good?

Clara *takes a pencil from beside her mattress. She looks at her notebook.*

Clara   That's too many questions.

Dad   Shall we stop talking then?

Clara   You called me.

Dad   Yeah, to say hello because you're all cooped up inside there. It's Sunday.

Clara   Exactly.

Dad   Do you want me to wake you up at a certain time?

Clara   I don't think so.

Dad   OK.

They both wait in silence.

Clara   It's as if I'm about to kill you.

Dad   Oh, you didn't get this dramatic way of seeing the world from me, it must be from your mother, life will throw enough at you as it is.

She throws her phone. She goes over to the edge of the bed; she takes a bottle of water. She comes out from underneath the quilt. She rests on the bed-head.

Playa Grande – The Beach

Clara   That summer, listening to Caetano and Maria Gadú on those January days when we barely even spoke a word to one another and I spend more time driving around the streets of Playa Grande than making love with you.

I speedily developed a special skill: an inability to ignore you. Everything you say makes me bored and tired. The void left by every word we fail to speak to one another, by every missed kiss, is filled with any kind of food.

I inhale it all as I steer blindly towards a break-up that I can't see coming my way, like grey clouds that engulf the sky in ten minutes and suddenly the front porch is soaked and my favourite smell in the whole world is damp earth. But neither of us is aware of what lies ahead. Or maybe we are, but we don't say anything. We shoot each other disgusted death stares but they aren't really aimed at the other person, they're aimed at us.

What I do really remember from that summer is holding you, but as you would a friend, without expecting anything more, just as a way to somehow say farewell to your body. I don't really know. I just hold you and holding you, spooning, or standing between the two single beds that we didn't even bother pushing together, I feel a deep sense of sadness at the realisation that I can love you like this, without physical intimacy but with an elevation of our souls.

We both believe that in February, just the two of us back in our tiny flat in the Old City, we can revive whatever it was that suddenly and unexpectedly died.

Don't ask me what, but something changed. Something broke. Don't ask me what. How can I go on loving you? We're not the same anymore. But that's not it. No. We can't go back. Don't ask me why. I can't explain it. Someone took away a piece of you and a piece of me and I don't know what that piece is. Don't ask me.

What are we supposed to do with this mess? My dress is pulled, torn, shredded.
It's impossible to purge myself of you.
It's unfathomable.
It's still unfathomable.

Music.

Hurt Settles In

Clara   I don't cry anymore
not as much as before.
It's true what they say
a week goes by and then
you start to realise that hurt comes in instalments
and so a bill turns up at the end of the month
only this bill is a photo or a Facebook post.

Hurt settles in
and then you don't cry any more.
You don't cry as much as before.
For one of two reasons
either it wasn't that hard to forget you, or I've already cried enough.

For me
I think it's a bit of both.
There's no doubt I've cried enough
and I'm not too sure about forgetting you.

But now it's time to fill my life with new things.

When we broke up, the first thing I said to myself was
this has to be the start of something else: a creative project.
My parents looked at me as if it was the first time they'd really understood that . . .

They don't get it.
But we are . . .

We are renewable energy for all the grief, heartbreak, and shit the world throws at us.

She writes in her notebook.

That moment when you realise
there's something in this
you can make something of this
that precise moment
may just be the moment that saves you.

We had our first big fight when I decided to stop arguing with him and start writing about arguing with him instead.

I carried on arguing a bit, but my mind was already elsewhere so instead of arguing about whatever we started arguing about, we were arguing about my (*she hesitates, picks up her notebook, reads something. She crosses it out. She writes again*) urgent need to write.

She writes it.

When you write you can lose yourself in love and everything else
I live life intensely and I'm overcome by a profound sense of weakness.
No-one taught me to be selfish
we should learn at school how to toughen up our ego.

An alarm goes off on her phone. **Clara** *says: "shit". She moves from the bed over to the chair covered in clothes. She takes off her summer clothes and puts on the clothes for autumn.*

AUTUMN

Gynae

Clara   I had a check-up with the gynaecologist.
While I wait my turn
I make a list of things to pack for a night away
to practice
like a shopping list
that you might have in your bag.
I list:
charger
floss
toothbrush
toothpaste.

I cross out toothpaste
perfume
deodorant
two pairs of knickers
jeans for the day after
fuchsia dress, just in case
my favourite sandals
something to eat
because the minibar might be overpriced
or because there might not even be a minibar
or because the void is so great that the only way to fill it is by eating
condoms with spermicide
an emergency morning-after pill.

Just as I write the two Ls of morning-after pill
there's a shadow
it's the gynaecologist.
What's she doing in the waiting room?
"You're my last one, in you go."

Does she just have resting bitch face or is it because she saw me write pill?
Did she read morning-after pill?
She's going to start asking all sorts of questions
she's going to assume I'm an irresponsible sort.

Recently
everything about women and our bodies makes me anxious
as if being a single woman activated a kind of safety alarm
so naïve.

The gynaecologist does the smear test.
She inserts the plastic device
and takes a small stick that I've never properly seen
the tiny stick they use to take a piece of you
I always imagined it was like the tiny wooden ones you get with your ice cream, like in La Cigale.
They do exactly the same action with the tiny stick as you do when you're scraping the ice cream out of the cone.
I ask her to give me a referral for a mammogram
because my usual doctor, who's on leave
sends me for one every year.

She says no
that I'm too young for that kind of screening.

So now I have to convince this woman about a decision that I took about my own body?

My usual gynaecologist is also my mum's gynaecologist
he brought me into this world
me and my brother as well
he adores us
I don't think he'd send me for that kind of screening once a year if he didn't think it was absolutely necessary.

When my mum got sick, I was the one who called him to read him the results
and he was the first one to say the word "cancer"
and then he said: "It's serious, Clara
I want to see you both in my surgery in an hour."

And I like going to see him.
He asks me about my life
if I'm single, or if I have a partner
if I bleed after sex
that sort of thing.
Look
I don't know how to make it any clearer to you that you need to make the referral and then I can get out of here.

I have a special bond with my gynaecologist.

Pause.

"There are different approaches", she says to me.

Approaches? Several of them? In gynaecology? Shouldn't there be just one? I think to myself.

My mum had breast cancer.
What?
Breast cancer.
My mum. She had it
breast cancer.
I know
that at some point
it's likely that I'll have it too.
I'd like to know as soon as possible
I'm not scared of cancer
or of dying
but I am scared of losing one of my boobs
not losing it
of them chopping it off
it would be a shock
because if you lose it, the surgeon can remove it and put in a plastic one at the same time.
I'd rather not do that
I don't like plastic
the thing is I'd rather not go through any of that.
I'm scared of the "chop",
the disfigurement, I suppose
my boobs are small, but I think they're fine
I suppose that's why I like them
because they're small and delicate
so I've never had to plump them up
or slim them down.
They are one of the only parts of my body that I've never had an issue with, ever.
Do you realise how important that is?

The gynaecologist puts on a resting gynaecologist's face.
Let's wait until Jaime comes back.
"Fine", I say with my eyes.
She opens the door for me.
I leave without the referral and think:

She could have at least examined my boobs
the gynaecologist didn't even touch my boobs
I don't really know how to examine myself in the shower
if I've got to spend hours waiting at the surgery
the very least she could do is touch my boobs.

Autumn

This can be a poem, a song, a rap or spoken word.

Clara Autumn is a rare dying beast which falls, lies, spits.
It foretells death and foreshadows light, it announces the fall.
Autumn.
Autumn doesn't know how to lie, autumn doesn't know how to reason, if you were
with me, it would say you're the love of my life and that's all that matters
it would speak of unclean sheets, love and champagne. It would speak
with a smile fixed on its face and say
autumn is so bold
autumn is so crazy
autumn is so wild
autumn is so bold
how lucky am I.

It's not true.
It's cold and you're gone.
Shitty autumn sneaks up on me and I'm helpless.
It arrives and I'm single, lover-less
it sneaks up on me, the autumn.

You're not here.
It's cold and you're gone.
What happened? What happened to us?
I left you, you
left me, you won't
face me, you
fell in love
I fell in love
we got bored
we got lost.

Yesterday I heard someone say
we've had so much rain this autumn.
It's true.
It's true. Autumn is shitty.
It rained non-stop and the water
washed over us
water washed over us.
It doesn't matter, it doesn't matter
smile
stay positive

like my friend tells me
it's what she tells me
stay positive
even when you don't feel like it
like staying
or being positive
it's what my friend tells me
it's what my friend tells me.

The sound of a storm.

Storm and Romance

Clara *comes back from some guy's place. She's made an attempt to dress up sort-of sexy but hasn't quite managed it.*

It's raining so she can come in soaked through.

On the screen, if images are being used, a scene or several from various classic romcoms can be projected.

Clara   It was because of the storm.
It's always the storm
you believe it from being a little girl because of the romcoms.
Whenever there's sex, there's rain.
The electric storm ruins everything.
When it rains you can't go out so it's better
to unplug everything and fuck
and not be scared
be inside someone else
and because we've been brainwashed
you think you're having the best sex ever
but it's the same, exactly the same
the only difference is that when there's lightening, we laugh
and one of you says: "Oh my God I'm so scared!"
And the other one holds you, but it's the same
exactly the same as on a boiling hot day
or in spring.

You think it's more passionate but it's not true
and that's what happened to you and me
the storm came and trapped us like two fools.
We just jumped aboard the ghost train of love and
now I feel uncomfortable and I want to go
but it's not your fault, or mine.
It's raining, there's a storm and sleeping alone is awful.

I'm a clutch of pinpricks.
That's how we are, isn't it
some of us feel perpetually perforated.

Break

Clara Someone said to me
start using Facebook to say what's on your mind
post on Facebook.
You have to write.

I'm going to ask the machine to tell me how I feel today
helpfully, it gives me loads of choice
a whole spectrum of states
helpfully, vast and wide-ranging.

I'm celebrating.
I'm living the dream.
I'm counting down the days till the weekend.

Pause.

I need more choice, please.
I'm eating.
I'm drinking.
I'm searching.

Like.
Love.
Sad face.
Angry face.
I'm so pissed off.

Your photo.
Get out of there.
A new photo of you
you so new and I'm here
far away
but also here, thanks to Facebook.
Get out of there.

They should really add "I'm stressed."
It's one of the emotions I learnt to understand at a young age because I have a
psychotherapist for a mother.
I'm stressed out.

Stop hiding.
Put on a revealing top.
Stop hiding.
Show off.
Stop hiding in life and in art.
Stand up straight.
No more massages.
Stand tall.
If you don't post it, do you really feel it?
You're not on the outside.
You're either a witness or an intruder
but you have to go in.
Go in.
Break up.
Your photo.
Get out of there.
But your photo.
I want to explode.
Get out of there.
I'm looking.
Big mistake!
I'm reading.
I'm remembering.
This isn't right.
Can Facebook just curate my nostalgia for me now?
Oh God, he unfriended me.
We are no longer friends.
Seven years gone to shit in one click.

Break up.
Log out.
That's not the way.

She looks at herself in the mirror.

Look at yourself.
This is not your voice.
Where is your voice?

(What's on your mind, Clara?)

Sacred Vanity

Clara   I've never waxed my whole lady garden
not the whole thing
I don't like the idea
or maybe I'm scared of it

I still remember my tiny twinkle from when I was a little girl
so that's enough.
They're slightly broken images but they're enough.
I remember it
and when the first hairs came through.

Hollywood wax is a terrible phrase
but more than the two words together
it's the way it's been degraded
that disturbs me.
A Hollywood wax as a commodity
as a necessary condition of my femininity
my poor pussy degraded in a waxing salon.
Besides, I don't like how it sounds
adding Hollywood to pussy
phonetically
it's really grating
and now I think about it
hair removal
grating
wax
grating
Hollywood
grating
Fascist
what did these words do in the past?
What did they mean at another moment in time?

The only memory I have of my pussy without a single hair is blurry.
Sometimes I try to remember it, but I get bored, so I just give up trying.

And not long ago my friend showed me hers
in the shower
shiny and new
her Hollywood pussy
and it just seemed a bit much to me
her Hollywood pussy.

I go for a wax quite regularly
but everyone's situation is different
so is where you're starting from
and who's looking at it.
Everything
in this world of relativism where beauty is in the eye of the fucking beholder.
I don't get excited by every new thing that everyone buys
the thing everyone has to have

I'd rather leave something behind
a trace
a part of me which can't be taken away.

Today I went to a different salon.
I ended up in one where everything was pastel
like someone had opened a tin of vintage and splashed it everywhere
and put up posters saying:
Freedom
Home
Sweet
Joy
Silvana is my therapist today.
She's friendly
I think it makes a difference when the person who's about to get up close to your pussy is friendly
it doesn't cost anything
it makes it less intense
and increases their tip.
Silvana is friendly and an expert
(or so it seems)
who loves nothing more than waxing.

Straight away she asks me to take off my knickers
she wants me to leave without a single hair down there
she asks me why I don't usually get it all removed
I explain to her that I find it too painful
that I have a low tolerance for pain
she tells me that if it's because of the pain then don't even mention it
if it's the pain I'm worried about, she'll make sure I leave here without even knowing I've had a wax.

I try to explain to her that, no, actually
I just don't want (besides the pain) what she's offering
it doesn't really appeal
I'm fine with my usual level of waxing and the max level, or whatever you want to call it
doesn't really appeal.
It's like going from weed to . . . It just doesn't appeal.

We must always want more.
I think that's perfect for life
but not for my pussy.
That's where I'm up to.
Someone is always trying to convince you of something based on the way they see the world

and if you use words like pain or fear, it just makes it worse.
Have no fear.
Have no fear.
Silvana respects my decision
she tells me she's going to take a little bit more than what I'm used to
just a bit more
and then next time, I'll leave without a single hair.

PSSHHP (*sound of pulling off wax*)
It doesn't hurt
she's waxing like never before and it doesn't hurt
I don't know how she did it
they must put something in the wax.
She finishes and before I know it
she's giving me a mirror
she grabs my hand
she puts the mirror in my hand
and she puts the mirror in front of me.
"Look at you",
she says, proud.
"What a difference, eh?
It's not the same
it's completely different
and did it hurt?"
Silvana is forcing me to look at my pussy.
I have to look at my pussy in the mirror with her next to me and say: wonderful, lovely.
For Silvana, the boundaries of my intimate space do not exist
and she makes me look at my pussy in front of her.
We are both looking at my vulva
and saying
much better
simpler
and she says
"You'll notice the difference next time you're on your period."

Just like at the hairdressers, I say, it's great
I think it's probably a good thing to normalise all of this
maybe we should act like we're at the hairdressers and
maybe I'm the weird one?

My Anarchist Boyfriend

Clara   I don't eat McDonalds anymore, since I met you
I've become a vegan.

Just fruit that has fallen from the tree, dying fruit
like that woman in *Notting Hill* who they try to set Hugh Grant up with after he's
been rejected by Julia Roberts
so they create (*she does air quotes*) "an ugly character with a mad face"
and make her a vegan.
Vegan/ugly/mad/scruffy/frigid.
Her body and brain pumped full of fruit
not a lot going on up there or down there
just a shit-ton of fruit.

I'm going out with a guy who's an anarchist
and he's principled.
He's the only man with principles left standing in the twenty-first century
he despises the ruling party, left or right
and he despises capitalism
and neoliberalism.

I don't wear clothes from any of the big brands since I've been with him
I buy everything in second-hand shops
and I recycle vegetable boxes that I buy from the man who has a small stall down the road
I pay him next to nothing and I turn them into furniture.
The house is full of furniture made from vegetable boxes and hand painted by me
and my parents are delighted.
Red boxes for bedside tables
blue boxes are bookshelves filled with vegan cookbooks and the diaries of Frida Kahlo, Alejandra Pizarnik and Idea Vilariño
green boxes are shelves where I keep all the utensils I need to make my vegan food
white boxes to put my records, weed and beer on, alongside all my weekend indulgences.

They're not so great for fucking, the boxes
they're weak
vintage culture is weak
pinky
aquamarine
women with red lips
polka-dot headscarves
and curves that are out of this world.
Weak but cool
just like the second-hand shop where I get all my clothes since I've been going out with my anarchist boyfriend.

I feel ugly
crap
I'm tired of eating seeds and watching rubbish TV

I feel stupid
I want to demolish a pack of Oreos
I'd give anything for a Zara jumper
and an overpriced jacket from Gap that I have to pay for in ten instalments
thanks to my shitty income as a private tutor.

I feel ugly but I know that the image I have of myself is distorted
it's defined by society
my own image of myself is defined by society
I feel ugly in society
and beautiful on the inside.
It's the image of myself that was imprinted on my brain
that's what my anarchist boyfriend tells me
do an experiment for a month by not looking at
the TV
your phone
or the massive ads in the street
or Hollywood films
or adverts on the side of the bus.
Do an experiment to cleanse your gaze
perfect your handwriting
that's what my anticapitalistic boyfriend says
anti-hegemony
anti-love
anti-affection
because commitment is for the weak
and there's no space for them.
My let's-fuck-now boyfriend.
My I-can-only-give-myself-to-you-now boyfriend.
"Now.
Sorry.
I'm just a fucking mess
but I'm not to blame
it's the system
and it's not my fault I can't love you
I'm broken
and I don't know how to build
what you want.
You're so kind and so geeky
like from another century."
I look at him
I despise him
I don't want this pain
I don't want any of it.

I'm raging
I'm going to max out my credit card in one go

I'm going to empty my current account
I'll be rich and poor at the same time
I'm going to eat five meal deals
bacon
cheddar
double-scoop ice cream which is what the love of my life would order
a lemon pie that tastes like plastic in La Cigale.

I'm going to sleep with a public finance accountant and fuck him till I can't fuck any more.
I'll get bored to death of talking to him about the latest Minions film
and this country which he says will be a country of poor people by 2050.
Men explain things to me
but maybe he looks at me with a look that's slightly less lost
and doesn't hurt me.

And then the anarchist guy turns up again and tells me forcefully, like it's an order: "Don't run away from your life's path, maybe I'm just the shit that you have to go through, get out of your working-class Disney film with your bourgeois dreams, your parents are going to die soon."

Rage

Clara   I don't want to hurt
to give what I get.
I want to go against the flow
against hegemony.
I don't want to be the person committing one micro-aggression after another
I don't want to perpetuate that.
We must do something.
Affection is no longer a gift
since when?
When fear filled our hearts with fear
I don't want to burn for the sake of it
or burn because it's expected.
Is that the goal?
I want to tear down a wall.
Give me one good reason why I shouldn't feel like the only thing we're doing in the midst of so much mediocrity is getting more and more stupid by the day
so much supermarket standard.
We just need two
you and me
lasting is a bad word.
We're going to say I love you the day we meet
that doesn't mean we're no longer cool or

that we're conforming
it's just about language
about speaking
speaking to one another so we heal.
Say it
say it to me
to me
you
start somewhere
from zero.
Take out the pencil
the revolution lies in recovering language, decolonising it.
It's written in the Bible
to name is to create
the Bible says it
try to be a bit less foolish
even the freedom to feel good because I love you has been taken away from me
don't leave me alone in this.
I want to buy you a birthday gift
and for you not to think I'm starting a war.

Take a risk, he used that word.
"A risk, I can't", he said.
Take a risk with this one.

WINTER

She turns on the heater. She makes her bed. "Ámbar Violeta" by Fito Páez is playing. She closes the window again. She takes a tablet with water. She plays with a ball of wool. She unravels it around her bedroom drawing a border around the edge of the mattress. She takes off her autumn clothes and is in her underwear. She wraps herself up in the quilt.

Dad Two

Clara Dad, I read a few scenes from *Emotional Terror* to a director.

Dad What's that?

Clara *Emotional Terror*.

Dad Oh, yes, the monologue.

Clara Would you please listen to me?

Dad I am listening.

Clara I was saying that I showed a few scenes from my monologue to a director.

Dad What did you show her?

Clara I showed her the Hollywood wax scene.

Dad The what?

Clara Nothing. I showed her a part of the text. It doesn't matter which. I showed her Scene X.

Dad Right.

Clara She says she loved it, that it's powerful, and very personal.

Dad But how long is the play?

Clara What, Dad?

Dad How long is it?

Clara I don't know, I've written about seventy pages.

Dad And the Hollywood wax scene, how long's that?

Clara It's funny hearing you say the Hollywood wax scene. I don't know, four.

Dad Four?

Clara Yes, what's wrong with that?

Dad You showed her a four-page scene from a seventy-page monologue.

Clara And?

Dad You didn't show her the whole text.

Clara No.

Dad And so, she doesn't know whether what you're writing is really any good or not.

Clara Well, no, but I showed her a sample. The Hollywood wax scene is a representative sample.

Dad I'm not sure, I'm not sure.

Clara What are you not sure about, Dad?

My dad puts his earphones in, but then he realises I'm carrying on the conversation, so he takes them out.

This director instantly started telling me where she could imagine the scene. She says it should be in a house.

Dad What do you mean in a house?

Clara Yes, that it's not for a theatre. It's a play that should be in a house. She sees it in a bathroom.

Dad In a bathroom?

Clara With a wave of his hands, my dad dismisses the whole conversation. He puts his earphones back in, but I start shouting as we're crossing the road, so he turns the volume down, but doesn't take them out this time.

Dad You take a shit in the bathroom, and you do a play in the theatre.

Clara We've reached the stage where nothing I say will make any difference.
He's done.
I know. I can feel it.
It's coming, it's coming, if he says it, I'll go mad.

Dad Here we are, Clara.

Clara He said it.

Dad, it's a play for a small audience.

Dad So?

Clara So you could say that we want to create a feeling of intimacy.

Dad You can fit six people in a bathroom, Clara.

Clara So?

Dad If you do it in a bathroom then I'm not going.

Clara I'm not going to argue about this with you anymore
no more
not about this

you can argue about other things with your parents.
Shit.
So you've decided you've got something to say about the staging of my play. No way!
Enough.
It's too much
it's my fault
it's all my fault.
Those months I spent living with you after the break-up
were wonderful
but a step backwards.
We became a tight-knit endogamic trio
you two are my favourite people in the whole world
it's not healthy
and the funniest thing about it is that no-one else even comes close
no-one
you're unbeatable.
You knocked everyone else out of the competition on day one.
Throw me out!

Pause. She's very tired.

My mother looks at me disappointed. I know what she's trying to tell me.

Mum, you're my favourite person. Then comes Dad. It was just a way of saying it. I wanted to finish my thought.

My mum smiles and I turn back to my dad.

I'm not going to carry on arguing with you because you think that art can only be Shakespeare or Lorca.

Dad You took me to see a play by Kartun, the Argentine writer, and I loved it.

Clara Shakespeare, Lorca and Kartun. All men, two of them dead. It's not a very broad artistic range, is it Dad.

My Fundamentalist Boyfriend

Clara I was going out with an accountant who
was able to start an argument about anything
just so he could maintain a sense of personal integrity.
A basic fundamentalist
who didn't understand that with some people you can be a bit less passionate
not so forceful.
Forcefulness makes some people uncomfortable
it makes them feel attacked
because well-made arguments
whether they're right or wrong, make people uncomfortable.

Strong opinions make people uncomfortable
certainty makes people uncomfortable
it's better to be amenable and swayable
open to being convinced
about anything.

That's what I liked about my fundamentalist boyfriend.
I suppose that was all I liked about him.

It was so hard to persuade him of anything.
He
who never spoke loudly
but his ideas spoke loud and clear.
I liked his conviction
his integrity
and his ingenuousness.
It didn't matter if he was talking to me, Žižek or my grandmother.
He was always the same
with his passion for arguing
even arguing for no good reason.
I really admire
people with convictions.

My fundamentalist boyfriend
would not let me pay the bill.
Who gets turned on by someone paying the bill for you?
I wonder if anyone ever got turned on by that.

We got to the point where we argued about every stupid little thing.

He didn't understand that my grandmother
fan of one of the big teams
wasn't interested in the sinister inner workings of football in our third-world country.
Big teams versus small teams
and the inherent inequalities of Uruguayan football
and I try to explain to him
that sometimes you have to give up a bit of your commitment
and compromise a little
it's the only way to survive
compromise, compromise, compromise, all the time.
And then he says to me that if we start compromising on everything
then everything will slip away.
"Well, it's not that we compromise on everything, my love
I mean the small things
like the stupid things that come up in conversation on a Sunday afternoon.
I'm asking you to not be so harsh

to not be so hostile."
"Keeping quiet is also hostile",
he tells me
and then I respond by saying that it's narrow-minded to try to change how someone thinks, especially if they are a seventy-year-old woman from a small town who was taken out of school to cook for her older brothers and roll their corn cigarettes in the middle of the countryside.
Not keeping your narrow-mindedness in check is also hostile
hers and his
the disparities caused by social inequality
it's stupid.
"You're calling me stupid", he says.
And that's when I become the attacker
and I ruin everything.
And our evening with a bottle of merlot that I barely touch and tapas with rocket
is replaced with an early night
without dinner
sleeping with our backs to each other
and tears of rage in our eyes.

Theatre

Clara I never wanted to be an actress
but I did take a drama course.
A short one.
More like a workshop.
A long time ago
I did a short three-month drama course in the neighbourhood my mum grew up in because I fell in love with the teacher in five seconds flat when I saw him at the vegetable stall.
I saw the drama teacher
ask the stall owner if he could put up a few posters for the course.
The owner looked pissed off
but he said yes
and the teacher left
and I saw the stall owner stick the poor poster
in a place where no-one was ever going to see it.
He stuck it on a crate of vegetables at the very back of the stall
where the vegetables that are about as enticing as a drama course end up.
I think I must have been the only person to see that poster.
When Robert, who owns the stall, turned around, I pulled it down and took it with me.
That means that the teacher, despite his initiative, had the bad luck of stumbling not only across Robert

but also, across me.
I thought that if posters were being pulled down at this rate
then there wouldn't be very many of us in the class
and so, I decided to go for it and put my name down.
I sent him a text which is what you did in those days
texts were somehow much less schizophrenic than WhatsApps.
I sent him a text.
Hi. My name is Clara. I'm interested in signing up for the drama course. I saw your poster at Robert's vegetable stall. I've never taken any classes . . . in acting, but I'm keen to learn more about it. Can people like me join? I'm very shy. Send me the cost and timings. Best wishes.
He replied immediately. Typical desperate teacher.
He only got half the message.
I wrote a new text.
Hi. I'm interested in the course. Timings and cost please. Thanks.
He replied and two weeks later I was getting started.
On the first day he asked us to prepare a monologue for the next class.
At that time, I didn't have a clue what I wanted to write
well maybe a clue
but not really
and I also wanted to ask something
because if you want to be in the smart-kid clique then you have to ask a question in the first class
besides, I hadn't dared to do any performing
and so I asked
and he wasn't very fair.

He said what was I doing in an acting class if I wasn't already familiar with the basics like not turning your back to the audience, playing the diagonal, and the art of the monologue.
I told him that the poster said: all welcome, no previous experience necessary.
It would take too long to explain why I never went back to his course.
Let's move on.

I never wanted to be an actress.
I was never interested in being on stage or performing.
If I'm being really honest, I get more and more nervous and awkward around people with each passing day.
However, between the ages of five and ten, I and every single one of my friends when we were asked what we wanted to do when we grew up would respond without fail: singing, acting and dancing.
The three things all at once.
Like an invincible trio
acting, singing, dancing
like it was a deal, as if these things, all of which are very difficult in their own right, were somehow easy all at once.

Cris Morena made them look easy on TV.
She took fifteen kids and made them act, dance and sing and you thought you could be just as good as them.
One day I even went to my mum's work in tears
and begged her to take me to Buenos Aires because
I wanted to be in *Chiquititas*, the soap about the little orphans
to spend the rest of my life in a world that was a mixture of their luminous mansion and Neverland.
I was born in the wrong city, I told my mum.

Deep down I never wanted that.
People in everyday life terrify me.
Can you imagine what it must be like up there?

Mother, driver, actress and trainee sniper.
I've always known that
those four things were not for me.
The thing is that sometimes
we get used to the idea of who we think we are.
It's simpler if we don't try to change who we are all the time.

Cats

Clara   I realised that I could be a mother when I met Ariadna.
Ariadna was a pretty dirty cat.
I hate cats
and I mean hate in the way Jack does in *As Good as It Gets*.
I hate cats
but I like my neighbour and so I said yes
that I'd look after her.
My neighbour was going away to San Andrés with his new girlfriend
and so he left me with this little lady and a lead that I never used, food, a few small bowls, and a ball of wool.
And his number (*she feels like she's said something to embarrass herself. She clarifies*) for WhatsApp, just in case.
Sometimes I thought about possible voice notes I could send him to strike up a conversation because of something to do with Ariadna, but thankfully, he wasn't needed.
The first few days I hated her.
I spent a lot of time fantasising about killing her and I wrote about my fantasy a lot.
I considered moving, leaving her with my parents
but it was too annoying, and it wasn't fair, on Ariadna.

And so, instead, I made friends with this little lady cat.
I'm lying

her dad didn't want our relationship to thrive.
We just became good housemates, concubines.
When it was time for food, I would open the balcony door for her
and she would come in and eat
and when she had finished eating, I put her back out on the balcony.
Until one day, without even really thinking about it
whilst we were eating lunch
I said: God this July has been freezing!
And she stopped chewing, swallowed and looked at me
and that's the moment I realised that it must be much colder outside on the balcony
than it is inside.
Ariadna was trying to tell me something . . .
and from that day on she didn't sleep outside anymore
and we started to chat at lunch
at dinner
I don't usually have a snack in the afternoon, but I started to have one so that I could talk to her.
I would talk and she looked at me. That's it. Each to their own. In their role. No egos.
Neither of us wanting to change the other; something that always happens in relationships.
And so, meals became the best part of the day.
And it seemed
that it was all becoming
a kind of routine which wasn't painful.
Things became a bit difficult when my neighbour came back
he saw that she was fatter, hollow-eyed
and a bit bald.
"This cat has been eating floury foods, Clara."
"A little", I said.
"A lot of floury foods", he responded.
I told him that when you eat together, you have to offer to share a taste of your food, it's good manners
and Ariadna always wanted a taste.
It's not my fault.
Now I have to be responsible for Ariadna's past traumas and her addiction to floury foods.
Did you even know that she was addicted to flour?
I didn't say that to him.
I also neglected to tell him that she almost froze to death, became a passive smoker, licked some moisturiser and swallowed a cherry stone.
"She's just a cat", he says!
There and then I lost all interest in our interaction
when someone reduces the other to the category of "cat"
I can't go on with the conversation.
I find it deeply hurtful.
I went to find the lead; I gave him what was left of the food.

I kept the ball of wall.
I cuddled Ariadna and I could tell from the way she looked at me that she was grateful.
It was strange.
Grateful but also nostalgic, as if she knew what she was going back to.

She mimics the cat.

She looked at me and I know exactly what she was saying to me.
It was: (*she does air quotes*)
"I'm going to miss licking the crumbs off the plate when you've finished eating your millefeuille, the smell, the horrible smell of your microwaveable hot water bottle, and . . . (*she gets emotional*) our conversations."
I closed the door and I cried
just like in a film
with my back against the door
I slid down to the floor
and my dressing gown snagged on all the nails sticking out the door that I'd never bothered to fix.
I cried for my own solitude, for Ariadna, and for my neighbour
but especially for my own solitude.
And that's when I realised that I loved cats.
Perhaps not all cats. But this cat.

Bags

She enters carrying two black binbags full of things.

Clara These bags were packed by my ex-boyfriend at his house and filled with the remnants of my life.
Yes.
I left it a bit late.
Extra-large bags like the kind you get at the supermarket when you collect your Christmas order.
Bags containing the remnants
of this story.
Everything can be reduced to four types of bags
things for the bin
things to keep
things that are maybes
things that hold no meaning whatsoever
but right now, are the most solid thing I have.
This.
Something like ashes
burnt out

there's no more
nothing.

He kept the things I'd have asked him for.
The only things I'd have asked for were the ones he kept.
It doesn't matter.
Let's be indifferent.

She starts taking things out of the bags. They are insignificant objects.

I'm never going through a break-up again I think to myself
I'm never falling in love again
as I'm going through the bags
I think to myself that I'm never going through a break-up again.
I'll hook the next one to my lovelorn heart
I'll bind him to my heart.

When I get back to my parents' house with the bags, they are in the living room drinking coffee.
Fortunately, they don't get up.
If they get up to hug me or ask what's the matter, then I'll start crying
if they come over to me, then I'll start crying
as I'm opening the first knot, I think
parents are the only constant in life.

I have an audience, so I add a touch of humour to it and as I'm unpacking the bags, I start telling them what's inside.

I'm a kind of menacing heartbreak Father Christmas
I'm Santa and they're the motherfucking children laughing at my jokes
and every now and then, when I go into the kitchen to throw something away, because my ex-boyfriend filled these bags with crap, I hear the boy played by my dad say to the girl played by my mum: "There's no going back now."

Poor naïve Dad. He still hoped there might be a make-up.

I don't get why he kept the magnets from places my brother travelled to
he kept the magnets
I realised when I walked past the fridge and saw all my magnets looking perfect stuck firmly to the side of the fridge
as if even they didn't want to come with me.

I know I'm going back to my parents' for a few months and so they'd be stuck in a bag for a while but it adds insult to injury!

Motherfuckers.
As if they were just waving me off

off you go.
As if they were leaving me as well
as if they were saying to me: hey fuck-face, good luck with it all, we magnets from Europe have decided it's best if we stay. Go and buy yourself a plastic fruit magnet at the flea market on Tristán.

She searches through the bags, finds just the kind of magnets of fruit and vegetables.

What I am taking, but he didn't give to me, was the photo of us from the fridge.
I think that was the thing that really broke me
not having a place on the fridge anymore.

SPRING

Healing

Clara The wound
the artist
who speaks
who cries
who tells of things greater than his being
something eternal
just for me.
How to follow?
How to follow?
The missing piece
you have it
you swallowed it.
Empty
lost
this knot
blood
heart
I don't know how to join my pieces together
assemble my mind.
Heal
heal on my own
just me alone
one must heal alone
one must heal by herself.
It's hard to feel the absence.
What do you fill it with?
The presence of others covers
they cover
they don't fill
they cover
it's not the same.
Let's start again.

I'm bones
fractured by your love which is love no longer
it's parting
dark, desolate land
a door slammed in my face
last night's dream where you were folding blankets

your back turned
with your back to me
and I was crying
and I was singing of how I lost you because I'm senseless
I lost you because I'm a fool.
Guys like you get lost
fool
they get lost.
I was the one who was lost
wandering through the void
with the lights of New York in my eyes.

I didn't see you
I didn't know how to see you
you were standing there
looking at me
with the same old eyes
always
waiting for me.
I'm sorry for being me.
Thank you for being you.

I'm telling you a secret
but I'm
enough
this is important
there's no story
there's no song
there was never enough.
This is serious
you
listen to me
I, I
want
I want to ask my love today
my fractured love
if you'll come back, I ask
ask the one who loves me today
and I love you
it doesn't matter.
That's what life is about, isn't it?
Isn't it about being more than just empty bones?
Being a sacred mountain
a soul that's not quite so faded.
Everything fades away on the journey.

Chau

Clara   This is a declaration of love.
Thank you for everything.
I'm finished.
Chau.
It's been a pleasure.
Sorry.
I didn't know how to keep up with the times.
I was trying to be a romantic in a hostile, all-consuming world.
I was trying to be a modernist in a world where everything was "post" something.
I was trying to leave a trace of myself on you so that
you'd leave a trace on me.
I was trying to survive
to be less finite
less immortal
less immoral.
I was trying to feel different.
I was trying not to feel guilty for wanting to be something for more than today
for wanting to be myself, with all my spiralling anxiety from the last century.
Thank you.
You help me realise
I don't fit together with you or many others
I'm desperately searching for a better version of my dad, and he doesn't exist.
Now we have to adjust
that's the worst word I've ever said in my life.
Adjust.
Adapt.
Assimilate.
Accept.
Fuck, all start with A.

We aren't cast from the same mould.
I've had enough of people telling me about my emotional dependence.
What's their problem with dependence?
Thank God, and who knows which god, that I depend on someone
some-ones, so many ones.

Luckily, I'm not a plant
I feel
I create
I imagine
I plan for the future
I plan for the future
I plan for the future. I plan for the future.
Another thing people don't say often enough.

Nothing.
You.
Yes.
I already know.
You can only give me this. Your hand. Now.
Now.
Like Richard III
the length of this scene and nothing more.

Dad Three

The phone rings. She answers.

Clara Gustavo. Yes, I left you a note on the fridge. I told you I was taking a few things with me. It's just a few things, Gustavo, don't be annoying.
It's nothing like the house. It's a reconstruction.
It's all just made up, Dad.
What are you really worried about?
It's just for a week, OK.
What do you mean lose them?
But you are not you, Gustavo.
Besides, I changed your name. This isn't about you, Dad.
What do you mean give you a share? What do you mean your artistic rights?
No, you're not coming to the opening night.
We'll do things the proper way. You'll come to the tenth show, once Mum has been five times and is in love with the performance, so she can persuade you that what I do is wonderful.
I've got to go. I have plans. No, don't get so worked up. Besides, you never like anything anyway.

Circle

Clara I made the mistake of listening to my friend who goes out with guys she meets on Tinder
and I agreed to a double date.

My homeopath says that I should do "crazy things"
and that's how I ended up
at a dinner with friends one night.
Friends who I don't know
who meet up to write
and read each other's work.

The group is led by my friend's Tinder boyfriend
and a friend of this Tinder boyfriend comes to pick me up.

Braulio.
Braulio seems like a relaxed kind of guy
as soon as I open the door
I just want to invite him in
and spend the evening there with him
but we have "plans".
We have to go to the Tinder guy's house.

They are meeting to read their poetry
and stories
there are no requirements
the idea is to write and share and discuss
I feel quite enthusiastic about it all
maybe I could read something I have on my phone.

Braulio and I arrive late
in the end I did ask him in.

We arrive.
I'm obviously the only new person
but everyone gets up and hugs me
as if I'm Braulio's wife
and that makes me feel nice.
All the girls in the group are dressed in the same way.
Their style is a mixture of clothes worn by
my homeopath, Ariadna's vet and the medium who called up my ancestors.

Braulio invites me to sit next to him.
Opposite, there is a red-haired woman who
won't stop staring at him.
Braulio tells me under his breath
that she's his ex-girlfriend.
She smiles at me.
Once we're all sitting down
the Tinder guy
invites us to continue reading around the circle.

And suddenly we're listening to
a red-haired woman talking about the only time she cheated on her husband.
It's a tale of guilt.
She has tears and snot all over her face.
I ask myself if this is the kind of opening
they expect in the circle
I ask myself again.
I look at the redhead.
Yes, this is what they expect.

Right away I want to leave
this is not for me.
This is not for me.
I have a front-row seat for a one-woman melodrama.
The redhead is hurting
everything is still
they're all listening to Montevideo's own Lena Dunham.

Gradually, the tale becomes punctuated with phrases like "I had to do it."
And "To deceive or to kill. That is the question."
And "All of us, at some point in our lives, must embrace the experience of infidelity."
And worst of all: "Because if this person doesn't cheat on you, the next one will so you should do it first."
And those were her closing words.
The Tinder guy asks for a round of applause for Elena
she's called Elena
there is a loud applause for Elena
whilst she's crying as if she's won the Pulitzer Prize
Elena pours herself a celebratory whisky
does a line of coke, and raises her glass saying:
"Let's demystify adultery."
Just like that
let's demystify adultery
and she only looks at the women.

I raise my hand and ask if that part is required
about adultery and myths
because if we have to think like that then
I can't be part of this.
First, I don't have a boyfriend
and second, if I did have one then I wouldn't like to demystify adultery
is what I say.
Some words together are the route into linguistic terrorism
the root cause of our deep emotional terror.
Myths exist for a reason
I try to explain to them
they are constructions but we need them
if we are going to destroy myths as well . . .

Everyone looks at me.
You're betraying the Greeks, for fuck's sake!

Braulio gets up
I sense he's making eyes at me to tell me to shut my mouth

but instead, he says:
"A healthy society is one where there is disagreement."

Tinder guy asks me to expand on my intervention
"What are you disagreeing with?"

I freeze.
Twenty eyes fixed on me.
I'm never listening to my homeopath again, ever.
I clear my throat
inside I'm dying.
I cry with rage at being so weak
for always saying yes to everything
for being so good at trying whatever it is in a quest to be happy
double date
literary circles for arsehole catharsis
Pilates
karaoke Thursdays
yoga
Zumba
upcycling workshop
theatre
sex as exercise
not talking to my dad for a week
not talking to the mirror for a week
giving up floury food
giving up weed
saying only what I think and not what I feel
stopping saving
taking up weed again
going running
going out with an accountant
going out with an anarchist
posting on social media to make the feelings more real
only reading contemporary philosophy
taking Bach Rescue Remedy again
giving up Bach Rescue Remedy
crying more
crying less.
Those cheap sites that let you shop like a millionaire were made for people like me,
I think
shop like a millionaire was made for me.

She breathes.

I think we're going about it all wrong
if from the get-go

we take it as given
that at some point I'm going to cheat on them
whatever happens.
It's as though everything is warped from the start, isn't it?
Elena assumes that we live in a world where subjectivity reigns and love conforms to certain conventions.
You're asking me to sell myself short
just like that, without putting up a fight.

I'd like to believe that's not all it is.
Love is the only thing that's not negotiable
don't forget that.
Love.
It's ours
and not only love. Romance.
Is it an anachronism? Is it over?
What the fuck is happening to us?
How has it become this complicated?
When did it become so complicated?
Aren't you all tired of being tired?

What would it mean to evolve?
I don't want anyone to ever to tell me what I have to do, let's live.

Someone laughs
I hear it.
I go on
even though someone just laughed, I believe partner is synonymous with honesty. And partner doesn't mean confinement. That's what we need to talk about. I think it's practically archaic to go on talking about love with two choices. And, Elena, what you're going through is good, what you're saying is that you're against passive female sexuality, and in that, I support you. But you confused things, Elena, the right to make choices about your sex life is nothing to do with romantic love or marriage contracts. It's just such a mess, Elena, it's all mixed up. And I do understand if you feel . . . overwhelmed.

Someone says something under their breath.

I ask this person to say it out loud
so that we can all hear.
They say:
"You turn up with that look on your face and that way of thinking."
I cut them off.
What about my face and my way of thinking?
What look do you have on your face?
Some idiot calls out from the kitchen

to say that he'll be my boyfriend so I can cheat on him.
They all laugh
Braulio forces a laugh.

I'm about to cry
once again at a totally inopportune moment.

I've just realised that I don't like literary circles.
In that moment, I realise that I don't want to see Braulio again
and that makes me happy
the small choices I can still make, make me happy.
In ten minutes, I'll be at home, far from this stupid fucking circle.

I get my things and start to leave.
I stop
I turn around
do I say it or not?
I say it
since this session started, I've been noting down a few phrases that you've said:

She takes her phone and reads.

"Right now, you couldn't convince me not to be single."
"I don't want to be with anyone."
"Me and him are just fine, with this slightly amorphous way of connecting."

Raise your hand if you'd want a hug in winter. At some point. Not always. Solitude is good, some of the time.

She raises her hand.

At the end of the day, life is just one long monologue, and you occasionally speak to others, but in the end, it's a monologue. Long stretches of being alone with fleeting moments where you are with someone else.

When I went to the toilet a bit ago, a girl was saying to her boyfriend, "Don't love me if you can't, but leave me alone. And let him love me if he wants to love me."

If I ran into him sometime, by chance, I'd say to him: let me love you. It's me. Nothing's changed. No, no, I changed, I changed, I mean, I'm not the same person I was before, something's different, something's different, you knew what I meant, but I'm the same, OK. There's not very many of us and we all know each other, and I find people extremely boring, but you, I never get bored of you. Do you know what that's like? To never get bored of someone? When I was with you, I got bored of me. That's why I went out, but I never went far.

And you, Braulio, you could be everything to me in five minutes flat, but I find you tiring. Not you, but all the paraphernalia of love. You're a good guy. But starting the whole machinery of love, I don't know what I want. I think I might not know for a while.

Yes, I want to get married and have four children. With curly hair. A love that promises happiness and eternity. Yes, I want to let off steam for a while and try everything. Disappear. I want to join a community of farmers in northern Chile. A house in the country. I want to dance. I want to die. I want to say I'm fine and for that to be true. I want to love everyone and just one person. I want you to come back. I never want you to come back. I want to make love to my childhood sweetheart. I want to burst with rage. I want everyone to stop and look at each other. I want everything to stop. I want you to change my life. For you to hold me. Squeeze me. Flee from me. Call me. Know me. Leave me. I want everything to stop being about everyone else. I want everything to stop being about me. I want a song that breaks me. I don't want it to hurt so much. I want to understand. I want to reset, disconnect, forget, I want . . .

What were we talking about? Oh yeah, monogamy. No. Not love either, or monogamy. I'm talking about honesty. Being honest with yourself. Not even with someone else. Maybe. Perhaps. Sometimes. What I mean is, I don't know what I mean anymore.

I'm leaving.
We can't go back
and that's fine
it's totally fine.
Even great loves die
and that's the hardest part, but it's also part of love.

Forgetting.
The farewell is slow.
Yes.
I should keep writing it all.

The lights start to lower. She goes to get her laptop. She opens it. The lights go down completely. Her face is lit only by the light from the screen. She starts writing. The light from the laptop turns off.

END